Domenico Quaranta

Beyond New Media Art

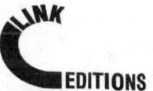

LINK EDITIONS

Domenico Quaranta
Beyond New Media Art

Publisher: LINK Editions, Brescia 2013
www.linkartcenter.eu

Translation and editing: Anna Rosemary Carruthers

Printed and distributed by: Lulu.com
www.lulu.com

ISBN 978-1-291-37697-5

Domenico Quaranta is an art critic and curator. His work focuses on the impact of the current techno-social developments on the arts.
He regularly writes for Flash Art and Artpulse.
In 2006 he edited (with M. Bittanti) the book "GameScenes. Art in the Age of Videogames"; in 2010, he published the book "Media, New Media, Postmedia".
As a curator, he organized various shows, including "Holy Fire. Art of the Digital Age" (Bruxelles 2008, with Y. Bernard), "Playlist" (Gijon 2009 and Bruxelles 2010) and "Collect the WWWorld. The Artist as Archivist in the Internet Age" (Brescia 2011; Basel and New York, 2012).
http://domenicoquaranta.com

«If all artists now, regardless of their preferred media, also routinely use digital computers to create, modify and produce works, do we need to have a special field of new media art? As digital and network media are rapidly became an omni-presence in our society, and as most artists came to routinely use it, new media field is facing a danger of becoming a ghetto whose participants would be united by their fetishism of latest computer technology, rather than by any deeper conceptual, ideological or aesthetic issues – a kind of local club for photo enthusiasts».

_ LEV MANOVICH

New Media as Grand Project has already been done, and arguing the transformative potential of technology should be superfluous in a world of smartphones.

_ MARIUS WATZ

Contents

A Brief History of the New Media Art World

45

Two Worlds Compared

81

The Boho Dance. New Media Art and Contemporary Art

121

The Postmedia Perspective

177

Appendix 1

225

Note to the English Edition

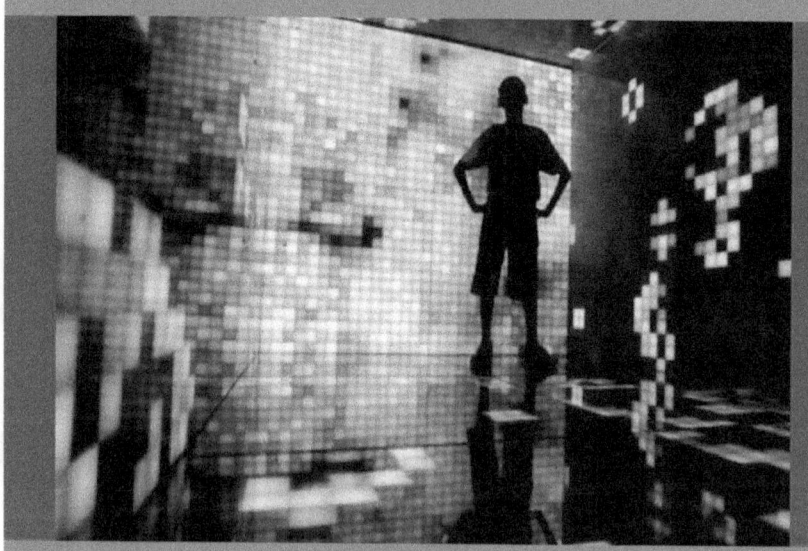

MEDIA
NEW MEDIA
POSTMEDIA

Domenico Quaranta

postmedia books

This book was first written in 2008 and 2009, as my Phd thesis at the University of Genoa, Italy. The title was *The War of Worlds. New Media Art and Contemporary Art.* In 2010, I cut it down considerably, I made some updates and I published it in Italian with Postmedia Books, an art publisher based in Milan. Upon suggestion of the editor, the title was changed into *Media, New Media, Postmedia.* [1]

At the time, I didn't think an English translation would be of any interest to an international audience. In Italy, there are no comprehensive histories of New Media Art, and *Media, New Media, Postmedia* was also intended to fill this gap in the local art publishing. English speakers, on the other hand, have access to many publications that provide this kind of historical overview, and better than I have here: from *Art and Electronic Media,* edited by Edward A. Shanken, to *Digital Art* by Christiane Paul, to name but a couple.

But *Media, New Media, Postmedia* was also an attempt to shape my own view of New Media Art, and to publicly intervene in the international debate on where it is placed in the broader field of contemporary arts. And this, thanks to a few lucky coincidences, turned out to be of interest to English speaking readers. In January 2011, I published an excerpt from the last chapter of the book on the online publishing platform of *Rhizome,* which led to some interesting discussions. [2] Later, in August 2011, art critic Régine Debatty published a review of the book on her blog *We Make Money Not Art.* [3] A few days later, Paddy Johnson, founder and editor of the influential online magazine *Art Fag City,* posted a comment on the blog that sparked more reactions. [4] It was Claire Bishop's article, published in the September 2012 issue of *Artforum,* and the debate it generated on mailing lists and on *Artforum* itself, [5] that finally convinced me of the topicality of the issues discussed in the book, and I asked my long time collaborator Anna Rosemary Carruthers to start working on the translation. She has my gratitude, for her speed and the quality of her work.

Writers will probably be in agreement with me on the fact that, after almost four years, you don't translate a book: you rewrite it, or you write another book. For a writer, it's incredibly hard to be respectful towards something you wrote years ago. In spite of what Gregory House may say, people change. Although I still believe in most of the things I wrote in this book, the temptation to rephrase them, to respond to criticism, to add further references, quotes and examples was hard to resist. But resist I did and, apart from some minor updates and a more sizeable addition to the last chapter, I tried to be as faithful as possible to the original text.

The note you are reading and the three appendices at the end of the book aim to cover the gap between the Italian edition (2010) and this English edition (2013). The first appendix is a medley of comments, quotes and notes connected to the editions of this book, sparked by the responses to the texts mentioned above. The second is a post about collecting that I wrote in 2012 for an online discussion about the subject on the mailing list *New Media Curating*. The last is a text on curating written at the end of 2012, which expands on and updates issues discussed in the last chapter of the book.

As for this note, it is a brief attempt to explain why – despite the interesting developments of the last few years – I think this book is still worth publishing (and reading). There is no doubt that things have moved on since I first published this book in 2010. There are interesting signals coming from the United States in particular. The increasing institutionalization of Rhizome, and the brilliant career of its former Executive Director Lauren Cornell, now curator for the New Museum and responsible, together with artist Ryan Trecartin, for the upcoming (2015) New Museum Triennial, is one example.

Cornell is the point woman for a new generation of "media literate" curators, with a background and a good network in the new media art world, who are successfully stepping up to the contemporary art world. Something similar is happening on the other side of the barricade. Massimiliano Gioni and Gary Carrion-Murayari, who curated the show *Ghost in the Machine*, also for the New Museum, proved that the whole of the contemporary art world does not share Nicolas Bourriaud and Francesco Bonami's resistance to art created using technology. The show dug deep into the "prehistory of the digital age", attempting to revisit some aspects of the relationship between art and technology that are usually sidestepped by mainstream art criticism. Another example is the work of Aaron Moulton, recently appointed Senior Curator of the Utah Museum of Contemporary Art. Former editor at *Flash Art* and freelance curator in Berlin, his curatorial and critical work manifests an increasing interest in the issues raised by the digital age, and the artists exploring those issues. His first group show for the museum was entitled *Analogital*, and included «artists who engage with concepts generated from the transitional space between analogue and digital». As Moulton explains:

«*Today's voracious image culture has led to a simulacrum of compounds where artists reference references of references and imagine the copy of the copy to be the original. New image vocabularies are emerging coupled with an unnostalgic condition where these new images appear, quickly evolve, disperse and disappear unarchived. Yet certain likenesses pervade our consciousness with no traceable reference, a kind of collective consciousness in an open-sourced handmade pixel. This combined with the virtual social conditions allow for a new way of considering sentimentality, sentience and sociality in the 21st century*». [6]

These are incredibly good signals, and they are not the only ones. Big museums finally seem to have realized that the exhibition model explored at the turn of the millennium was a dead end, and are now presenting "new media art" in a more "tactical" way. After a few years of inactivity, Christiane Paul organized a big solo show of Cory Arcangel at the Whitney Museum, and relaunched the museum's online initiatives. The curatorial work of Paola Antonelli at MoMA is bringing a lot of "new media art" into the museum and its collections, albeit in the Design department. Furthermore, as Paddy Johnson noted in her 2011 post on *Art Fag City*, "new media art" now features more in mainstream contemporary art magazines, and keeps producing a lot of online debate. Despite the demise of Expanded Box at Arco Madrid, and the closing of some commercial galleries with an interest in new media, its presence in the contemporary art market is growing, slowly but surely.

That said, one swallow doesn't make a summer. A single event does not necessarily indicate a trend. Neither do five or even ten events. The art world is too big, and too layered, for this to happen. And the old mistakes can always resurface, here and there. Two years ago the Arte Laguna Prize, one of the biggest art prizes in Italy, added a section called "virtual art". [7] The name appears to have been "suggested" by its main sponsor, the Italian company Telecom. Unsurprisingly, the quality of the applications is usually very bad, and hardly representative of developments in the new media art field. Which is a pity, when you think that the winner gets 7,000 euros.

In October 2010, with *YouTube Play. A Biennial of Creative Video*, [8] the Guggenheim Museum looked all set to relaunch the big museum – big technological sponsor alliance to organize an uncritical celebration of new media. The event was developed by YouTube and the Guggenheim Museum in collaboration with HP, and boasted an impressive line-up of artists and curators (including Laurie Anderson, Douglas Gordon, Takashi Murakami and Nancy Spector) appointed to endorse the creative potential of YouTube.

It's 2013 now, and luckily this biennial turned out to be a one-hit wonder.

But apart from all this, the most important thing is that most of the artistic production that takes place in the "new media art world" has as yet little or no visibility in the contemporary art world. And what *is* visible is not visible to everybody. The September 2012 issue of *Artforum* sums up the current state of play. The fact that *Artforum*, arguably the most important art criticism platform in the contemporary art world, decided to dedicate the issue marking its fiftieth anniversary to the subject "Art's New Media", looks like something of a turning point. Michelle Kuo, the editor of the issue, starts her introduction with a reference to an infamous letter that the magazine's editor, Philip Leider, sent to a contributor who submitted an essay on Charles Csuri in 1967. Rejecting the submission, Leider adds: «I can't imagine *Artforum* ever doing a special issue on electronics or computers in art, but one never knows». If this rejection can be seen as the starting point of the story told in this book, the 2012 special issue on art's new media should mark its happy ending. So does it?

Michelle Kuo's introduction is quite promising. She writes:

«*Today we still cringe at manufactured genres like "computer art," even if art as we know it could barely exist without computers. Technophilia and technophobia alike pervade museums, galleries, and art-fair booths; the language of new media and social media – platform, network, algorithm, sharing – abounds in press releases and exhibition titles, slaking our thirst for 1960s-cum-1990s cyber-euphoria. At the same time, Leider's doubt echoes in the distance, a critical reminder that art's affair with media is always prone to historical amnesia, to lazy conflations of vastly different positions and practices, to abrupt shifts from the faddish embrace of progress to a pining for the obsolete. We are nostalgic; we want to move on».* [9]

«This special issue of *Artforum* aims to move on but not forget», Kuo adds, introducing a series of essays and reviews that dig deep into history as well as discussing present developments. At the same time, however, *Artforum* focuses mostly on what is already canonized, instead of trying to bring new things into the contemporary art canon; and it doesn't distinguish between digital media and other "new" media such as video, photography, language and publishing, featuring artists like Tacita Dean, Wolfgang Tillmans and Barbara Kruger, and commissioning a cover from Lawrence Weiner. In other words, it doesn't forget, but it doesn't really move on either.

This becomes particularly clear when we consider Claire Bishop's essay "Digital Divide", one of the most hotly discussed articles in the issue (thanks also to its availability online). Intended as an «examination of contemporary art's repressed relationship to the digital», Bishop's essay is extremely interesting, because it shows the point of view of a clever, open-minded and well informed mainstream contemporary art critic on the topics we are about to explore in the following pages. Bishop opens her essay by pointing to the failure of what we will call the "boho dance" between new media art and the contemporary art world:

«WHATEVER HAPPENED TO DIGITAL ART? Cast your mind back to the late 1990s, when we got our first e-mail accounts. Wasn't there a pervasive sense that visual art was going to get digital, too, harnessing the new technologies that were just beginning to transform our lives? But somehow the venture never really gained traction – which is not to say that digital media have failed to infiltrate contemporary art. Most art today deploys new technology at one if not most stages of its production, dissemination, and consumption. Multichannel video installations, Photoshopped images, digital prints, cut-and-pasted files [...]: These are ubiquitous forms, their omnipresence facilitated by the accessibility and affordability of digital cameras and editing software». [10]

Then she goes on to sum up the core issue that her essay wants to explore:

«So why do I have a sense that the appearance and content of contemporary art have been curiously unresponsive to the total upheaval in our labor and leisure inaugurated by the digital revolution? While many artists use digital technology, how many really confront the question of what it means to think, see, and filter affect through the digital? How many thematize this, or reflect deeply on how we experience, and are altered by, the digitization of our existence? I find it strange that I can count on one hand the works of art that do seem to undertake this task».

There are two extremely interesting things in this paragraph. The first is Bishop's genuine interest in an art dealing with the socio-cultural consequences of the information age. This has rarely been a requirement for mainstream art criticism throughout the last two decades. The fact that Bishop is starting to look for art that «confront[s] the question of what it means to think, see, and filter affect through the digital» proves that something is finally changing. At the same time, however, the fact that she hasn't yet comes across any of this art shows that all the efforts to lend it visibility have not been as successful as insiders might assume. In the comments to the essay Bishop has often been flamed for being uninformed, for not being aware of this, that or the other. But in my view this lack of information merely proves that those who – like me – believe that the art Bishop is looking for is already here, still have a lot of work to do in terms of showing that it exists and has something to say.

This becomes particularly clear in the following passage, when Bishop explains:

In fact, the most prevalent trends in contemporary art since the '90s seem united in their apparent eschewal of the digital and the virtual. Performance art, social practice, assemblage-

9

*based sculpture, painting on canvas, the "archival impulse,"
analog film, and the fascination with modernist design and
architecture: At first glance, none of these formats appear to
have anything to do with digital media, and when they are
discussed, it is typically in relation to previous artistic
practices across the twentieth century. But when we examine
these dominant forms of contemporary art more closely, their
operational logic and systems of spectatorship prove intimately
connected to the technological revolution we are undergoing.
[...] I am suggesting that the digital is, on a deep level, the
shaping condition – even the structuring paradox – that
determines artistic decisions to work with certain formats and
media. [...] One word that might be used to describe this
dynamic – a preoccupation that is present but denied,
perpetually active but apparently buried – is disavowal: I
know, but all the same... [...] My point is that mainstream
contemporary art simultaneously disavows and depends on the
digital revolution, even – especially – when this art declines to
speak overtly about the conditions of living in and through new
media. But why is contemporary art so reluctant to describe
our experience of digitized life?*

It would be hard to find a more lucid diagnosis of the
relationship between contemporary art and the digital revolution.
There are two things we should note, however. The first is that
reactionary responses are always a symptom of revolutionary
change. Just as exhausted academicism was a response to the
industrial revolution and new media such as photography – "a
preoccupation that was present but denied, perpetually active but
apparently buried" – mainstream contemporary art is a response to
the digital revolution and new media such as the computer. Bishop
should have been honest enough to admit that mainstream
contemporary art is the contemporary form of exhausted
academicism. The second is that progressive responses to this
change do exist – you simply have to look elsewhere to find them,
just as in the nineteenth century you had to look outside the Salon,
at the Salon des Indépendants, or in a photographer's studio. And

sometimes these responses develop and challenge the very "most prevalent trends in contemporary art" that Bishop discusses. The interest in obsolete media is also a key trend in "digital aware" art, where it becomes a way to explore medium specificity, reject the rhetoric of the new, resist planned obsolescence, revisit the history of media (taking a stand against the "historical amnesia" described by Kuo) and regain control over the machine. [11] Social practices have been explored and improved by online performances like the Toywar and by the activity of platforms and collectives as diverse as The Yes Men, Runme.org, F.A.T Lab and Dump.fm, and by many individual artists who tackle online social networking. As for "the archival impulse", my traveling exhibition and online research blog *Collect the WWWorld. The Artist as Archivist in the Internet Age* might be seen as an unintended, anticipated response to Bishop, and a demonstration of how these issues resonate in "internet aware" art. [12]

Even if all this is left out of her essay, Bishop's conclusions actually seem to converge toward what we are saying here:

Is there a sense of fear underlying visual art's disavowal of new media? Faced with the infinite multiplicity of digital files, the uniqueness of the art object needs to be reasserted in the face of its infinite, uncontrollable dissemination via Instagram, Facebook, Tumblr, etc. [...] visual art's ongoing double attachment to intellectual property and physicality threatens to jeopardize its own relevance in the forthcoming decades. In a hundred years' time, will visual art have suffered the same fate as theater in the age of cinema? [...] If the digital means anything for visual art, it is the need to take stock of this orientation and to question art's most treasured assumptions. At its most utopian, the digital revolution opens up a new dematerialized, deauthored, and unmarketable reality of collective culture; at its worst, it signals the impending obsolescence of visual art itself.

Utopia and obsolescence are actually two sides of the same coin: the obsolescence of that visual art that is unable to respond to the challenges of the digital age goes hand in hand with the emergence of a new paradigm. This is not a utopian future: it's already happening. But it's happening mainly outside of the mainstream art world, in those very places where Bishop, at the beginning of her essay, says she doesn't want to look:

«*There is, of course, an entire sphere of "new media" art, but this is a specialized field of its own: It rarely overlaps with the mainstream art world (commercial galleries, the Turner Prize, national pavilions at Venice). While this split is itself undoubtedly symptomatic, the mainstream art world and its response to the digital are the focus of this essay.*»

Instead of putting this "symptomatic split" aside, this book traces its roots in recent history, tries to understand why it exists, asks if the time has come to move past it, and thinks about how to do so.

I hope you enjoy reading it.

Domenico Quaranta
March 29, 2013

Notes

[1] Domenico Quaranta, *Media, New Media, Postmedia*, Postmedia Books, Milan 2010.

[2] Domenico Quaranta, "The Postmedia Perspective", in *Rhizome,* January 12, 2011, online at http://rhizome.org/editorial/2011/jan/12/the-postmedia-perspective/ (last visit March 2013).

[3] Régine Debatty, "Book review – Media, New Media, Postmedia", in *We Make Money Not Art*, August 27, 2011, online at http://we-make-money-not-art.com/archives/2011/08/media-new-media-postmedia.php (last visit March 2013).

[4] Paddy Johnson, "Is New Media Accepted in the Art World? Domenico Quaranta's Media, New Media, PostMedia", in *Art Fag City*, August 30, 2011, online at www.artfagcity.com/2011/08/30/is-new-media-accepted-in-the-art-world-domenico-quarantas-media-new-media-postmedia/ (last visit March 2013).

[5] Claire Bishop, "Digital Divide. Claire Bishop on Contemporary Art and New Media", in *Artforum*, September 2012, online at http://artforum.com/inprint/issue=201207&id=31944&pagenum=0 (last visit March 2013).

[6] From the exhibition's press release, online at www.utahmoca.org/analogital-page/ (last visit March 2013).

[7] Cf. www.artelagunaprize.com (last visit March 2013).

[8] For more information, visit www.guggenheim.org/new-york/interact/participate/youtube-play (last visit March 2013).

[9] Michelle Kuo, "Art's New Media", in *Artforum*, September 2012, online at http://artforum.com/inprint/id=31950 (last visit March 2013).

[10] Claire Bishop, "Digital Divide. Claire Bishop on Contemporary Art and New Media", cit.

[11] Cf. Domenico Quaranta (Ed.), *Playlist. Playing Games, Music, Art*. Exh. Cat., LABoral Centro de Arte y Creación Industrial, Gijon, Spain, December 18, 2009 – May 17, 2010. Online at: http://domenicoquaranta.com/public/pdf/LABoral_Revista_PLAYLIST.pdf (last visit March 2013).

[12] Cf. Domenico Quaranta (ed.), *Collect the WWWorld. The Artist as Archivist in the Internet Age*. Exh. cat. Brescia, Spazio Contemporanea, September 24 – October 15, 2011. LINK Editions, Brescia 2011. Online at http://editions.linkartcenter.eu/ (last visit March 2013).

Prologue

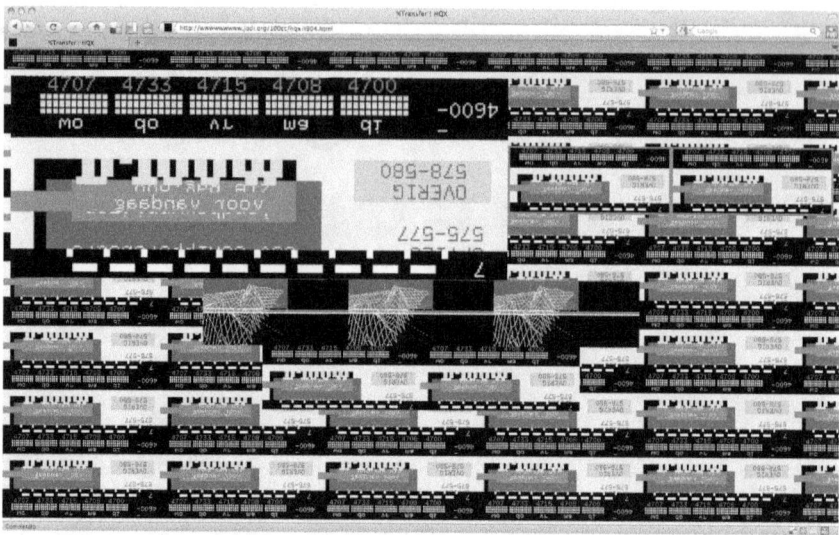

Jodi, *http://wwwwwwwww.jodi.org/*, 1995. Web project, screenshot.

«What is the need of new media as a separate domain if the computer is being integrated in all existing art forms anyway?» Geert Lovink [1]

If Arthur C. Danto's intellectual career kicked off when he saw Andy Warhol's *Brillo Box*, my much more modest story starts with another dazzling encounter, with the site *jodi.org*. Ever since then I have looked to artistic practice for a response to the challenges and questions posed by the changes shaping our world, that the Spanish sociologist Manuel Castells defined in a monumental, significantly titled book: "the information age". [2] Unfortunately I do not share Castells' gift of brevity, and so despite having a very good idea of what it is I do, when people ask me to sum it up in a word, I turn red and start stammering, reeling off the expressions on the spines of the many books that have made their way onto my shelves in the meantime: New Media Art, Digital Art, Media Art. None of these really covers exactly what I do though. What I am interested in, in art, goes beyond these definitions, and these definitions go beyond what I am interested in, taking in for example the hulking electronic toys that can be seen at the Ars Electronica Center in Linz, the monstrosities produced by old painters who have taken it upon themselves to start tinkering about with Photoshop filters, and the virtuoso flights of fancy undertaken by many software artisans. My sparring partners know this, and – depending on who they are, but always for the wrong reasons – either get worked up about it or don't take me seriously. So lately I have taken to saying just "contemporary art" and cutting out the stuttering. When all is said and done, if art reflects its era, everything I have just said can easily be summed up in these two words. For at least the last fifteen years contemporary art has been the art of the information age.

But if things were that simple, there would be no need for this book. The expression "New Media Art", which is deemed inadequate even by those who use it, has turned out to be a particularly resistant one, just like the point of view it embodies. The art that it represents has a limited presence in the world where contemporary art is produced, exhibited and talked about. It rarely appears in shows, museum collections and magazines, where it might sometimes get a little space, almost under the heading "other stuff". This is due to this very term and the perspective it represents – viewed as obsolete, and rejected by contemporary art criticism – and it happens in spite of the extraordinary success of works that should by rights fall into this category but which, luckily for them, are presented and discussed in a different way.

What we really need to do, then, is take this label by the horns and go back to its roots in order to understand what it hides and move past it once and for all. So what is New Media Art? What does this term *really* describe? And what has occasioned the schism between this term and the art scene it is supposed to describe? And lastly, what accounts for the limited presence in critical debate of an artistic practice that appears to have all the credentials for representing an era in which digital media are powerfully reshaping the political, economic, social and cultural organization of the world we live in? *Beyond New Media Art* is an attempt to respond to all these questions. It does not set out to challenge one term and replace it with another. It does not aim to do away with a category, but to explain the origins of that category and reveal its current lack of substance. It sets out to identify a number of artists already burdened with the label "New Media artists", and to put a line through that and free them into a wider arena where they can simply be considered "artists".

Notes

[1] Geert Lovink, "New Media Arts: In Search of the Cool Obscure. Explorations beyond the Official Discourse", in *Diagonal Thoughts*, 2007. Online at www.diagonalthoughts.com/?p=204 (last visit March 2013).
[2] Manuel Castells, *The Information Age*, Blackwell, Cambridge, MA – Oxford, UK, 1996 – 1998.

New
Media
Art

19

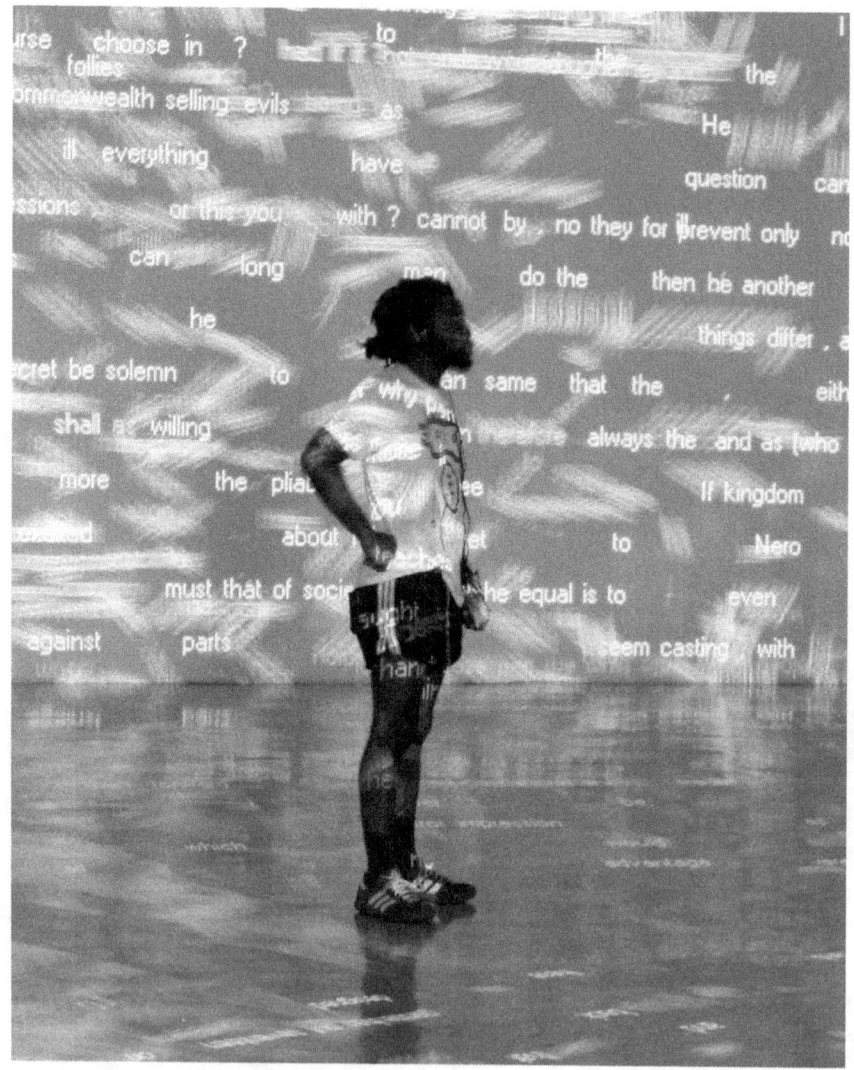

Charles Sandison, *Utopia*, 2006. Installation. Copyright Charles Sandison, courtesy the artist.

«Add the word 'art' and you instantly create a problem».
Geert Lovink [1]

16 October 2003. As part of the "Unilever Series", the Tate Modern in London presented *The Weather Project*, the latest spectacular work by the Danish artist Olafur Eliasson. In the immense Turbine Hall, converted from a former power station, Eliasson staged a spectacular environmental simulation. From the back wall, sun bathed the venue in yellow light, slowly clearing the fog that filled it. When the fog disappeared viewers realised that the space, already huge, was dizzyingly doubled by a mirror covering the entire ceiling. The mirror also created the impression of the sun, actually a semicircle of single frequency light bulbs. Both the light cycle and the fog production were controlled by a complex technological system hidden from view.

From 16 October 2003 to 21 March 2004, this installation was visited by more than two million people, making Eliasson one of the world's best known living artists. Many people went more than once, lying on the floor of the Turbine Hall to savour this exceptional simulation of the solar cycle.

Olafur Eliasson loves working in close contact with specialists from a wide range of disciplines: architects, scientists, designers, meteorologists and computer scientists. His studio is a sort of ever-changing laboratory, and many of his projects use computers to control installations that can be viewed as complex perceptive mechanisms. Eliasson works with light and the mechanisms of perception, digging into the history of technology in search of instruments – from panoramas to kaleidoscopes – and phenomena – like light refraction – to create situations that are enveloping, magical, disorientating.

2006. Three years after the success of *The Weather Project*, the American critics Mark Tribe and Reena Jana wrote a book for the publisher Taschen entitled *New Media Art*. «[...] we use the term

New Media art to describe projects that make use of emerging media technologies and are concerned with the cultural, political and aesthetics possibilities of these tools», they write in the introduction. [2] This definition looks perfect for *The Weather Project*. Yet in the book neither the work nor the artist are even mentioned – and it is hard to believe this is an oversight. It is also hard to believe that well-known artists like Mariko Mori, Carsten Höller, Carsten Nicolai and Pierre Huyghe, who often use "emerging technologies", focusing on their "cultural, political and aesthetic function", have merely been overlooked. Even if they were not among the authors' favourites, they surely could have been included for strategic purposes – also due to the fact that this so-called New Media Art appears to enjoy a popularity inversely proportional to that achieved by Eliasson et al. Like its peers (Media Art, Digital Art), the term New Media Art is carefully avoided in all the main narrations on recent art: there is no trace of it, for example, in *Art Since 1900*, the book by Hal Foster, Rosalind Krauss, Yve-Alain Bois and Benjamin H.D. Buchloh that efficiently sums up the vision of twentieth century art offered by American academic criticism. [3] And it is all too easy to come across damning statements like that of a *Frankfurter Allgemeine* journalist in 2008: «Media Art was an episode. There's a lot of good art that uses the media. But there's no Media Art». [4]

Clearly there is something else that Tribe and Jana aren't telling us. Something that goes beyond the use and exploration of emerging technologies, and that functions, in their view, as a distinguishing factor, and for others as an element of discredit.

To identify that "something" we need to take the expression "New Media Art" seriously and tackle the literature that regards it in search of distinguishing characteristics. In the chapters that follow we will look at four key questions posed by this term. If New Media Art is an artistic category, does it define a "genre" or a "movement"? What historic limits apply to the term? What does

"New Media" mean? And lastly: what do we mean by "medium"?

Although these four questions are closely connected, for the sake of clarity we will try to keep them separate. But not before clearing up one preliminary question that would otherwise plague our endeavors: the terminology issue.

The Terminology Issue

The term "New Media Art" is the product of a fierce, almost Darwinian process of natural selection. This has not prevented a number of competing terms, like Digital Art and Media Art, from surviving, or the winning term from being abused by its users. The complicated background of the term New Media Art reflects both the uncertain definition of the arena it applies to, and the weakness of its affirmation strategies. For now, however, it is important to point out that while different terms will be used in this book, we are always talking about the same thing. Indeed this term-related confusion has led to a situation in which different terms are often used synonymously, even in the same text.

Yet it is not *always* the same thing. The expression Digital Art, for example, narrows the field to digital media, while the expression Media Art, particularly popular in German academic literature, extends the reach to all media: press, radio, fax, telephone, satellite communications, video and television, light, electricity, film, photography, *and also* computers, software, the web and video games. As underlined in the online encyclopedia *Medien Kunst Netz*, launched in 2004 and edited by the German scholars Rudolf Frieling and Dieter Daniels, the term Media Art forges a tradition that goes from Man Ray to Nam June Paik to the current use of computers and the web, while Digital Art covers at most a story that begins in the late sixties, the period of the first experiments that used computers to make art. Lastly, the term

Digital Art shifts the focus unduly "low", namely towards any kind of creative use of digital media: from digital illustration to concept design to Photoshop virtuosities and 3D modeling, on a professional or an amateur level. At least according to Google, digital art has more to do with deviantArt (an online community of wannabe artists) than with actual art. Both Media Art and New Media Art, on the other hand, are saved from these base associations by their "high" origins.

There are similar issues with other, now obsolete alternatives that rose to the fore for varying periods between the sixties and the nineties: Electronic Art, Computer Art, Multimedia Art, Interactive Art, Virtual Art, Cyberart, etc. Electronic Art, in particular, came into being in the sixties in the context of video, establishing itself in the subsequent decades for anything to do with electronics, as can be evinced from the names of the events that started up in that period: from Ars Electronica (an annual festival that has been held in the city of Linz since 1979) to ISEA (the International Symposium for Electronic Art, a touring festival launched in 1988) to the Dutch Electronic Art Festival (DEAF) in Rotterdam, established in 1994. The other terms tended to highlight the hottest feature of digital media of a given period, and usually didn't survive the downward curve of the hype cycle.

Genre or Movement?

All of these terms, like New Media Art, stress the medium used for making the art, or the characteristic held to be decisive. Which should be enough to deem New Media Art a genre rather than an art movement. This view appears to be particularly congenial to Christiane Paul, Adjunct Curator of New Media Arts at the Whitney Museum in New York:

«*A lowest common denominator for defining new media art seems to be that it is computational and based on algorithms. [...] New Media Art is often characterized as process-oriented, time-based, dynamic, and real-time; participatory, collaborative and performative; modular, variable, generative, and customizable*». [5]

The definition proposed by Mark Tribe and Reena Jana also seems to allude to a genre with a precise technological basis. Yet in the follow-up to their book, Tribe and Jana link the term New Media Art to a specific period and a specific community. In one interview they were even more explicit:

«*I do think that New Media art was one of the few historically significant art movements of the late 20th century. There were a lot of other historically significant practices, but none of them galvanized as movements per se. (Tribe) Our point is that during the 1990s, with the dawn of the Internet's popular rise as a mass-market communication medium coupled with the increasing presence of PCs among households, a specific art movement started to take shape that both used these tools as primary artistic media to comment on the effect of these media on society and culture. (Jana)*». [6]

Chronological Limits

Tribe and Jana's statement also underlines how difficult it is to link New Media Art to a set period of time. The two writers circumscribe the phenomenon to the 1990s, merely acknowledging the existence of precedents that in their view belong in the categories of "art and technology" and "Media Art" (that in their view pertain to media – radio, video, TV etc. – that were no longer new in the 1990s). The inherent perspective of the term Digital Art takes us back at least to the 1960s, and the first experiments with Computer Art and cybernetic art exhibited in the historic exhibition at the ICA in London, entitled *Cybernetic Serendipity* (1968). Terms like "art and technology" and "electronic art" take us even further back, to the age of the avant-garde movements.

This is the perspective adopted, among others, by Edward A. Shanken in his book *Art and Electronic Media* (2009), [7] itself a perfect exemplification of the contradictions we are discussing: the selection of artists includes avant-garde artists, such as Lazlo Moholy-Nagy and Naum Gabo; successful contemporary artists who made occasional use of electronic media, like Mario Merz and Bruce Nauman, or a regular use of well accepted electronic media, such as neon lights (Dan Flavin) or video (Bill Viola); and younger art stars such as Olafur Eliasson, Mariko Mori and Pierre Huyghe. Shanken carefully avoids the term New Media Art. He draws a timeline that goes back to the avant-gardes; and even if he doesn't explicitly talk about art and electronic media as a genre, which art movement can be so broad as to include, let's say, Mario Merz and Bill Viola? And in any case the main issue raised in the very short preface to the book is that of the under-recognition of electronic art in mainstream art discourses. But just what is under-recognized? Electronic art? The cultural perspective implicit in this very label? Or most of the artists he lists alongside these few well known names? What is Shanken really talking about? What lies beyond this apparent schizophrenia?

What Does "New Media" Mean?

In an essay of 2000, [8] Steve Dietz, then head of New Media Initiatives at the Walker Art Center in Minneapolis, ironically recalled how in the century of the media, each separate medium went from being "new", to irrevocably getting old. The rhetoric of novelty no doubt poses a number of problems, the first being that of taking for granted that every use of a new medium produces art that is in turn "new", without entering into the merits of its aesthetic and cultural content. At the same time, it holds true that every new medium, when it bursts onto the scene, is revolutionary in its own way, heralding new, hitherto inexistent possibilities for communication and expression and often forcing the traditional disciplines to rethink their own nature and function. As Michael Rush writes, for example: «The final avant-garde, if one should call it that, of the twentieth century is that art which engages the most enduring revolution in a century of revolutions: the technological revolution». In his book *New Media in Late 20th Century Art*, Rush dwells on the period following the Second World War, but adopts a perspective that embraces the entire technological revolution of the twentieth century, from photography to virtual reality. But in this more generic sense the expression "new media" remains a rather weak category – undoubtedly functional in terms of a "technological" history of twentieth century art, but not when it comes to describing a specific phenomenon. It is no coincidence that Rush talks about the new media of art, but not New Media Art. [9]

Towards the mid nineties, the expression "New Media" started to be used by the big names in publishing to distinguish the newly opened divisions producing interactive CD-ROMs and websites from those working with relatively more traditional platforms like newspapers, radio and TV. It was then that the expression "New Media" went from being a generic one (any kind of new medium), to having a more specific meaning, closely connected to digital media.

At the same time this interpretation of the term began to circulate in art circles and among media theorists. In 2001, Lev Manovich published *The Language of New Media* with the MIT Press, a book destined to become a cornerstone of studies on digital languages. [10] According to Manovich, "new media" became a conceptual category when computers first began to be used not only to produce, but also to store and distribute contents. New Media is therefore the result of the encounter between two technologies which came into being in the same period: mass media and data processing. This encounter changed the identity of the media as much as that of the computer, transformed from simple calculator into a "media processor". [11]

The success of the term "New Media" went hand in hand with the rise of its related academic discipline: New Media Studies, and with the appearance of the first, temporary anthology, in the form of the weighty tome *The New Media Reader* (2003). [12] Manovich's introduction to this book [13] proves most instructive, in its deliberate refusal to make a distinction between "New Media" and "New Media Art", opting instead for the generic notion of the "new media field", which does not separate the technological and commercial aspects of the new media from those concerned purely with art. According to Manovich, art and media are the product of a single arena where artists and developers work in close contact. Manovich goes even further, asserting that the new media, and not art, are the true heirs of the revolution sparked by the avant-garde movements, and that the story of new media is the true story of contemporary art, because it is there that the hypotheses posited by the avant-garde movements come to fruition – not in Joyce's novels, Brecht's dramas, Pollock's paintings or Rauschenberg's art – but in the mouse, the graphic interface, the World Wide Web and Photoshop.

For the purposes of this book, however, the most interesting thing is the assertion that New Media Art and the culture of new media are an integral part of the story of new media, and that they can (or rather must) continue to exist as a sector, distinct from contemporary art in virtue of the fact that they genuinely do differ from it.

What Does "Medium" Mean?

Further complicating the notion of "New Media" is the substantial ambiguity that surrounds the very concept of medium in the contemporary debate. The two aspects of "New Media" – the generic and the specific – indeed overshadow another distinction: that between medium as "artistic medium" and medium as a generic means of communication. The first can be traced to Clement Greenberg and the tradition of art criticism. The second is linked to Marshall McLuhan and the tradition of Media Studies. These two concepts are radically different yet regularly get confused in art criticism, with terms like "Media Art", "New Media Art", "media specific" and "post media era".

In the sixties Clement Greenberg notably defined Modernism as the irreducible tension of every art form towards its "specific" nature, its unique and irreducible characteristics. In his view this «coincided with all that was unique in the nature of its medium». Every art form has to be rendered pure, «and in its "purity" find the guarantee of its standards of quality as well as of its independence». For example, in painting this means concentrating on the intrinsic characteristics of the painterly medium: flatness, the shape of the canvas, and the properties of the pigment. [14] Post-Greenberghian criticism tends to crystallize this definition and radicalise its reductive stance even beyond the intentions of Greenberg himself. As Rosalind Krauss notes, «from the '60s on, to utter the word "medium" meant invoking "Greenberg"». [15] But even when Rosalind Krauss, in the same text, attempted to move beyond the reductive stance of this conception (medium as mere material support), [16] to examine the complex relationships that arise between work and medium, and the set of conventions that determine the "medium specificity" of a work, she stayed firmly within Greenberg's interpretation of medium as "artistic medium".

From another angle, the concept of medium that the Canadian sociologist Marshall McLuhan introduced in the same period regarded "any extension of ourselves", albeit predominantly in regard to the electronic means of communication that rose to the fore in the previous decades, radio and TV in particular, turning the world into a sort of "global village". The impact of these media has been overwhelming, as can be seen in the explanation that McLuhan offers of his famous maxim, "the medium is the message": «the "message" of any medium or technology is the change of scale or pace or pattern that it introduces into human affairs». [17]

It goes without saying that the confusion between these two notions gives rise to undue and unacceptable simplifications. The accusations of formalism often levelled at the art that uses new technologies is one example: neither the enthusiastic exploration of the medium's potential, or the critical testing of its limits, or the examination of its social and cultural consequences, can be attributed to Greenberg's formalism. When Nam June Paik distorts a TV signal, or Jodi remixes the code of a web page, they are not just working on the inherent characteristics of the medium (the flow of electrons in the cathode ray tube, or HTML): they are interfering with a means of communication in order to highlight its conventions and potential, and to explore "the change of scale or pace or pattern that it introduces into human affairs".

This is a glaring misconception, yet one that fooled everyone.

A Medium-Based Definition?

At the end of this brief exploration, however, we have not yet pinpointed the meaning of the expression New Media Art. Critics do not seem to have come to any kind of agreement on the chronological, philosophical or practical boundaries of the phenomenon: some focus on the last decade, others go back to the avant-garde movements; some restrict it to the visual arts, others extend it to all art forms and even the history of the technologies themselves. Even the precise nature of these "new media" is up for discussion. As things currently stand, New Media Art recalls the mythological Phoenix: "everyone knows it exists, no-one knows where it is". The term corresponds to an indistinct cloud of meanings that turn every debate on its true nature into a comic parody of itself.

The only fact that seems to garner pretty much unanimous accord is the point we started out from: New Media Art is defined in relation to the media it uses, and it sets out to draw forth the social, political and cultural implications of those media. It would be easy to infer from this that the concept of New Media Art is based on the aforementioned question of formalism. Indeed this is something that both its detractors and supporters for once appear to agree on. For the former it is patently obvious that we entered a post-media phase in the sixties, with art no longer focusing on the specific characteristics of a medium but taking an open, nomadic approach. For contemporary art criticism, this makes New Media Art's claim to focus on a medium absurd, naive and obsolete. We will examine the notion of post-mediality further on. For now, Francesco Bonami's derisive comment sums it up pretty well: "those who talk about computer art haven't a clue what they're talking about, and confuse the medium with the content, the idea, the result, mistaking the tool for the work of art. Art is not like Formula One, where the car counts more than the driver". [18]

This approach also influenced the fortunes of the expression "Video Art". It is telling that this expression is now rejected even by those who contributed to establishing it in the past. In 1971 David Ross was the first curator hired by a museum in the role of "Curator of Video Art" (at the Everson Museum of Art in Siracuse, New York). Thirty four years on, he writes:

«Simply put, as an art historical category, video art does not actually exist. It is provisional – a simple category of convenience [...] To restate the problem, video is not a movement or the label for a shared aesthetic – it is simply a set of tools; tools capable of producing extraordinary works of art». [19]

On the other hand, among supporters of New Media Art, there is the idea that the new technologies have had a significant impact on artistic practice, and that art has the duty to explore this potential.

In a text regarding Ars Electronica in Linz in 2003, Lev Manovich once again lucidly summarises the state of play. Manovich explains that since the sixties, contemporary art has been a predominantly conceptual activity, and that the typical artist trained in the last two decades no longer works on paintings, photographs or videos, but "projects". He continues:

«when Ars Electronica program asks "In which direction is artists' work with the new instruments like algorithms and dynamic systems transforming the process of artistic creativity?" (festival program, p. 9), the very assumptions behind such a question put it outside of the paradigm of contemporary art». [20]

Taken out of context, this statement might appear to be in line with that of Bonami, and indeed it is, albeit from a diametrically opposed viewpoint. Both are saying that New Media Art has nothing to do with contemporary art. But for Manovich this is positive, and should be acknowledged by abandoning the term art altogether.

Yet if New Media Art was a category based purely on the use of a medium, putting it out of action would be easy, as Ross found with the expression Video Art. And its consistency would be ensured: in the period that Video Art enjoyed the consensus it subsequently lost, it was still all about video.

As we have seen, however, there are many works that use the new media that no-one would ever dream of calling New Media Art. Furthermore, despite the considerable efforts made by critics and artists to shrug off this perspective, it is still around: why so?

The answer lies implicitly in many of the protests against the idea that an artistic category can be based on the use of a medium. According to the English artist Charles Sandison, [21] an expression like Media Art

«can lead to an art ghetto, where artists, whose only common link is that they are faced with the same criticism. Their isolation is re-enforced when they are forced to create a universal defence. the fact that their defence is based on a misunderstood appreciation of an emergent medium inevitably leads 'full-circle' resulting in greater suspicion and rejection».

In one interview the American artist Brody Condon asserted:

«Every time you describe these artists by material, you are hurting, and not helping them [...] It's about ideas, not material. I don't give a shit about new media». [22]

Personalities like Steve Dietz and Andreas Broeckmann, who made a name for themselves as curators of New Media Art, have on various occasions taken their distance from that term and the approach that it implies. The former, for an exhibition curated in 2005 with the English curator Sarah Cook, coined the expression "the art formerly known as New Media" and has reiterated on various occasions that «while the technology may be enabling, to the extent that it's only about an instrumentalization of those capabilities, it's probably not very interesting»; but he has never stopped wondering why many "new media artists" with a solid pedigree receive little or no consideration in the art world. [23] The latter, in the catalogue of an exhibition he curated at the Stedelijk Museum in Amsterdam in 2008, called the underlying assumption of the expression New Media Art a "grave misconception", going on to say: «Entire artistic careers were ruined by the stigma of doing 'art with a plug'. (Others were made by the exclusivity which that stigma offered in certain circles)». [24] Lastly, the critic Régine Debatty has said: «the "new media" label [...] fits the genre like a straitjacket and sends it to a ghetto without even a flicker of compassion. Forget the new, drop the media, enjoy art». [25]

All of these positions challenge not only the idea of finding a satisfactory definition, but also the existence of a socio-cultural context that can be identified with it, but which a growing number of artists feel imprisoned by and wish to break out of. That the existence of this "context" is the real Gordian knot here, when it comes to understanding what lies behind the term New Media Art, emerges clearly in the definition put forward by Beryl Graham and Sarah Cook in the recent book *Rethinking Curating* (2010). While – it goes without saying – the two writers are critical of the term, they continue to feel that it has a place in debate on curatorial practice, as long as the focus of attention is shifted from the "media" to the "behaviour". In line with this they define New Media Art as

«art that is made using electronic media technology and that displays any or all of the three behaviors of interactivity, connectivity, and computability in any combination».

Yet the brief list of provisos that follows this definition is rather revealing, in so far as the authors feel it necessary to exclude «artworks that may have science and technology as a theme, but that do not use electronic media technology for their production and distribution» and vice versa, to include «artworks showing these behaviors, but that may be from the wider fields of contemporary art or from life in technological times». [26]

These strange distinctions do not ring true because – in the light of the definition that precedes them – they appear to be entirely superfluous. Yet they are included. Why is that? It would appear that Graham and Cook are attempting to combat a general idea that includes certain works in the category of New Media Art and excludes others, based on criteria not connected to the languages used and the behaviour manifested. A criteria that, according to what we have said so far, could be linked to the idea of "belonging".

But belonging to what, exactly? Terms like "niche" or "ghetto" are often bandied about, but a niche inside the contemporary art world surely implies a minimum of shared ideas, and common means of production and distribution. On the contrary, most New Media Art appears able to exist and persist completely outside of the art world, and do perfectly well without it.

New Media Art: a World Unto Itself

All of this, and everything we have not yet managed to account for, can be taken care of with a simple theorem: that the expression New Media Art identifies an "art world" that is entirely independent, both from the world of contemporary art and any other "art world". To be comprehensible, the definition of New Media Art must be based on sociology rather than technology.

In other words, the expression New Media Art – like those which preceded it and those which will sooner or later follow it – does not indicate the art that uses digital technology as an artistic medium; it is not an artistic genre or an aesthetic category; it does not describe a movement or an avant-garde. What the expression New Media Art really describes is the art that is produced, discussed, critiqued and viewed in a specific "art world", that we will call the "New Media Art world".

The idea that to define New Media Art we need to refer to a "context" rather than a movement or a given use of the medium is not new. In actual fact it appears to be implicit in almost all critical discourse on New Media Art, with all those references to the ghetto, scene or community of New Media Art.

The media critic Geert Lovink, for example, devotes a whole chapter of his book *Zero Comments* to the "crisis of New Media Art". The essay opens with a few unsettling questions:

«Why is new media art perceived as an obscure and self-referential subculture that is in the process of disappearing? Why is it so hard for artists that experiment with the latest technologies to be part of pop culture or 'contemporary arts'? [...] New media art has positioned itself in between commercial demo design and museum strategies, and instead of being crushed, it has fallen into an abyss of misunderstanding». [27]

A few pages in, Lovink explains that «New media arts can best be described as a transitional, hybrid art form, a multi-disciplinary 'cloud' of micro-practices». In another passage, New Media Art is described as a community that does not produce art, but tests and explores the artistic medium (of the future) for the benefit of (future) generations. Lastly, the view espoused by Jon Ippolito and Joline Blais in *At the Edge of Art*, published in 2006, [28] is particularly interesting: the duo asserts that some of the most significant "artistic" developments of recent years happened outside the art world, often involving figures who do not see themselves first and foremost as artists, but researchers, scientists, activists. In view of this, if we want the term "art" to continue to mean something, we need to reconsider what it actually means, and above all we need to set aside the Duchampian concept of art as being something that happens in the art world. Blais and Ippolito encourage us to look for art in the "wrong places", namely outside of the art world: on the net, in labs, in scientific and technological research facilities. What can be found there, and what according to Blais and Ippolito forces us to redefine the very notion of art, coincides for the most part with what others class under the umbrella term of New Media Art.

Lev Manovich talks openly of two different socio-cultural contexts, and in 1997 he came up with two significant names for them: Duchamp Land and Turing Land (Marcel Duchamp being the father of contemporary art and Alan Turing one of the fathers of the computer).

Art Worlds

«New media, to its credit, has been one of the very few art forms that has taken the programmatic wish to blow up the walls of the white cube seriously. This was done in such a systematic manner that it moved itself outside of the art system altogether». Geert Lovink [29]

So can this ghetto, this "Turing land", this arena outside the world of contemporary art, be viewed as an "art world" in its own right? *Art Worlds* is the title of an essay published in 1982 by the American sociologist Howard S. Becker. [30] Becker starts out from the notion that any work of art, be it a painting, a novel, a play or a poem, is not the product of an individual (the artist) but that of a social system in which the artist is just one of the players. For a work to exist, it takes more than an individual with an idea who brings that to fruition: to produce a work artists need materials, tools, support. And for something to exist as a "work of art" there has to be someone to appreciate it and a philosophical system that justifies it as art. Each of these activities also requires special training, and therefore a system of education, and more broadly, there needs to be a social order that makes art possible. This set of players and factors is what makes up an "art world". Obviously, Becker notes, works of art can come about even without one or more of these factors: what counts is that the resulting work will differ from what it might have been had all of these factors come into play. In other words, the "art world" radically influences the nature of the work of art.

Each "art world", therefore, is based on a precise division of labour, within which the artist plays a very special role. The artist is the person with that special gift that enables him or her to create a work of art; but the artist's creative act takes place within a cooperative system, respecting certain *standards* that the system is able to manage and certain *conventions* that are shared by both the producers and consumers of a work of art. If these standards and conventions are not respected it does not mean that the work of art is not possible, just that everything is more difficult: the artist has to find non-conventional distribution channels, brave investors, an open-minded audience. As for the conventions, they facilitate the artist's work and interaction with the public, but often impose powerful limitations.

If the standards and conventions of a given art world are not respected the result is isolation: opting for freedom can cause problems and limit success, at least in the immediate timeframe. As Becker writes:

«*Systems change and accomodate to artists as artists change and accomodate to systems. Furthermore, artists can secede from the contemporary system and create a new one, or attempt to, or do without the constraining benefits of distribution. Art worlds often have more than one distribution systems operating at the same time*». [31]

This is what happened to Video Art, which often was not distributed, or was distributed using alternative channels, some created ad hoc by artists or curators. The same applies to the systems involved in producing works of art, and systems for criticism and training. If existing educational facilities do not offer

the right tools to develop a given artistic language, people can opt to be self-taught, or found new schools and faculties. If the existing production structures are not sufficient, new ones can be founded, or the artists can move from the academies and studios into specialised labs; if the media that host the critical debate do not suffice, alternative ways can be found.

If these structures of production, distribution, training and criticism take shape and come together, they can give rise to a new art world. According to Becker an art world is a network of relationships that attempts to stand out from other worlds, but at the same time forges relationships with them. What's more: sometimes

«[...] art worlds provoke some of their members to create innovations they then will not accept. Some of these innovations develop small worlds of their own; some remain dormant and then find acceptance from a larger art world years or generations later; some remain magnificent curiosities of little more than antiquarian interest». [32]

This short paragraph, in my view, unpacks the whole question, from the origins of New Media Art to current debate on its presence in the contemporary art world, and whether it belongs to the latter. In the sixties and seventies the advent of languages that challenged the standards and conventions of their respective "art worlds" drove visual artists, writers, set designers, musicians, choreographers and directors to seek a form of freedom that ended up relegating them to a niche. To support and develop their work, between the sixties and the nineties these creatives came up with new systems to create, distribute and criticise their output, and new educational programs. All of this gradually transformed that niche into an independent art world, the New Media Art world, which inevitably introduced its own conventions and standards. The next chapter looks at how this new world took shape.

Yet the linearity of this story was challenged in the mid nineties, when the digital media, which for thirty years has been confined to universities and research bodies, developed the means for mass distribution, influencing artistic production on all levels and giving rise to new art forms, like Net Art. This undermined the conditions which led to the creation of the New Media Art world: nowadays, works which make extensive use of digital media can also be created, distributed and appreciated in the contemporary art world, as the high profile examples of Olafur Eliasson, Mariko Mori and many others show. Furthermore, the digital medium no longer requires specific training, absolute dedication, access to tools and labs, etc.: more often than not, a home computer equipped with consumer software is more than enough to make art. And a home computer is just one of the many tools available in any artist's studio.

The consequences of this shift in art production and dissemination are enormous, and far from being completely understood. Right now, it may be enough to notice that art that deals with digital media is now being exhibited and appreciated in both the New Media Art world and the contemporary art world, because, as Becker says, it fulfils the concept of art held by both, and because it adapts to the distribution systems and discourse of both. At this point, a clash is inevitable. On one side, we have the New Media Art world, with its own tradition, its institutions, its jargon, its idea of art: an idea that's starting to be too narrow to provide a good understanding of what's going on, but that's still the only one available. On the other, we have the contemporary art world, which is genuinely interested in what's going on, but doesn't yet have the conceptual tools to understand it, and is slowly developing the practical tools required to deal with it; and that, at the same time, does not acknowledge the research undertaken in the New Media Art world. In between the two, there are the artists, with their different approaches to the medium and to the ideas revolving around it. Some are happy with the New Media Art world; some aren't, and they also resist the economic structures of the contemporary art world. But most of them want to be free to use both traditional and new media; they are looking for a different understanding, a wider platform, a longer history, a new economic model. They want to be understood as art, not as New Media Art. And they are embarking on a difficult process of migration toward the contemporary art world.

While the third chapter explores this "war of the worlds" and the elements that underpin it, the two subsequent chapters look at the dynamics of this migration. To be seriously considered on the platform of contemporary art, New Media Art must rid itself of this term, the perspective it embodies and the associations that it implies. Going from one world to another poses not only problems of translation, but also obliges this art to give up its specific characteristics, and its history. As an independent category or sector, New Media Art is not conceivable inside the world of contemporary art. As we will see in the fourth chapter, the failure to acknowledge the need for this transition has doomed all attempts to promote the art known as New Media Art within the contemporary art world. A new perspective is needed, as we will discuss in the fifth chapter.

Notes

[1] Geert Lovink, "New Media Arts: In Search of the Cool Obscure. Explorations beyond the Official Discourse", in *Diagonal Thoughts*, 2007. Online at www.diagonalthoughts.com/?p=204 (last visit March 2013).

[2] Mark Tribe, Reena Jana, *New Media Art*, Taschen, Köln 2006, p. 6.

[3] Hal Foster, Rosalind Krauss, Yve-Alain Bois, Benjamin H.D. Buchloh, *Art since 1900. Modernism, Antimodernism, Postmodernism*, Thames & Hudson, London 2004.

[4] Stefan Heidenreich, "Es gibt gar keine Medienkunst!", in *Frankfurter Allgemeine Sonntagszeitung*, January 27, 2008.

[5] Christiane Paul (ed.), *New Media in the White Cube and Beyond*, University of California Press, Berkeley and Los Angeles, 2008, pp. 3 – 4.

[6] Domenico Quaranta, "The Last Avant-garde. Interview with Mark Tribe & Reena Jana", in *Nettime*, October 30, 2006.

[7] Edward A. Shanken, *Art and Electronic Media*, Phaidon Press, London – New York 2009.

[8] Steve Dietz, "Curating New Media", August 2000, in *Yproductions*, online at www.yproductions.com/writing/archives/curating_new_media.html (last visit March 2013).

[9] Michael Rush, *New Media in Late 20th-Century Art*, Thames & Hudson, London 1999 [2001], p. 8.

[10] Lev Manovich, *The Language of New Media*, The MIT Press, Cambridge (Massachusetts), 2001.

[11] Ibid., p. 44.

[12] Noah Wardrip-Fruin, Nick Montfort (eds.), *The New Media Reader*, The MIT Press, Cambridge – Massachusetts, London – England 2003.

[13] Lev Manovich, "New Media from Borges to HTML", 2002. In Noah Wardrip-Fruin, Nick Montfort (eds.), *The New Media Reader*, cit., p. 14.

[14] Clement Greenberg, "Modernist Painting", in *Forum Lectures*, Voice of America, Washington, D. C. 1960. Also available in: Francis Frascina, Charles Harrison (eds.), *Modern Art and Modernism: A Critical Anthology*, 1982.

[15] Rosalind Krauss, *A Voyage in the North Sea. Art in the Age of the Post-Medium Condition*, Thames & Hudson, London 1999, p. 6.

[16] In the recent *Under Blue Cup* (2011), Krauss actually considers some media theory – specifically the ideas of Marshall McLuhan and Friedrich

Kittler – with consequences that we will discuss in Chapter 5. Notably, she introduces this section writing: «*Medium* and *media* are what the French would call "false friends" – French look-alikes for English words that are strictly *not* synonymous». In Rosalind Krauss, *Under Blue Cup*, The MIT Press, Cambridge – London 2011, p. 33.

[17] Marshall McLuhan, *Understanding Media. The Extensions of Man*, 1964.

[18] Francesco Bonami, *Lo potevo fare anch'io. Perché l'arte contemporanea è davvero arte*, Mondadori, Milano 2007, p. 24.

[19] David A. Ross, "The History Remains Provisional", in Ida Gianelli, Marcella Beccaria (eds.), *Video Art. The Castello di Rivoli Collection*, Skira, Milano 2005, p. 4.

[20] Lev Manovich, "Don't Call it Art: Ars Electronica 2003", in *Nettime*, September 2003.

[21] Cf. "charles sandison on charles sandison!", in *Designboom*, 2002, online at www.designboom.com/portrait/sandison.html (last visit March 2013).

[22] Brody Condon, pers.comm., 2008. In Domenico Quaranta, Yves Bernard (eds.), *Holy Fire. Art of the Digital Age*, exhibition catalogue, iMAL, Bruxelles, April 2008. Brescia, FPEditions 2008, p. 91.

[23] Steve Dietz, "'Just Art': Contemporary Art After the Art Formerly Known As New Media", October 27, 2006. Online at www.yproductions.com/writing/archives/just_art_contemporary_art_afte.html (last visit March 2013).

[24] In AAVV, *Deep Screen. Art in Digital Culture*, exhibition catalogue, Stedelijk Museum, Amsterdam, May 30 – September 30 2008, pp. 154 – 155.

[25] Pers. Comm., in Domenico Quaranta, Yves Bernard (eds.), *Holy Fire...*, cit., p. 94.

[26] Beryl Graham, Sarah Cook, *Rethinking Curating. Art after New Media*, MIT Press, Cambridge, Massachusetts – London, England 2010, p. 10.

[27] Geert Lovink, *Zero Comments, Blogging and Critical Internet Culture*, Routledge, New York 2007.

[28] Joline Blais, Jon Ippolito, *At the Edge of Art*, Thames and Hudson, London 2006.

[29] Geert Lovink, "New Media Arts: In Search of the Cool Obscure. Explorations beyond the Official Discourse", cit.

[30] Howard S. Becker, *Art Worlds*, University of California Press, Berkeley – Los Angeles – London 1982 [1984].

[31] Ibid., p. 95.

[32] Ibid., p. 36.

A Brief History of the New Media Art World

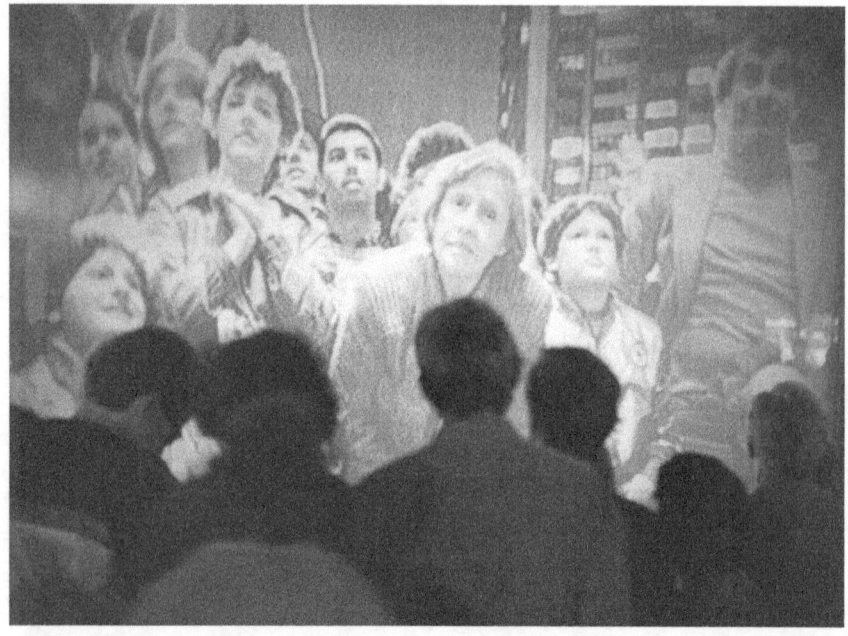

Kit Galloway and Sherrie Rabinowitz, *Hole-in-Space* (photographic documentation), 1980. Courtesy the artists; photo: courtesy Kit Galloway; © 2008 Kit Galloway and Sherrie Rabinowitz

This chapter aims to provide a historiographic background for the hypothesis advanced in the previous one: namely that a multidisciplinary, varied set of practices evolved into a niche and then established itself as an entirely autonomous "art world". To do so we will take a bird's eye view of the history of New Media Art, overlooking the aesthetic and cultural aspects in order to focus, with a number of case studies, on its social history. It goes without saying that, being presented for this specific purpose, this history does not set out to be an exhaustive one.

The Sixties

Our story begins between the end of the 1950s and the beginning of the 1960s, when technological progress on one hand and developments in art on the other created the conditions for art, science and technology to intertwine once more. Such an encounter was anything but new in the history of art, having been vigorously embraced by the avant-garde movements: see Lazlo Moholy-Nagy, often invoked as one of the founding fathers of New Media Art, above all for his *Licht-raum-modulator* (1930), a kinetic sculpture that produces fascinating light effects. And it was the historic avant-garde movements that informed the new artistic experiences that sought to go beyond what then looked like the dead end of Abstract Expressionism: New Dada, Nouveau Réalisme, Gutai, Happening, Fluxus, Kinetic Art, Arte Programmata, Optical Art, Pop Art and Video Art. Reality, in the shape of real or represented objects, entered artworks; the pop culture conveyed by the media began to capture the attention of artists; art appropriated all media, from the human body to consumer products, from advertising to television sets to cars, and theoretical developments like cybernetics and information theory informed the lexicon of art. This is, for example, what John Brockman says about John Cage:

«He convened weekly dinners during which he tried out his ideas, as well as his mushroom recipes, on a group of young artists, poets, and writers [...] we talked about media, communications, art, music, philosophy, the ideas of McLuhan and Norbert Wiener. McLuhan had pointed out that by inventing electric technology, we had externalized our central nervous system: that is, our mind. Cage went further to say that we now had to presume that "there is only one mind, the one we all share". Cage pointed out that we had to go beyond private and personal mindsets and understand how radically things had changed. Mind had become socialized. "We can't

*change our minds without changing the world", he said. Mind
as a man-made environment became our environment, which
he characterized as "the collective consciousness," which we
could tap into by creating "a global utilities network."» [1]*

For the first and only time in the history of art, the implicit
perspective in the most generic interpretation of the expression
New Media Art became a mass strategy, common to all the avant-
garde art of the period. This situation was short-lived: while a few
"new media" and artistic strategies, from assemblage to
photography, performance and conceptual interventions on
mechanically reproduced images rapidly became the stuff of the
establishment, the more radically technophile or science-based
expressions, like Kinetic and Optical art, were put out of action,
and video entered a splendid isolation of its own that was to last
until the early 1990s.

At the same time, in the States, the spectre of permanent war
gave an incredible boost to scientific and technological research.
In 1946 the University of Pennsylvania presented the first digital
calculator, ENIAC (Electronic Numerical Integrator and
Computer); 1951 saw the launch of UNIVAC, the first computer to
hit the market, capable of processing both numerical data and text.
These were huge machines without any kind of user interface, that
accepted programs in the shape of perforated cards and could only
be operated by highly skilled users. Accessibility was also very
restricted: developed for military applications, they resided mostly
in research centers and universities. It was in Bell Laboratories in
Murray Hill (New Jersey) in particular that the first studies on the
algorithmic production of text, music and images were carried out,
and not by artists, but engineers and researchers who saw these
experiments as more or less necessary diversions to their research
work. The electronic engineer A. Michael Noll, for example, was
taken on by Bell Labs in 1961 and worked there for 15 years. In
the summer of 1962 he created his first works of "Computer Art",

abstract images generated by algorithms and mathematical functions that were an evident tribute to Piet Mondrian and Cubism. Around 1963 many pioneers began working in this direction, including Lillian Schwartz, Herbert Franke, Manfred Mohr, Jean-Pierre Hébert and Roman Verotsko. In April 1965 the Howard Wise Gallery in New York, the same venue that brought Gruppo Zero and Kinetic Art to America, staged the exhibition *Computer-Generated Pictures by Bela Julesz and Michael Noll.* Computer Art appeared in a number of group shows, including *Cybernetic Serendipity* (ICA, London 1968), *Tendencija 4* (Zagreb 1969) and *Computerkunst* (Hannover 1969). [2] At the same time, potential uses of computers in literature and music were also being studied: on one hand there was the combinatory literature developed by Alison Knowles at Bell Labs and the members of the European group OuLiPo (Ouvroir de Littérature Potentielle), founded in 1960 by Raymond Queneau and François Le Lionnais; and on the other the work of the composer James Tenney at Bell Labs. [3]

This initial foray into Computer Art therefore came about in an extremely restricted context, in both sociological and technological terms. From an aesthetic point of view the massive mainframes of the sixties placed great limitations on artists and were extremely difficult to use, and the result was that in this niche engineers vastly outnumbered genuine artists. In view of this, much Computer Art of the sixties is exceptionally ingenuous aesthetically speaking – in the words of Jim Pomeroy, it rolled out «flashy geometric logos tunneling through twirling 'wire-frames,' graphic nudes, adolescent sci-fi fantasies, and endless variations on the Mona Lisa». [4] A. Michael Noll candidly confesses:

«In the early 1960s, the digital computer offered great promise as a new tool and medium for the arts. In the past ten years, however, little has actually been accomplished in computer art. I've come to the conclusion that most computer art done by

engineers and scientists, my own work included, would benefit from an artist's touch». [5]

Yet dismissing Computer Art as merely ingenuous would be a simplistic way of looking at things. Even supposing that the only achievement of Noll and the first computer artists was to show it was possible to make art with a computer, their contribution to the evolution of the medium was crucial. For Computer Art not only paved the way for New Media Art, but the whole of computer graphics, which over the years has progressed to photorealistic videogames and 3D animation. Even considering merely this dual legacy we can appreciate the scope of its contribution to the culture of the twentieth century. And the success, however fleeting, of Computer Art also points up something else: the openness of the art world of the sixties to the most advanced, precarious fringes of cultural experimentation, its acceptance of ideas that would be hard pressed to find a welcome elsewhere.

The best demonstration of this was probably the 1968 exhibition *Cybernetic Serendipity* curated by Jasia Reichardt at the Institute of Contemporary Art in London. This show was part of the work of the Independent Group and resulted from the 1965 encounter between Reichardt and Max Bense, the German philosopher, a key figure of the Stuttgart school, who studied the relationships between maths, language and art, and coined the term "information aesthetics". According to Brent MacGregor, it was Bense who told Reichardt to "look into computers". [6] In 1966 the exhibition was announced at a public conference, and fund-raising began. Despite initial expectations, the only private company to invest significantly in it was IBM; the rest was covered by the Arts Council. *Cybernetic Serendipity* was not an exhibition of Computer Art, but a multidisciplinary event that explored the impact of information technology and cybernetic theory on life and contemporary creativity. It was divided into three sections: the first featured works – images, but also music, animations and texts – generated by computers, the second contained cybernetic robots and "painting machines", and the third explored the social uses of computers and the history of cybernetics. Alongside the pioneers of Computer Art and cybernetic art, from Charles Csuri to Michael Noll, John Whitney to Edward Ihnatowicz to the Computer Technique Group of Tokyo, were artists who shared aesthetic, thematic or formal characteristics with the latter (Nam June Paik, Jean Tinguely and his machines, James Seawright, the Optical painter Bridget Riley, and avant-garde musicians like John Cage and Jannis Xenakis). But there were also explanatory elements and even a computer, provided by IBM, that offered a service for booking flights. According to the curator:

«Cybernetic Serendipity deals with possibilities rather than achievements, and in this sense it is prematurely optimistic. There are no heroic claims to be made because computers have so far neither revolutionized music, nor art, nor poetry, in the same way that they have revolutionized science [...] The computer is only a tool which, at the moment, still seems far removed from those polemic preoccupations which concern art [...] The possibilities inherent in the computer as a creative tool will do little to change those idioms of art which rely primarily on the dialogue between the artist, his ideas and the canvas. They will, however, increase the scope of the art and contribute to its diversity». [7]

Cybernetic Serendipity came about in a context, the British context, which was of great interest. Catherine Mason's research [8] has in fact shown that Britain's distinctive education system facilitated the development of relationships between art, science and technology between the sixties and the eighties. A legacy of the Victorian education system, Britain's design schools provided both artistic education and training in the applied arts. In the 1950s, the Independent Group addressed, among other things, the implications of science, technology and the mass media on art and

society, culminating in the exhibition *This Is Tomorrow*
(Whitechapel Art Gallery, 1956). In 1953 Richard Hamilton went
to teach at King's College in Newcastle, where, together with
Victor Pasmore, he held a Basic Design course. Among their
students was Roy Ascott, who was encouraged to cultivate his
interest in communication, interactivity and cybernetics.

In 1961, Ascott was asked by the Ealing Art School to create a
two-year course based on the principles of cybernetics: his Ground
Course, along with his subsequent appointments, was to play a
crucial role in the education of a new generation of artists and
designers. In 1967 the first polytechnics appeared, thanks to
sizeable government investments in technology in the post war
period, which also led to the creation of a Ministry of Technology.
In the polytechnics, as Catherine Mason notes, an art student could
also learn programming. In the seventies this led to a wide network
of schools engaged in Computer Art, yielding interesting results
above all in computer graphics for television and advertising. At
the same time, these academic roots enabled students and lecturers
to develop their own creative work, despite the relative lack of
interest in digital art from the art world.

And while British Computer Art survived in the world of
academe, it soon developed systems of support and critical debate.
In 1968, in connection with the British Computer Society, the
Computer Arts Society (CAS) was founded. In 1969, CAS
launched its own publication, *Page*, as a platform for debate and
critical engagement. Equally early on, CAS began to look beyond
the United Kingdom, setting up chapters in various European
countries and coming to the States in 1971. In 1970 the association
had 377 members, including libraries and institutions, in 17
countries. In this period it put together a collection that included
works by pioneers like Manuel Barbadillo, Charles Csuri, Herbert
W. Franke, Edward Ihnatowicz, Ken Knowlton, Manfred Mohr,
Georg Nees, Frieder Nake, Lillian Schwartz and Alan Sutcliffe,

and in 2007, with Mason's involvement, this collection was bought by the Victoria and Albert Museum in London.

Just how receptive the art world of the sixties was to the "art and technology" pairing is also proved by the milieu that sprung up around the distinctive figure of Billy Klüver (1927 – 2004). An electronic engineer of Swedish origin, in 1958 Klüver was hired by Bell Labs in Murray Hill. With a life-long interest in art, in the early seventies he began to work with artists. In 1960 he provided technical support to the Swiss artist Jean Tinguely (after being introduced to him by Pontus Hultén) for his spectacular *Homage to New York* (1960), a kinetic machine that self-destructed in the Sculpture Garden of the MoMA in New York. Robert Rauschenberg was also involved in this project. Following that, Klüver provided technical support to various artists: he worked with Rauschenberg on the installation *Oracle* (1962 – 1965) supplying the artist with remote controlled radios, and he helped Jasper Johns and Andy Warhol, providing the material for the latter's famous *Silver Clouds*, the helium-filled pillows that accompanied his temporary break from painting, presented in a solo show at the Leo Castelli gallery in 1966.

1966 also saw Klüver's first major production, the outcome of a collaboration with Rauschenberg. From 14 to 23 October 1966, at the 69th Regiment Armory in New York, he presented the event *9 Evenings: Theatre and Engineering*, a series of multimedia performances featuring ten artists working with thirty engineers and scientists from Bell Labs. Participants included Robert Rauschenberg, John Cage, David Tudor, Yvonne Rainer, Robert Whitman and Öyvind Fahlström. During the event Klüver discussed the idea of giving this collaboration between artists and engineers more stable foundations, and this was what led to the establishment of Experiments in Arts and Technology (E.A.T.), a no-profit association launched at the start of the following year that promoted collaborations between artists and engineers with both technical and financial input, thanks to ongoing links with the technology industry. By 1969 E.A.T boasted 4,000 members and various chapters throughout the United States. [9]

Klüver's collaborative model was in fact a two-way process: while on one hand he was convinced that technicians could help artists achieve their objectives, on the other he believed that artists, as visionaries and active agents of social change, could influence the development of technology. This is Barbara Rose's take on the matter:

«That aesthetic needs can have practical consequences by introducing new variables into technology signifies that artists may be, potentially, the most useful personnel of future research and development laboratories». [10]

Yet artists remained the central focus of E.A.T., and their point of view prevailed. It is no coincidence that lack of function and criticism of technology were recurrent elements in E.A.T. productions: as Klüver writes in the press release of *9 Evenings*: «All the projects I have worked on have at least one thing in common: from an engineer's point of view they are ridiculous. That is their value.»

E.A.T. debuted in grand style, following *9 Evenings* with the exhibition *Some More Beginnings* (1968) at the Brooklyn Museum in New York, and, for Expo 70 in Osaka (1970), producing the Pepsi Pavilion, [11] an ambitious immersive environment that was ten years ahead of future interest in virtual reality and interactive installations. A significant sample of installations produced by E.A.T. also featured in the 1968 exhibition *The Machine as Seen at the End of the Mechanical Age*, curated by Pontus Hultén for the MoMA in New York. E.A.T.'s activities continued in the 70s and 80s but its projects in that period were considerably less ambitious, at least from an artistic point of view. The association began to pour its energies into social or service projects, like *Children and*

Communication (1972), which enabled the children of New York to communicate by telephone, fax or telex, or the development of a large screen for outdoor television broadcasts for the Pompidou Centre in Paris. As of the 80s E.A.T.'s main occupation was that of documenting and cataloguing its past work: a self-historicization project that culminated in 2000 in the digitalization of its documentary material and subsequently the organization of celebratory events. [12]

The Seventies

If some kind of follow-up had materialized, these early experiments, and the model pursued by E.A.T. – to get acknowledged exponents of the artistic avant-garde working in close contact with engineers, while keeping their respective roles distinct – could feasibly be attributed a key role in the history of contemporary art. So how did it come to pass that the great emphasis placed in the sixties on the "art and technology" pairing by key figures like Jasia Reichardt, Roy Ascott, Billy Klüver, Robert Rauschenberg and Pontus Hultén, as well as Jack Burnham, gradually waned in subsequent years, leaving only the faintest of traces in the official historiography of art? How was it that one of the most significant components of the neo avant-garde ended up as an underground phenomenon, carving out a niche that enabled it to go unnoticed for the next thirty years?

There is no single answer to this question: we must rather look to a series of circumstances that emerged during the seventies. In the first place, in this period the "art and technology" pairing found itself up against ideological and political opposition connected to the military purposes of technological research and the considerable financial interests involved. The Vietnam war, and the protests against it from artistic and intellectual quarters, fuelled opposition to the "art and technology" model. "Technology is what we do to the Black Panthers and Vietnamese", Richard Serra asserted in 1969. [13]

Beyond the political sphere, other academics have highlighted the emergence in the late sixties of "anti-computer" sentiment, bound up with enduring concepts such as the romantic vision of the artists and the fear that technology might supersede the individual and undermine the central role of the artist in the creative act. [14] It has also been observed that the critical model underpinning the acknowledgement of the importance of the "art and technology" pairing has encountered varying fortunes. In a 2007 essay, [15] in line with Jack Burnham, Edward A. Shanken asserts that the hermeneutic approach imposed by Alois Riegl and summed up in the concept of Kunstwollen, quashed the theories of Gottfried Semper, according to whom art reflects "economic, technical and social relationships". In Shanken's opinion, this approach still endures today, helping to keep New Media Art outside the canons of contemporary art.

In the short term, these two prejudices conspired against the operative and interpretative model of the "art and technology" pairing, with a number of significant results: video retired into a niche, despite continuing to have (limited) critical success, above all in works that put formal exploration of the medium in second place, as per the "narcissistic" line plotted by Rosalind Krauss; Kinetic Art and Optical Art, also steeped in technophile rhetoric, vanished completely from the scene, after an initial period of great success, to be rediscovered only relatively recently; even a certain interpretative approach to Conceptual Art – as put forward by Jack Burnham in *Software* (New York, Jewish Museum 1970) and Kynaston McShine in *Information* (New York, MoMA 1970) – that relates conceptual work to the advent of information technologies, surrendered to other approaches with less of a technological vein. As for the nascent field of New Media Art, the collaborative model developed by Klüver was well suited to the organization of one-off events, but less to facilitating continuity in artists' work. Lastly, Computer Art had to come to terms with its aesthetic limitations and the problems involved in actually accessing the machines, which continued to be expensive and bulky.

During the seventies computers became more accessible, albeit gradually. Research into increasingly intuitive forms of man-machine interaction made enormous progress, and in 1969 the first distributed network made its appearance, in the shape of Arpanet. In 1971, thanks to the creation of a common protocol among various university and corporate networks, the internet was born. In parallel to this, alongside the cumbersome mainframes, cheaper, more manageable computers appeared: minicomputers (like the PDP-8, distributed as of 1968); microcomputers, like the famed Altair 8800, distributed as of 1975; and home computers, headed up by the equally legendary Apple II (1977), produced by the start-up Apple Computer (founded by Steve Wozniak and Steve Jobs in 1976).

With the arrival of home computers on the scene, computing branched out of research centers and universities and entered offices and households. A complex, variegated culture sprung up around them, with contributions not only from engineers and high level researchers, but also amateurs and enthusiasts. Many of them had radical political ideas, influenced by Californian counter-culture.

Much of the New Media Art of the seventies was an expression of this complex cultural milieu. In this context it is not easy to identify figures who can be described simply as "artists": most of them worked across the disciplines, researchers and employees of the hi-tech industry with an artistic sideline. Douglas Kahn relates, for example, that the first serious attempt to make music with an Altair 8800 was undertaken between 1970 and 1975 by Ned Lagin, who was doing astronaut training at the MIT, but also studied jazz and composition. This work earned him a temporary collaboration with the Grateful Dead. In the same enclave of enthusiasts in the Bay Area there was Paul De Marinis, who worked with Jim Pomeroy and David Tudor on a number of sound installations before starting out on his own artistic career. [16]

Visual experimentation received impetus from university and corporate circles. In Stanford University in 1970, the Xerox Corporation opened the Palo Alto Research Centre (PARC), devoted to the development of graphic applications; in the same year, General Electric presented Genigraphics, a graphic system designed for the business world, but used extensively by artists. In 1973, the main computing association in the United States, the ACM (Association for Computing Machinery), set up SIGGRAPH, its "Special Interest Group on GRAPHics and Interactive Techniques", which organized its first conference in 1974. From then on SIGGRAPH became the main international showcase for developments in computer graphics. This field was to be heavily influenced by the discovery of fractals, described in 1975 by the French-American mathematician Benoît Mandelbrot, then researcher at IBM, as geometric forms that can be split into parts, each a small scale copy of the whole. [17] Throughout the decade, thanks to institutional and corporate support, research into the algorithmic generation of images thus developed, between the more aesthetically and conceptually conscious work of such artists as Charles Csuri, Manfred Mohr and Vera Molnar on the one hand, and the simple deployment of the productive and aesthetic potential of the new tools on the other.

Something similar happened with robotics. In 1973 at the University of California San Diego (UCSD), Harold Cohen launched the AARON project, which consisted in developing a form of artificial intelligence capable of painting. Having trained as a painter, over the years Cohen attempted to teach AARON the basic rules of painting, developing its "aesthetic tastes" and decision-making power. The painting done by AARON naturally closely resembles that of Cohen, though the machine did gradually develop its own style over time. In Britain Edward Ihnatowicz, who in 1971 began working as a Research Assistant in the Department of Mechanical Engineering at University College in London, produced his most ambitious project, the cybernetic sculpture *The Senster* (1970 – 1974), thanks to a commission from Philips, which exhibited it for four years in its permanent exhibition space in Eindhoven, before dismantling it. The sculpture, a 4 meter aluminium structure controlled by a computer, responded to the voices and movements of viewers.

In the late seventies and early eighties it was above all telecommunications that lent New Media Art a presence and a profile outside of the corporate/university world. While one to one communication systems (like the telephone) and one to many systems (like mail) elicited the attention of the avant-garde movements and Fluxus, before the advent of the Internet satellite broadcasting was the technology that afforded concrete opportunities to explore the field of communications. In 1973, for the first time in history, satellite technology succeeded in broadcasting a cultural event – Elvis Presley's concert in Hawaii – to the whole world. On 29 December 1976, with the support of the Contemporary Arts Museum in Houston, the video artist Douglas Davis broadcast the closing minutes of his performance *Seven Thoughts* to all the IntelSat channels. The following year, thanks to funding from NASA, the Californian artists Kit Galloway and Sherrie Rabinowitz produced *Satellite Arts Project '77,* which connected two NASA centers, one on the East Coast and one on the West Coast, via satellite: images of dancers performing in the two centers were filmed and edited, using a simple chroma-key, to form a single live image. In this way, performers physically 3,000 miles apart could act as if dancing together on the same stage. Dance was adopted as a traditional performing art capable of exploring the limitations and potential of technology. [18]

In the same year Documenta 6, curated by Manfred Schneckenburger, was devoted to means of communication, with the aim of exploring the position of art in the media society. The exhibition presented photography, video and video installations, and opened up to television by means of satellite broadcasts of performances by Davis, Nam June Paik and Joseph Beuys.

The Eighties

It was above all in the 1980s that artistic work on communication gathered pace, extending to telematics too. 1980 saw two major events, the conference *Artists' Use of Telecommunications*, organized by Carl Eugene Loeffler at the Museum of Modern Art in San Francisco, and *Hole in Space*, a public art project by Galloway and Rabinowitz. The former was an international event that connected up participants in different areas of the globe by satellite, Slow-Scan TV (video broadcast via telephone) or telematic network: from the Center for Advanced Visual Studies at the M.I.T. in Cambridge (USA) to Japan's Tsukuba University; from the Alternative Media Center of New York to the Trinity Video and Ontario College of Art in Toronto; from the Western Front Society in Vancouver to the Museum des 20 Jahrhunderts in Vienna. Participants included Robert Adrian, Bill Bartlett, Douglas Davis, Carl Loeffler, David Ross, Aldo Tambellini, Norman White, Gene Youngblood and Peter Weibel. The event highlighted the presence of a solid network of traditional art institutions, research centers and media centers. *Hole in Space,* on the other hand, created a satellite bridge between public areas in two cities (New York and Los Angeles), with large screens installed at the Lincoln Center for the Performing Arts in New York City and the Broadway Department Store in Century

City, Los Angeles, respectively. The screens showed live footage from a camera placed beside each one, enabling people in the street, most of whom were unaware that the event was taking place, to interact with others thousands of miles away. The result was a highly participative, spectacular event, that attracted various audiences who explored different levels of interaction and remote communication: relational aesthetics ante-litteram – but also, as it has been defined on YouTube, "the mother of all video chats".

In 1982 it was the turn of *The World in 24 Hours*, coordinated by Robert Adrian from the Ars Electronica Festival in Linz and featuring a wide range of communications technologies: from phone to fax, Slow-Scan TV and telematic networks, followed in 1983 by *La Plissure du Texte* by Roy Ascott (Paris, Musée d'Art Moderne de la Ville de Paris), a collaborative text produced by various users connected by BBS, and in 1984 by *Good Morning Mr Orwell*, a satellite broadcast of video pieces and live performances coordinated by Nam June Paik and produced by WNET TV in New York in collaboration with the Pompidou Center in Paris, seen by more than 10 million people. All these events reveal both the upsurge in interest from traditional art institutions and the great ferment of the field, with the involvement of both companies and specialized centers, some of which came into being in that very decade.

The interest from traditional art institutions must however be seen in context. The nascent technologies were the hot topic of the day, and it was not difficult to get sponsorship from the hi-tech industry and television networks. By the early eighties the latter enjoyed an unprecedented presence in society, and critical reflections on the media and their power to manipulate were advanced by artists and intellectuals, and reached the public at large (Sidney Lumet's film *Network*, on the power of television, was released in 1976). Moreover, in the decade that saw the return of painting and the explosion of the art market, the institutions took it upon themselves to support less stable, less marketable artistic genres like video, photography and performance.

In other words, while conditions were favorable, the reappearance of New Media Art in the establishment art world during the 1980s was conditioned by external factors and was on the whole too fleeting to lead to lasting continuity. All of this emerges clearly if we consider two key events in this decade: the exhibition *Les Immateriaux*, curated by Jean Francois Lyotard and Thierry Chaput for the Pompidou Center in Paris in 1985; and the 1986 Venice Biennale, coordinated by Maurizio Calvesi and entitled "Art and Science".

The first was not actually an exhibition devoted to the New Media or *art numerique*, as it is known in France. It started life as a project on the "new materials of creativity", but the involvement – at a late stage – of Lyotard transformed it into an exploration of post-modern sensibility. As Lyotard said: «It is not our intention to sum up the new technologies in this exhibition [...] or to explain how they work. All it attempts is to discover and raise a sensibility that is specific to post-modernism, and we assume that it exists already». [19] Its press release described it as a "non-exhibition", and one of its stated aims was to challenge the modern, "prescriptive" model of the exhibition, connected to the 19th century salon and the gallery. In *Les Immateriaux* works were not hung on the walls: cables attached to the floor and ceiling divided up a decentralised setting, which could be explored in various ways. Visitors were given a walkman with the soundtrack of the exhibition, which played according to their position in the venue: this collage of music, sounds and texts, only some of which actually related to the exhibition, aimed to create a powerful sensation of instability. The event also featured works by conceptual and minimal artists, from Joseph Kosuth to Dan Flavin and Robert Ryman, precursors like Marcel Duchamp and Moholy-Nagy, and artists working with communication technologies, such as Roy Ascott and Rolf Gelhaar; yet it was the exhibition itself that was designed "as a work of art", to the point that the actual works on show are rarely mentioned in the numerous comments that the event elicited. [20]

Once again, we are faced with a singular contrast: while on one hand *Les Immateriaux* was of seminal importance for New Media Art, configuring the aesthetic and philosophic categories that were to be its focus in subsequent decades, on the other hand it showed the art crowd that, as Jasia Reichardt commented with regard to *Cybernetic Serendipity*, this area was yet to produce any definitive outcomes, comparable with those of other artistic tendencies, and was as yet mainly to be appreciated for its aspect of research and experimentation.

Similar observations could be made with regard to the 1986 Venice Biennale, where the "Technology and Computing" section curated by Roy Ascott, Don Foresta, Tom Sherman and Tommaso Trini was given a deliberately "workshop" style layout. The central nucleus of this was the Planetary Network, coordinated by Roy Ascott: for three weeks in this workshop in the heart of the Corderie venue, the artists present conducted communicational exchanges of various kinds with other artists in twenty different locations, from Canada to Australia, using three communications protocols: email, fax and Slow-Scan TV. The networking aspect – artists across the globe working together – clearly prevailed over the actual material exchanged: video, images faxed with manual interventions by the artists involved, computer-generated images and texts. According to Ascott, networking and working within a telematic network – with meetings, interactions, negotiations, and visualizations in the electronic arena – was at the core of this show. [21] In the exhibition catalogue, Tom Sherman [22] also returns to the idea of interaction as a founding element of the electronic arts, in an illuminating text that also dwells on their exclusion from the art world in the 1970s and their radical "difference" that continues to make them unpalatable today: their love of machines, feared by the public at large; their propensity for collaborations, which clashes with the rampant careerism of the art world, and the notion of interaction (between artist and machine, between artists via machine, and between machine and public).

The 1986 Biennale was undoubtedly a great platform for New Media Art, which in Venice found a unique opportunity to network and succeeded in exploring a large part of its potential. Around the Planetary Network the event featured the most groundbreaking work in computer graphics, as well as less technological, more amateur images; the "first interactive art videodisc" by Lynn Hershman Leeson; a fascinating installation of sounds and coloured lights by Brian Eno, and the sound environment *Very Nervous System* (1984) by the Canadian David Rokeby: a space controlled by a system of sensors that perceived the presence of the viewer and his or her movements in the area, translated into sounds by a computer.

From the 1980s onwards this vast, variegated scene found its first, privileged point of encounter at the Ars Electronica festival in Linz, Austria. [23] Ars Electronica came about in 1979 as a renewed version of the Bruckner Festival, an event devoted to contemporary music accompanied by an academic symposium. The initial idea was to dedicate the symposium to electronic music. But the involvement of the Austrian Broadcasting Corporation (ORF), directed locally by Hannes Leopoldseder, raised the bar. Leopoldseder proposed going beyond the limits of the symposium and creating a permanent festival devoted to technology and its impact on art and society. On 18 September 1979 the first edition of the Ars Electronica festival opened with a spectacular open-air event, in front of an audience of 100,000. The success of this first edition excited the organisers, who began to think about making it a stable thing. The business model behind it had not yet firmed up, and the following editions, up to 1986, took place on a biennial basis. In the meantime the Austrian artist and curator Peter Weibel joined the artistic committee, and from 1986 the event was scheduled to take place every year, with a common theme for the festival and symposium. 1987 saw the launch of the Prix Ars Electronica, a prize – divided into different categories – that was to play a fundamental role in stimulating creativity, as well as establishing a series of critical and qualitative criteria, and developing a hierarchy of merit within the artistic community. In the early 1990s, feasibility studies were undertaken into founding a permanent center, the Ars Electronica Center in Linz, which got off the ground in 1995, accompanied by Ars Electronica Futurelab. The former was conceived as a "Museum of the Future", gathering and hosting emerging results from the digital medium, while the latter was devoted to production and research, involving artists in courses and workshops and putting the most advanced technologies at their disposal.

As emerges from this brief overview, Ars Electronica and the people involved in it were to play a decisive role in establishing New Media Art world as an independent arena. By stimulating debate, proposing categories and criteria of value, facilitating the production and circulation of works, developing a strategic network with other centers, universities and companies and contributing to the development of an economy and model of sustainability for New Media Art, Ars Electronica became its undisputed mecca. Locally, the Ars Electronica model was made possible by the fact that the post-industrial city of Linz was attempting to reinvent itself as the cultural and technological capital of Austria and central Europe. But its success was above all linked to the existence of a flourishing art scene in search of a stable platform for producing and exhibiting its work, not linked to one-off events like the aforementioned 1986 Biennale, and to the slow but ongoing development of an alternative system of festivals and centers like V2_, launched in Hertogenbosch, Holland in 1981 before moving to Rotterdam in 1994, where it stages a biennial festival called the Dutch Electronic Art Festival (DEAF).

All these developments are obviously a product of the inexorable progress of technology, which was gradually seeping into everyday life. After the Apple II, various models of home computer appeared on the market: from the Atari 400 to the Commodore VIC-20, the first computer to achieve sales of over a million; from the Sinclair ZX Spectrum to the Commodore 64 and the IBM PC. In 1984, Apple Computer launched the Macintosh, a genuine revolution in the history of the personal computer: relatively cheap (at almost 2,500 dollars), the computer functioned with keyboard and mouse, and featured a graphic interface that replaced the customary green text against a black background. This graphic interface heralded the introduction of common metaphors inspired by the world of the office that the computer was destined for: desktop, wastebasket, windows, files and documents. Lastly, the computer featured a modem, a device that enabled it to connect up to a telematic network via a simple telephone line. Telematic networks also began to spread, and while Internet remained mainly linked to the American university system, some countries (like France with Minitel) created a national network, and on an amateur level BBS (Bulletin Board Systems) took off. These computer systems functioned like electronic noticeboards, with users connecting to them to share or download files and exchange messages. BBS technology first appeared in 1977 and became popular above all thanks to Fidonet, (invented by the American Tom Jennings in 1984), a network of different BBS.

But computing did not make its way into households (and the everyday lives of millions) only by means of home computers and networks. In 1961 the MIT labs created *Spacewar!*, the first videogame in history. It did not take long for the business world to realise that this very basic interactive interface could be the start of a profitable sector of cultural entertainment. In the second half of the 1970s arcade games took off, along with the first home platforms for videogames. From *Pong* (1972) to *Space Invaders* (1978) and *Pacman* (1980), the videogames industry expanded exponentially, and the advent in 1983 of the NES (Nintendo Entertainment System) was to make an indelible mark on the collective consciousness.

These developments had conspicuous consequences on the cultural sphere. The 1980s were the decade of hackers, cyberpunk, basic telematics, virtual reality and the start of the free software movement: phenomena which are too complex to be explored in detail here. Cyberpunk, for example, came about as a literary movement in the United States in the early 80s, thanks to the science fiction successes of William Gibson and Bruce Sterling, and the rediscovery of Philip K. Dick, but in Italy it developed as a political movement, attaching onto the substrate of punk, the ferment of the social centers and the left-wing protest movements in 1977. [24] Likewise in California, where a pivotal role was played by figures like Timothy Leary, exponent of counterculture and advocate for psychedelic drugs, who went on to develop videogames, use BBS and become a leading figure of "cyberculture", and scholar of virtual reality. Both the hacker movement and the Free Software philosophy were rooted in this complex milieu.

Artists played an active role in shaping this culture, and enriching its imagery with their works. It is often difficult, if not impossible, to separate the art from the context it is an active, integral part of. The association between New Media and New Media Art formed in the previous decades, but consolidated in the 1980s. This arose perhaps because on one hand, these artists were excluded from – or deliberately avoided – traditional artistic contexts, and on the other because there was a proliferation of hybrid, multidisciplinary figures who did not separate their art from their political activism, or their contribution to the network. In 1986, reviewing an Italian festival, Vittorio Fagone wrote about a "third culture", distinguishing digital culture from humanistic and scientific culture: a culture in which «engineers, mathematicians, information technologists, architects, musicians and artists (or, if we wish, "visual operators") and graphic designers live and work together, often exchange not roles but models and objectives. Electronic art occupies this space». [25]

In parallel, the system of relationships, events and production centers that conveyed and supported "electronic art", also firmed up. While in previous decades New Media Art was rooted in the universities and research centers, in the 80s New Media Art became an independent "art world" in its own right and laid the foundations for its continued existence. On the networks debate was conveyed above all on the BBS, while in the real world New Media Art was distributed at temporary events like technology and electronic art festivals, in line with the Linz model. Towards the end of the decade the first "New Media Centers" appeared, really taking off in the early 90s. The advent of these new distribution channels outside of the traditional art world gave the "third culture" fairly sound foundations in terms of visibility, critical debate and preservation. Yet in this regard Italy remained a fairly isolated case. Despite the presence of an active, vibrant art scene (with artists and groups like Tommaso Tozzi, the Giovanotti Mondani Meccanici, Correnti Magnetiche, Mario Canali, Studio Azzurro, Giacomo Verde and, later on, Piero Gilardi and Maurizio Bolognini), the lack of institutional involvement led to a proliferation of autonomous, isolated initiatives, the result of voluntary efforts by curators like Mario Costa and Maria Grazia Mattei, conducted mostly in private venues or peripheral institutional settings. Even now Italy has no Media Centers, and its few active festivals struggle to make a name for themselves internationally.

The Early Nineties

1989 is a pivotal year in terms of gaining insight into the subsequent fate of New Media Art, and could indeed be taken as the symbolic date in its process of institutionalisation. The initial setting for this was Europe, where specialized institutions (art centers, museums, workshops, archives and festivals) flourished at an unprecedented rate. It was in 1989 that the ZKM (Zentrum für Kunst und Medientechnologie) of Karlsruhe (Germany) was founded, a center that could, broadly-speaking, be seen as the leader of this process. In the same year the fall of the Berlin Wall and the Soviet empire opened an entirely new season, for art too. Russia, together with the countries of Eastern Europe, was obliged to speedily institutionalize contemporary art, which to date had been developing in unofficial situations like squats and private homes. This process was heavily influenced by the billionaire philanthropist George Soros with his Soros Centers of Contemporary Art (SCCA).

As Lioudmila Voropai writes, [26] there were some interesting aspects to this process of institutionalization. In the first place, New Media Art had always stressed its "social utility" and contribution to the creative development of the New Media, thus adding to the legacy of confusion between the development of the medium and its use for artistic purposes, between "New Media" and "New Media Art". This confusion was accompanied by the ambiguous and conflictual relationship between New Media Art and contemporary art, and was indeed one of the reasons behind the conflict: the social utility of New Media Art implicitly opposed the non-utility of contemporary art, which not coincidentally bases its economy on a luxury market.

«On the one hand, Media Art intended to be integrated as a subsystem into the art system. On the other hand, its discourse of legitimisation – i.e. Media Art is "more than just art" – led

to its actual 'art qualities' being sacrificed to endless technological 'try-outs' and experiments. With the result, that Media Art has obtained an image of being "insufficient" art».

The conflict between the two became even more pronounced when they were made to coexist in the same institution. The institution in question was the ZKM, the very notion of which speaks volumes about the nature of the relationship between contemporary art and New Media Art in the early 1990s. The two different art worlds coexist here, like a separated couple still sharing the same roof, thanks to an apparently virtuous division into a series of "institutes" and departments, coordinated since 1999 by the director Peter Weibel: the Museum of Contemporary Art, founded in 1999 and also a venue for temporary exhibitions; the Media Museum, which has a permanent, and unique, collection of "interactive media art", accompanied in recent years by a number of "permanent exhibitions" on the latest developments in New Media Art; the Institute for Visual Media, the center's "research and development" division (founded and directed by the artist Jeffrey Shaw until 2003); the Institute for Music and Acoustics, the Institute for Media, Education, and Economics, and the Filminstitute.

In reality the ZKM only opened its premises, in a converted industrial area, in 1997, but it prepared the terrain with a series of temporary initiatives, like the Multimedia festival of 1989. Its vocation, linked to the orientation of its director (or rather the duo Weibel – Shaw) and its origins in the early 90s, made it into a temple for the interactive, immersive and technologically groundbreaking installations of the last decade of the century, so much so that in Europe the expression "ZKM art" is normally used, tongue in cheek, to refer to this kind of art. [27]

Criticism aside, the ZKM has the undisputed merit of being the first in the 90s to raise the question of the "museification" of New Media Art, and issues related to how to preserve it and create a canon, in this way establishing a model for other international players, like Tokyo's Intercommunication Center (ICC), founded in 1990 and given a permanent venue in 1997.

Back in Europe, we have already seen how in the 90s various long-standing institutions like Ars Electronica and V2_ reinforced their position. In the Netherlands sizeable institutional investments in the new media led to the foundation in 1990 of the Inter-Society for the Electronic Arts, or ISEA, that organizes the International Symposium on Electronic Art. This association, which moved its headquarters to Montreal in Québec from 1996 to 2001, before returning to Holland, has an extremely international outlook, as evinced by the itinerant nature of the symposium, always staged in a different location.

In Germany, the Institute for New Media (INM) in Frankfurt was set up in 1989 as an experimental workshop in the context of the Art School, before evolving into an independent research platform for post-graduate students. 1988 saw the founding in Britain of the FACT in Liverpool (then known as Moviola), which remains the country's most important New Media Art institution.

These are just a few examples on an international panorama in constant expansion. In this context it is inevitable to take a brief look at what was going on in Eastern Europe, not only for the significant contribution it gave to the development of New Media Art in the 90s, but because what went on there in the space of a decade appears to encapsulate the entire history of New Media Art.

In Eastern Europe, up to the 90s, avant-garde art existed entirely outside of the institutional sphere. The Open Society Institute & Soros Foundation Network was the first to make a serious move in this direction. As of 1991 SCCAs were set up in 17 former Soviet block countries. These were relatively short-lived: in 1999, after the Soros foundations were restructured, all the SCCAs became independent non-governmental organizations. For many of them this meant tackling the crucial issue of funding, not always an easy task where public funds for culture were in relatively short supply. But some managed to survive.

Supporting New Media Art was one of the key missions of the SCCAs. This came about because in an area where the personal computer was still a rarity and a status symbol, the social utility of the centers lay in their ability to guarantee the population (and the artists) access to the network and the new technologies. In post-socialist countries there was no tradition of New Media Art: information technology was linked to military uses and scientific research, and the embargo which followed the war with Afghanistan effectively prevented Western-made technologies from arriving in Russia. Yet the networking that got under way, and the widespread use of the network, enabled New Media Art to flourish.

In 1993 the SCCA in Moscow set up its New Media Art Laboratory, led by Alexei Isaev and Olga Shishko. In 1994 the artist Alexei Shulgin established the Moscow-WWW-Art-Lab, and in the same year Gallery 21, a no-profit venue in the famous quarter of Pushkinaskaya 10 – a squat converted into an art center – opened its doors in St. Petersburg. Leaving Russia, Budapest saw the opening of the C3, the Center for Culture and Communication, which is still up and running, and which combined the traditional functions of an art center with teaching activities, holding courses and workshops on Internet and the new technologies, while Ljubljana opened the Ljudmila Digital Media Lab, promoting festivals and events, and supporting the artistic activities of Vuk Ćosić, one of the pioneers of Net Art.

As Voropai notes, the post-Soros era began during the golden age of New Media Art in the West. 1999 was the year of *net_condition*, a travelling exhibition organised by the ZKM, which opened the season of the major museum exhibitions, destined to continue – above all in the States – until 2002. In Russia the decline of the New Media institutions gave rise to a difficult situation. The affirmation of an uncertain, poorly regulated art market, buoyed up by the new rich, who saw art as a way of laying claim to elite status, did not favour New Media Art, which was held – rightly or wrongly – to be an institutional art form.

«These days in Russia –Voropai explains – it's not easy to find an artist who would explicitly call himself a media artist. Those from the old media art guard who didn't completely sink from the art scene into advertising agencies, TV productions and so on, continue to produce artworks, which do not need the label "media art" to be sold at the art market.»

This is the situation that has come to pass, in a more recent period, and with the same dynamics, in the West. Here the development of a system of New Media Art, by means of the dynamics we have attempted to illustrate, has gone hand in hand with increasing interest from traditional artistic institutions. Yet the latter tend to be uninterested in the underground tradition of New Media Art, and focus their attention on its most recent results, connected to the mass spread of digital technologies and the advent of the web in the second half of the 90s.

Indeed at the start of the decade there were as yet few artists using "domestic" technologies with some degree of awareness, to make art: figures like the Italian Maurizio Bolognini, who in the early 1990s produced installations in a highly conceptual vein by reprogramming and "sealing" personal computers in such a way that their vitality and continued functioning, perceptible as a monotonous hum, could be detected but not visualised through any output devices; [28] or like the German artist Wolfgang Staehle, who in New York in 1991 used various BBS to found *The Thing*, conceived as a "social sculpture" à la Beuys. And while home computing remained the main arena for the formation of the digital cultures of the 90s, at the start of the decade New Media Art focused above all on immersive systems and virtual reality, telepresence and interactivity (with figures like Jeffrey Shaw, David Rokeby, Paul Sermon and, back in Italy, Mario Canali, Piero Gilardi and Studio Azzurro), technological prostheses and robotics (Eduardo Kac, Stelarc), and 3D graphics and generative algorithms (Karl Sims). But this work involved the use of cutting edge technologies, and was too focused on the latest developments in technology and too detached from the developments in contemporary art in that period to be properly interesting in this context.

With the advent of the World Wide Web (Mosaic, the first commercial browser, appeared in 1994), and the mass distribution of the personal computer (1995), this situation changed radically. The computers of the 90s were cheap and featured an intuitive interface; anyone, with a minimum of instruction (which was often undertaken in universities, in the workplace or, for the young generations, by means of videogames) could use them. Processing text, modifying images, and creating sound and video files were relatively simple matters. At the same time the web gave the internet network a multimedia, hypertext interface based on a programming language (html), the basics of which can be picked up in a few days. Making art with a computer no longer required technological training, access to research labs, collaborations with engineers and professionals. Anyone could do it, and not necessarily to make art that was accessible only via computer. So while on one hand computers could be used by any artist, they could also be employed by anyone wishing to exploit the extraordinary communicative, aesthetic and narrative potential of the web. Net Art came about in this very way. It was no longer a question of creating the finest image possible with a given tool, or generating an immersive interface, but about exploring and subverting an elementary language, creating a short circuit in communication, infiltrating a global communications medium. The first net artists did not come from the New Media Art of previous years, but from photography (Alexei Shulgin), post-conceptual art (Vuk Ćosić), film (Olia Lialina), street art (Heath Bunting), painting (Mark Napier) and video (Jodi); they had an artistic, rather than a technological training; some turned to the web out of frustration with the contemporary art world, others were fresh out of art school, and others had links with political activism, which in that very period was beginning to realise the web's unprecedented potential for media impact (Ricardo Dominguez). Net Art was ironic, subversive and played with the limits of meaning; it looked to the avant-garde and neo avant-garde movements; it practiced pastiche, collage and linguistic games, and it was the output of an era of cultural production that eliminated the difference between original and copy.

Net Art originated between 1995 and 1997. In 1997 Documenta, one of the most important dates in the contemporary art calendar, had a section devoted to Net Art. The year before, the Swiss collective etoy won a Golden Nica at the Prix Ars Electronica, in the "World Wide Web" category, for the work *Digital Hijack*, a spectacular operation of search engine manipulation that diverted hundreds of thousands of internet users onto their site. [29] In the "Computer Animation" category, the first prize went to Pixar, for the animated movie *Toy Story* (1995), the first movie produced entirely using computer graphics. In the photograph that commemorates the event, an etoy agent with a shaved head and mirror sunglasses, in an orange jacket and black trousers, shares the stage with Japanese interactive artist Masaki Fujihata, Canadian electroacoustic music composer Robert Normandeau, and writer and film director Pete Docter from Pixar: they are all smiling, but they seem to be wondering what they are doing on the same stage. And the question is by no means irrelevant: while 1989 was the key year for consolidating the New Media Art world, 1997 was the *annus horribilis* of the split between the art and its world: the moment when so called "new media artists" started wondering what they had in common, besides the medium and their under-recognition by mainstream art worlds.

The events that we have described, from the eighties onwards, appear to be entirely concentrated in Europe. So what was going on with the States, the homeland of the new technologies and the first artistic experiments in this direction? Lev Manovich accounts for [30] the American delay on this front with two simple considerations. In the first place, the rapidity with which the new technologies were assimilated in the States made them invisible in a very short space of time. In other words, in the US there was no hiatus between the arrival of a new technology and its normalization, the hiatus that enables artists to develop a critical distance from the medium. Secondly, Manovich blames the lack of institutional support, at least compared to areas like Western Europe, Australia and Japan, where the New Media Art world leaned heavily on public funding in the 80s and 90s. In the States the art world is market-driven, and in that context an artistic practice that had always professed its unsaleability had trouble getting by for many years.

This, at least, was the case until the late 90s, when the situation changed completely. Universities and art schools set up courses and programs of New Media Art and New Media Design; prestigious academic publishers like the MIT Press began producing books on the subject; renowned institutions like the Princeton Institute for Advanced Studies, the Rockefeller Foundation and the Social Science Research Council set about organizing conferences, prizes and funding, and the major contemporary art museums, from the Whitney Museum of American Art in New York to MoMA, from the San Francisco Museum of Modern Art to the Walker Art Center in Minneapolis to the Guggenheim in New York, together with numerous university museums, got involved with exhibitions, programs and curatorial positions. Even some private galleries, like the Postmasters Gallery in New York, staged solo and group shows of New Media Art. Various no-profit organizations (often led by artists) also appeared, along with specialized institutions like Eyebeam in New York, while existing structures like the Electronic Arts Intermix (EAI) founded by Howard Wise in 1971 and mainly focussed on video, opened up more substantially to the digital media. In other words, interest in New Media Art exploded in the States at a period in which the New Media sector was gaining financial thrust, and New Media Art was becoming financially and technically sustainable for any artist.

This phenomenon, however, was fairly short-lived: after the collapse of the New Economy, and the consequent disappearance of the funding that had boosted interest in it, the enthusiasm of American museum system cooled off considerably. At this point the American New Media Art scene was faced with two alternatives, both of which it explored. On one hand it attempted to tackle the arduous task of integrating into the contemporary art system and its market. On the other it looked to Europe with interest, attempting to come up with an alternative model for survival that would enable it to preserve its specific characteristics.

Notes

[1] In John Brockman, *Digerati. Encounters with the CyberElite*, HardWired, New York 1996, p. xxiii.

[2] For more on early computer art, check out Wolf Lieser, *The World of Digital Art*, h.f.ullmann, Potsdam 2010.

[3] Cf. Douglas Kahn, "Between a Bach and a Bard Place: Productive Constraint in Early Computer Arts", in Oliver Grau (ed.), *Media Art Histories*, MIT Press (Leonardo Books), Cambridge, Massachusetts and London, England, 2007, pp. 422 – 451.

[4] Ibid., p. 427.

[5] Ivi.

[6] Brent MacGregor, "Cybernetic Serendipity Revisited", undated (2008), online at http://design.osu.edu/carlson/history/PDFs/cyberserendipity.pdf (last visit March 2013).

[7] Ivi.

[8] Cf. Catherine Mason, *A computer in the Art Room: the Origins of British Computer Arts 1950 – 80*, Norfolk, JJG Publishing 2008.

[9] Billy Klüver, "E.A.T. – Archive of published documents", 2000, online at www.fondation-langlois.org/html/e/page.php?NumPage=306 (last visit March 2013).

[10] Cit. in Branden W. Joseph, "Engineering Marvel: Branden W. Joseph on Billy Klüver", in *Artforum*, March 2004.

[11] Cf. Billy Klüver, J. Martin, Barbara Rose (eds.), *Pavilion: Experiments in Art and Technology*, New York, E. P. Dutton 1972.

[12] E.A.T.'s archives are now available on the website of the Daniel Langlois Foundation for Art, Science, and Technology, based in Montreal (Canada), which actively contributed to their digitalization.

[13] Cf. Anne Collins Goodyear, "From Technophilia to Technophobia: The Impact of the Vietnam War on the Reception of "Art and Technology"", in *Leonardo*, April 2008, Vol. 41, No. 2, pp. 169-173; and Sylvie Lacerte, "Experiments in Art and Technology: a Gap to Fill in Art History's Recent Chronicles", in *Refresh!*, September 2008, online at www.fondation-langlois.org/html/e/page.php?NumPage=1716 (last visit March 2013).

[14] Cf. Taylor Grant, "How Anti-Computer Sentiment Shaped Early Computer Art", in *Refresh!*, September 2008.

[15] Edward A Shanken, "Historicizing Art and Technology: Forging a Method and Firing a Canon", in Oliver Grau (ed.), *Media Art Histories*, cit., p. 48.

[16] Cf. Douglas Kahn, cit., pp. 440 and following.

[17] Cf. Benoît B. Mandelbrot, *The Fractal Geometry of Nature*, New York, W. H. Freeman and Co., 1982.

[18] Cf. Annmarie Chandler, "Animating the Social. Mobile Image / Kit Galloway and Sherrie Rabinowitz", in Annmarie Chandler e Norie Neumark (eds.), *At a Distance. Precursors to Art and Activism on the Internet*, The MIT Press, Cambridge, Massachusetts and London, England 2005 [2006], pp. 153 – 174.

[19] Cit. in Tilman Baumgärtel, "Immaterial Material: Physicality, Corporality, and Dematerialization in Telecommunication Artworks", in Annmarie Chandler e Norie Neumark (eds.), *At a Distance...*, cit., p. 63.

[20] Cf. Bernard Blistène, "Les Immatériaux: A Conversation with Jean-François Lyotard", in *Flash Art*, Issue 121, March 1985, available online at www.kether.com/words/lyotard/index.html (last visit March 2013).

[21] Cf. Roy Ascott, "Arte, tecnologia e computer", in AAVV, *XLII Esposizione Internazionale d'Arte La Biennale di Venezia. Arte e scienza. Biologia / Tecnologia e informatica*, exhibition catalogue, Electa, Venezia 1986, p. 33.

[22] Tom Sherman, "Amare la macchina è naturale", in AAVV, *XLII Esposizione Internazionale d'Arte...*, cit., pp. 43 – 45.

[23] Cf. Hannes Leopoldseder, Christine Schöpf, Gerfried Stocker, *1979 – 2004 Ars Electronica*, Hatje Cantz Verlag 2004.

[24] Cf. Tatiana Bazzichelli, *Networking. The Net As Artwork*, Digital Aesthetics Research Center, Aarhus University 2008. Available for download at http://darc.imv.au.dk/wp-content/files/networking_bazzichelli.pdf (last visit March 2013).

[25] Vittorio Fagone, in *VideoMagazine*, 1986. Cit. in Tatiana Bazzichelli, *Networking...*, cit., p. 95.

[26] Lioudmila Voropai, "Institutionalisation of Media Art in the Post-Soviet Space: The Role of Cultural Policy and Socioeconomic Factors", in *Re:place*, November 2007, online at http://pl02.donau-uni.ac.at/jspui/handle/10002/449 (last visit March 2013).

[27] Cf. Inke Arns, in "Media Art Undone", conference panel at transmediale07, Berlin, February 3, 2007. Full transcript of the presentations is available here: www.mikro.in-berlin.de/wiki/tiki-index.php?page=MAU (last visit March 2013).

[28] Cf. AAVV, *Maurizio Bolognini. Infinito personale*, Edizioni Nuovi Strumenti

2007.

[29] Cf. Nico Piro (ed.), *Etoy – Cyberterrorismo. Come si organizza un rapimento virtuale*, Castelvecchi, Roma 1998.

[30] Lev Manovich, "New Media from Borges to HTML", cit.

Two Worlds Compared

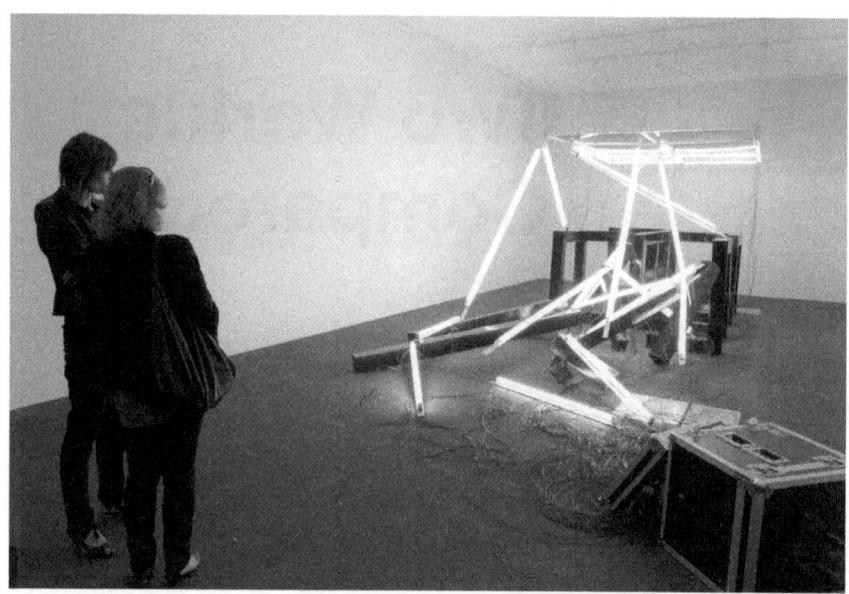

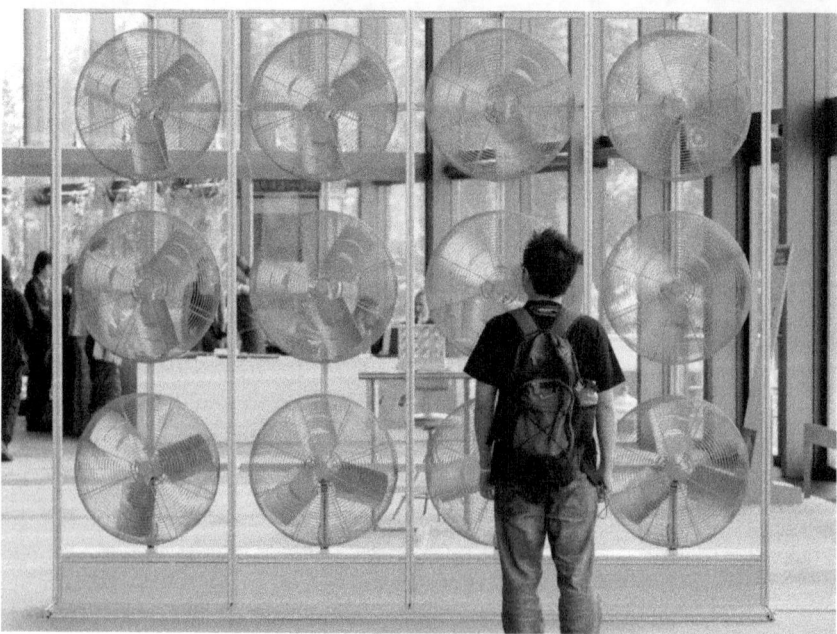

Top: Art Unlimited 2009. Courtesy of Art Basel. Bottom: Scott Snibbe, *Blow Up*, 2005. Interactive installation, Ars Electronica 2005. Source: rubra. Courtesy Ars Electronica Archive.

«If you are going to call yourself an artist then talk in the language of an artist. Too many in new media have forgotten this». Warren Neidich [1]

The 1990s witnessed the advent of an artistic practice that straddled the contemporary art world and the New Media Art world; a practice that was a paid-up member of the latter but has recently developed characteristics that makes it suitable for the former, along with a keen desire to overcome the distinction between the two. Both worlds have their positives and negatives; both have to mediate between conservative tendencies and innovative energies, and in both, as the critics Inke Arns and Jacob Lillemose write, «forces are working against an integration of the two worlds that actually both would benefit from». [2]

This chapter sets out to compare and contrast these two worlds. The comparison is based on a number of conceptual nodes summed up by Howard S. Becker in his book *Art Worlds*: the idea of art that a given art world is based on, the type of artist who thrives there, the system for attributing value to works of art, the level of tolerance for and openness to ideas that stray from the classic canons. Some simplification is inevitable: in any system there are rules that guarantee its specific nature, while exceptions make it permeable and adaptable to a topic, art, which is impossible to pin down and ever-changing.

The introduction of a third section, regarding the internet, is necessary because the advent of the internet and consumer electronics formed a seedbed for the mutant gene that led to the artistic practice that engages with the new media becoming a practice that shifts between the two worlds, going beyond and spilling over the confines of both.

A useful starting point for our comparison is the distinction introduced by Lev Manovich in a 1997 text, between Duchamp Land (the contemporary art world) and Turing Land (the New Media Art world). [3] According to Manovich, the canonical art object of Duchamp Land displays the following characteristics: it is "content-oriented", be that content beauty, "metaphors for the human condition", rule breaking, etc; it is "complicated", in the sense that understanding the object involves using various cultural codes and adopting an irreverent, post-modern stance; it is ironic, self-referential and often adopts a destructive approach to the material it uses.

Vice versa, the canonical art object of Turing Land is held to display entirely opposite characteristics: it is technology oriented, or rather oriented at experimenting with the latest technologies available on the market; it is simple and mainly lacking in irony, and it takes the technology it uses very seriously – thus being closer to the computer industry than art.

Dwelling on this last point, Manovich goes on to note that Turing Land hardly ever reflects on the limitations of the machine, its flaws and crashes; here computers are required to work, and when they do not the result is shock (like at an industrial demonstration), rather than being interpreted as a "marvellous Dadaist accident". Manovich notes that some artists are starting to work on this, but he does not believe that the art of Turing Land will ever spill over into Duchamp Land, because the latter «wants art, not research into new aesthetic possibilities of new media».

Manovich's mistake lies in confusing the idea of art supported by Turing Land with the artistic practice that actually manifests itself there. In 1997 this was as yet a pardonable error, given that much New Media Art in that period had no problem describing itself as "research into new aesthetic possibilities of new media"; but it became a cardinal sin in 2003, when Manovich, writing about Ars Electronica, developed similar ideas. [4] That was the period when the dissociation between the idea of art supported by contexts like Ars Electronica, and the idea of art implicit in much of the "New Media Art" of the day was in full swing.

Contemporary Art: the Idea of Art

As Arthur Danto wrote, [5] from the sixties onwards (namely from the acceptance of the new "paradigm" introduced by Marcel Duchamp in the 1910s with his first readymades) anything and everything could be art, as long as there was an internal reason for which a given thing should be considered art. Identifying this reason, however, is not always easy. Francesco Bonami, in a book that sets out to explain to the man in the street "why contemporary art really is art", spectacularly fails in this mission by adopting oblique strategies that constantly avoid the question. In the introduction, Bonami explains that to understand a work of art «all you need is an open-minded approach», curiosity and courage, and that the important thing in art is not the technique, but the idea, which has to be "new" and "right": «The important thing, in any case and if possible before others get there before you, is to think the right thing at the right time». [6] Yet Bonami does not explain the concept of "new". In this complete absence of rules, the only one that appears to withstand scrutiny, and that Bonami returns to frequently, is the central role of the idea. The "right idea", "good contents", is the only thing that links Duchamp, who «learned how to generate hot air better than others», and the "reactionary" art of Lucian Freud, who paints «as if Duchamp and Warhol had never existed».

I have mentioned Bonami's dumbed-down aesthetics, rather than more structured theories, because I think it reveals something significant about the arena we are analyzing. One of the most renowned international critics and curators, Bonami does not seem to base his work on a specific "idea of art". He seems to operate more like a water-diviner, who can see art where others cannot – and is almost always in the right place. Obviously this is possible because when Bonami makes his choice, he has the authority and the means to impose it as the "right" choice to other members of the art world: a consideration that implies a contextual definition of art, according to which art is art because there is a surrounding context that says it is. As Blais and Ippolito explain, [7] this idea is nothing more than intellectual provocation (that of Duchamp) turned intellectual inertia (that of today's art world). If a work of art is defined by its aura, and if in the age of its technical reproducibility that aura is no longer an integral part of it, the process of "conferring" that aura – namely the work of critics, museums, gallerists and dealers – does not follow but actually precedes the recognition of an object as a work of art. Art is art because critics write about it, museums exhibit it and collectors collect it, not vice versa; the aura is the *consequence* of this intellectual attention, the interest of the museums, the investments made by collectors, and so on, rather than the cause. [8]

This theory, which crops up not infrequently among both those within the art world, and those criticizing it from the outside, is undoubtedly an enthralling one. Also because, once embraced, it is very easy to find evidence to back it up, and very difficult to find arguments against it. By way of example, it is all too easy to look at Damien Hirst, one of the stars of today's art world, and see the results of canny investments made by an advertising mogul (Charles Saatchi), an extremely solid art world (the English establishment), an unprecedented eye for business (that of the artist) and the concerted efforts of museums, collectors, galleries, critics and curators. It is more difficult to explain why his colored dots mesmerize us, why his butterfly wings fascinate us and why his pharmacies and animals in formaldehyde embody our angst more than many other present day works of art. In other words, it is more difficult to understand whether we would have recognised these pieces as works of art before the art world lent them an aura, variously boosted by the torrents of words used to describe them, the floods of money spent on buying them and the sacral ambiance of the white cube.

This problem obviously arises from the weak nature of the few attempts that have been made to come up with a definition of art that transcends the contextual theory. Bonami's "theory of the right idea" encapsulates this weakness fairly well. Even a vastly more sophisticated theory, like that of the philosopher Mario Perniola (2000) does not seem to yield the results hoped for. Today «we consider it "natural" that some objects are works of art and that some people are artists; any other question seems superfluous», [9] Perniola writes. But just what is it, aside from economic worth and communicative value, that makes art art?

According to the philosopher, the answer to this question lies in *art's shadow*, «a shady form which contains the most unsettling and enigmatic elements that belong to it». Yet Perniola refuses to define this shadow, conscious that by nature it «disappears when exposed to the light». We can at best identify only a few components of that shadow – the "splendour of the real", the "sex appeal of the inorganic", the "logic of dissent". But shedding light on it necessarily means making it vanish.

What seems to emerge from all these "weak" theories is the need for strong contents, art's ability to home in on an issue, objectivize it and present it for our analysis. This also gives rise to prejudice against media specificity, and art that is not "just art". This prejudice is linked on one hand to the "damnatio memoriae" that struck Clement Greenberg in the States, and on the other to the fact that art appears to have entered a "postmedia" phase that best manifests itself in multimedia installations, and the nomadic shifting between different media that characterizes the work of many artists. In particular, according to Rosalind Krauss, medium specificity was overcome around the 1970s, on one hand by Marcel Broodthaers with his "eagle principle", that «simultaneously implodes the idea of an aesthetic medium and turns everything equally into a readymade that collapses the difference between the aesthetic and the commodified»; [10] and on the other by video that, sharing the «television's "constitutive heterogeneity"», proclaimed the end of medium specificity. «In the age of television, so it broadcast – Krauss writes – we inhabit a post-medium condition». [11] Which does not mean that staying with one medium is inappropriate, or that exploring the specific characteristics of that medium is a cardinal sin. Krauss tries to explain this in another essay, significantly entitled "Reinventing the medium". According to Krauss, a medium can be rediscovered and reinvented by artists in the post-medium phase when it has fallen into obsolescence: not to explore its creative and aesthetic potential, but to examine it as a "theoretical object" of art. [12]

Contemporary Art: the Artist

In *Remainder*, the first novel by the English artist and writer Tom McCarthy, the main character has survived an accident, followed by a grueling rehabilitation process, that has left him with partial memory loss, but compensation of several million pounds. With this money the character attempts relentlessly to regain the authenticity of some brief episodes of his past and present life by faithfully reconstructing and reenacting them. His first project involves reproducing the atmosphere of a house he believes he has lived in. The setting is reconstructed in great detail (down to the cracks in the walls, the black cats on the roof in front, the sounds and the smells), and various "reenactors" are hired full-time to enable him to relive these moments whenever he feels like it. This is followed by other "projects", staged with the involvement of hundreds of professionals and "reenactors": the obsessive reconstruction of a minor accident he once had in a gas station, a murder, a bank robbery. All of this is done to enable him to relive the tingling feeling he experiences when authenticity is achieved.

At one point someone asks him: «Does he, perhaps, [...] consider himself to be some kind of artist?» To which he replies: «No. I wasn't any good at art. In school». [13] These lines are telling. They reveal that today's art is not something you learn at school, and is not necessarily associated with traditional artistic techniques. They also say that art is something visionary and gratuitous; it is not to do with objects, but projects, and it does not produce anything of use, but requires total dedication, generous funds and the involvement of many different kinds of professionals.

The artist figure that emerges from this picture is still firmly anchored to the romantic vision of the genius, obviously updated to today's standards. Figures like Olafur Eliasson, who created waterfalls cascading down the struts of New York's bridges, and Matthew Barney, who spent five years of his life producing an unprecedented cycle of films, conceived in its entirety as a sophisticated allegory of male genitalia, embody this idea to perfection. The romantic genius acquires celebrity status, and is required to be an excellent entrepreneur of him or herself: think of figures like Damien Hirst, Maurizio Cattelan and Francesco Vezzoli, and further back Jeff Koons and Andy Warhol. If we descend gradually from art's lofty pinnacles into the complex, variegated fauna of artists, many of these aspects fade away, but the one constant, the one thing we always expect from an artist, is absolute devotion to a project, an idea. With this one lodestar established, everything else is up for discussion, renegotiation. The mythos of complete freedom also admits the option of choosing an entirely reactionary path – that of manual skill, technical prowess, obsessively nurturing a single language. Artists can hide their identities behind a pseudonym or a collective: in this way an academic painter like John Currin can rub shoulders with the likes of Jeff Koons, who has skilled craftsman producing his marble busts. And while the latter, who places himself at the center of many of his works, explores – and reinforces – the cult of the personality of the artist, in contemporary art it is not difficult to come across collaborative platforms, in which individual contributions merge into collective output: the existence of collectives like the Indian RAQS Media Collective – a platform that operates on an artistic, critical and curatorial level – comes as no surprise.

Contemporary Art: the Confines

In *Mercanti d'aura*, Alessandro Dal Lago and Serena Giordano assert that the notion of "purpose" represents an insurmountable barrier to an object being a work of art. If an object has a purpose, it cannot be art, because art serves no purpose; it exists unto itself. And the writers go one further, maintaining that objects created to serve a purpose (therefore the products of worlds such as that of fashion, design and the entire cultural industry) possess disturbing properties that make opposition to them particularly vehement. These objects disturb us because they are artworks in all respects, but also «services marked by the stigma of subordinate work». [14]

This theory is undoubtedly a fairly convincing one. Conceived by the aesthetes of the late nineteenth century, the idea of art for art's sake has stayed with us, in various different forms, in the art and criticism of the twentieth century. Yet continuing to envisage the world of contemporary art as an ivory tower under constant threat from base, secondary practices, is frankly anachronistic. All of the arts have their own "art world", and most of the artifacts they generate can only be appreciated according to the canons of those worlds. Yet each of these worlds can produce – has produced and continues to produce – a series of artifacts (usually a fairly limited series) able to fulfil the conditions of another world, for example that of contemporary art. This happens for various reasons: because the historic schism between some of these "art worlds" is actually a fairly recent thing, and because certain phenomena that are part of the mythology of contemporary art, like modernism, envisaged a reconciliation that continues to crop up at regular intervals – and, lastly – because the contemporary art world, intended as an arena of free experimentation, unfettered by ulterior motives, has always been particularly receptive to approaches and figures viewed as anomalous by the other art worlds.

In other words, the skin of the contemporary art world is much more porous and permeable than that of other worlds, and while it may have proved slightly less porous at some periods in its history, the period that began in 1989, with the fall of the Berlin wall and the recovery of the art market after the recession at the end of the 80s, was undoubtedly particularly open to contamination. In his critical and curatorial work Germano Celant has often highlighted this: [15]

«Art [...] finally understood that in order to express and present itself as a process of relentless reinvention and encounter, it not only has to accept intertwining and merging into other languages, from architecture to fashion, from design to cinema, it also has to express itself flexibly with all media».

This situation has given rise to two movements: one of appropriation, which encourages artists to engage with other media, be it importing them into the contemporary art world or shifting towards those others worlds, and one of convergence, which sees many hybrid, borderline figures (filmmakers, designers, musicians, etc.) bringing their works into the arena of contemporary art. This does not happen, as might be expected, only on the "borders of the empire", but at its summit, involving figures of prime importance. Think of Matthew Barney and Shirin Neshat, who have taken works to the Venice Film Festival; think of the numerous artists who have directed Hollywood movies (from Robert Longo to Kathryn Bigelow to Julian Schnabel); or Pierre Bismuth, who won an Oscar for his screenplay for the film *Eternal Sunshine Of The Spotless Mind* (2004), written with the director Michael Gondry. And think, too, of Takashi Murakami's collaboration with Vuitton, the double identity of Carsten Nicolai (who also works as a musician, going by the name of Alva Noto), and Peter Greenaway's nomadism.

All of this is also facilitated by internal developments in the contemporary art world, which is increasingly forging a presence as one of the sectors of the cultural industry and show business. And museums and institutions, traditionally more conservative, are facilitating this process, hosting exhibitions devoted to fashion and design, in ways that can be debatable and are indeed debated, but are undeniably forging a trend.

Contemporary Art: the Value

The question of how all this is to be reconciled with the traditional conception of the visual work of art, intended as an artifact that is unique (or reproduced in limited editions), collectible, and therefore financially valuable, is constantly being renegotiated, and obviously entails some interesting compromises.

In the contemporary art world value is attributed by means of a complex system that includes criticism, museums and other institutions, prizes, exhibitions and the market. Not being able to deal with each of these players singly, I will consider above all the market, which, in my analysis, represents the missing link in the world of New Media Art.

The art market has played a key role in the world of visual arts since the nineteenth century, when the arts began gradually severing their ties with the nobility and institutional powers, becoming a private activity mainly destined for the cultured bourgeoisie in search of the social prestige that only a productive relationship with the world of culture can confer. Particularly after the Second World War, art became increasingly bound up with the market: in this way, while the "dematerialization of art" became possible in a period when the market was relatively weak, when the market recovered in the 1980s, and there was a resurgence in demand for marketable artifacts, traditional practices like painting and sculpture rose to the fore once more. The collapse of the stock market in 1989, together with other crucial factors – the new geopolitical situation, and AIDS wiping out an entire generation of artists – played a key role in changing the lie of the land in the early nineties.

The phase which followed this, and which is still under way, is a complex one for various reasons. Globalization is bringing forth new art scenarios, new exhibiting platforms and new markets; major temporary art events, like the biennales, are springing up, creating new destinations for cultural tourism; contemporary art museums are being revamped, testing the terrain of the global museum, and becoming artistic objects in their own right, with containers that are often more appealing than their contents, boosting the number of services on offer and becoming focal points of a society in which the services sector, media and culture play a key role; and lastly, the advent of the information society has generated an exponential increase in platforms for criticism, with the launch of dozens of new magazines.

The art market spearheads this transformation. Private galleries

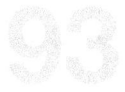

stage events; by means of contemporary art fairs they increasingly condition the construction of museum collections; by paying for advertising space in art magazines they finance art criticism, and even if the relationship forged between the two is not, at least in the most virtuous cases, a genuine exchange, they inevitably end up conditioning the choices made. Art fairs have grown exponentially in the last decade and some of them (like Art Basel, Frieze or New York's Armory Show) have established themselves as primary cultural events, key destinations for global tourism, on a par with museum exhibitions and biennales. Lastly, auctions, the main arena for the so-called "secondary market", have gradually opened up to contemporary art and the so-called "primary market", their fluctuations influencing the careers of artists.

In *The Art Fair Age* (2008), the Spanish critic Paco Barragán defines art fairs as «Urban Entertainment Centers», [16] and contemporary collecting as a pyramid: on the bottom layer, art is sought after as "social capital", a source of prestige and affirmation; on the next level art is collected as "financial capital", namely for its investment value; on the third level of the pyramid we find companies who view art as a "brand" of sure-fire appeal, and include it in their market strategies, while at the top we come to private collectors who seek intellectual fulfillment from art. And the latter are increasingly putting their collections into the public domain, by means of donations to museums (like Giuseppe Panza di Biumo), taking over established institutions (like the new Palazzo Grassi owned by the French entrepreneur François Pinault) or setting up their own foundations (like the Fondazione Sandretto Re Rebaudengo in Turin), thus boosting their influence over the process of institutionalization.

The close bond between the contemporary art world and its economy was incisively analysed by the English critic Julian Stallabrass in his book *Art Incorporated* (2004), which explicitly focuses on the «regulation and incorporation of art in the new world order». [17] According to Stallabrass, art's micro-economy, governed by a handful of dealers, critics and collectors, is precisely what ensures its freedom from the rules of global capitalism and mass culture. Yet at the same time contemporary art can be seen as a giant metaphor for the capitalist system, with which it has more than one affinity.

After demonstrating that the salient characteristics of the art of the 90s – multiculturalism, the success of the installation and the emphasis on youth – are closely linked to its economy, Stallabrass dwells on the way in which the economy of the art world conditions production. The author explains that, while most other art worlds are based on an economy of usage, the core business of contemporary art consists in the «production of rare or unique objects that can only be owned by the very wealthy, whether they are states, businesses or individuals» (p. 102). In recent decades this idiosyncratic economy has had to come to terms with the existence of technically reproducible languages, giving rise to some bizarre compromises: while on one hand photographic works and video exist on the market in very limited series, highly-priced and accompanied by an authentication, on the other, artists like Jeff Koons and Takashi Murakami create digital images which they then get professionals to paint, transforming an infinitely reproducible file into a unique artwork, using a practice (painting) that is manual and entirely traditional.

And the ups and downs of the market also obviously influence the type of art that is produced. In the eternal struggle between traditional (and easily marketable) languages, and more difficult forms, the former experience a predictable revival at every economic boom, while the latter emerge more forcefully in every recession, in a «predictable and mechanical process» (p. 107).

As for the artists, the idiosyncrasies of the system almost always relegate them to poverty. While there are a few big names who manage to make a killing, most artists are at the lower end of the earning scale. Poverty is at once a side-effect of the particular workings of the system, a contradiction and an ideal: poverty suits art. The artist's is a high level profession, usually practised by people of high social extraction but low income, who often fund their art with other activities. As Stallabrass concludes: «As a whole, the art market is an archaic, protected enclave, so far immune from the gales of neoliberal modernization that have swept aside so many other less commercial practices. Its status grants it social distinction and a degree of autonomy, even sometimes from the odd market that is at its basis» (p. 114).

We might object by asserting that Stallabrass' vision is a bit too prosaic, that art is something else altogether, something not so exclusively tied to the fortunes of the market. We could object that the present period as it will be reconstructed in two hundred years' time will have little to do with auction prices, corporate investments and collectors. This is true up to a point, given that the fluctuations of the art economy influence critical debate and the construction of museum collections, as Stallabrass warned us right from the beginning: «the art world is layered vertically and heterogeneous horizontally, comprising many overlapping spheres of association and commerce» (p. 25).

This can also be said of the other art worlds, and it is exactly what makes it difficult to reason systematically. At the same time, it is on this horizontal plane that the various worlds intersect, mutually influencing their respective fates.

New Media Art: the Idea of Art

As we have seen, the world of New Media Art came about to offer artists wishing to experiment with technologies of all kinds the opportunity to do so, removed from the constrictions and limits of a world, the contemporary art world, which is strongly conditioned by its economy and a critical predilection for contents above the exploration of a medium. Far from challenging this configuration, New Media Art criticism merely takes it for granted, and replicates it ad infinitum, to the point of asserting, as Edward Shanken does in *Media Art Histories*, that contemporary art has never accepted New Media Art because it has always rejected the interpretative model based on the relationship between art, science and technology. [18] Which would imply that it can only be interpreted in this way.

In 2006 Gerfried Stocker, director of the Ars Electronica Center and the yearly festival connected to it, returned to discuss this idea of art. The text, rhetorically entitled "The Art of Tomorrow", [19] is significant from various points of view. Indeed Stocker acknowledges that the current developments in new technologies call for a rethink of the structure and functioning of a festival like Ars Electronica, but does so basically without challenging the idea of art it is based on, namely that art is «a test-drive of the future» (p. 7); that Media Art is «an experiment […] that often brings the creators and proponents of this "new art" into an association with engineers and researchers» (p. 11); and that its basic characteristic is its ability to go beyond an instrumental use of the media as a «medium of representation», making the media not only its tool and medium, but also its subject matter, triumphantly concluding:

«Media art thus does not reign supreme as a result of the images and sounds that it is able to marshal and dispatch, but rather due to the quality with which the explicit characteristics of the employed media are orchestrated. It is no great achievement to transfer traditional artistic patterns and behavioral schema into media art; the challenge is to invent new ones» (p. 13).

Stocker's target is contemporary art, which in his view addresses new media only to «transfer traditional artistic patterns and behavioral schema into media art». In Stocker's view Media

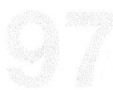

Art, on the other hand, deploys the various media in a conscious way. Stocker is clearly acting territorial, taking a stand against the traditional porosity of the contemporary art world, artists' hunger for recognition and the work of those who, starting from an analogous stance, are intent on facilitating the entrance of New Media Art into the contemporary art world. He adopts a simplistic conception of the latter that downplays the importance of the widespread, non-professional and non self-referential use of the new media, and has a fixed vision of New Media Art as a testbed and arena for research into the technologies of the future. But aside from its defensive attitude, it is important to observe how this vision actually ends up bringing two different strands together: exploration of the medium, which has some affinities with media and design and industrial research, and an approach to the new technologies that is concerned with their social, political and cultural consequences –prioritizing the former to the detriment of the latter. The obvious risk is that the tendency for spectacle, entertainment, works of art that look like giant toys or prototypes for the cultural industry can end up taking over. When this happens, New Media Art events risk resembling what is described in this amusing excerpt quoted by Geert Lovink in *Zero Comments* and written as a comment on the 2006 ISEA festival: [20]

«*The festival's imagination of the "Interactive City" seemed to be characterized by a spirit of play which feels increasingly oriented towards middle-class consumer spectacle and the experience economy. To give you an example of some art experiences that were possible at ISEA:*

- eating ice cream and singing karaoke
- calling an old person in San Jose to talk about whatever you might have in common with them
- pressing a button on a machine and getting an artsy plane ticket with your photo on it
- drifting through the city as if it were a sports field via applying sports plays in urban space

- visualizing your social network via bluetooth as you go around the conference and talk to your friends
- watching/listening to noise music made by people riding skateboards around the conference
- listening to an erotic sci-fi narrative about san jose on your cell phone while riding the train

- flipping light switches to make a one-word message in public space
- viewing colorful 3D representations of wireless digital data».

If this represents the *mainstream* of New Media Art, can we really be surprised that critics, curators and above all artists are migrating en masse towards the contemporary art world, severing their connections with a term that conjures up such questionable associations with the world of entertainment?

We might object that the New Media Art world does not entirely identify with Stocker's stance, neither with the "irrelevant mobile entertainment" stigmatized by kanarinka. In the next chapter we will take a brief look at the experience of the Hartware MedienKunstVerein in Dortmund, directed by Inke Arns, which embodies a diametrically opposed view. Between one extreme and the other we can make out a myriad nuances, to the point that Stocker's take on things could even be a minority viewpoint. Yet it is in any case a leading minority, ambiguously positioned between «commercial demo design and museum strategies», as Geert Lovink puts it, that influences all of the artistic production circulating in this sphere.

New Media Art: the Artist

In *Art of the Digital Age*, Bruce Wands [21] depicts the digital artist as someone equipped with technological skills and a good dose of «technological curiosity»; often a programmer, used to working in collaboration with other programmers and IT engineers; attracted to new technologies and viewing art in terms of research and experimentation; a risk-taker who readily veers off the beaten track of established languages and forms to venture into new terrain.

Though this definition does not add anything new to what we have said so far, it is an interesting one from various points of view. In the first place, New Media Art appears to have entirely overcome the romantic conception of the artist as genius, and seems to be more interested in returning to the Renaissance models of artist as artisan and artist as scientist. Familiarity with programming also takes the New Media artist into another sociologically interesting terrain: that of hacking (used here in its original sense, freed from the negative connotations attributed by the mass media).

It goes without saying that many New Media artists are, and consider themselves to be hackers, to all intents and purposes, and have much in common with hacker ethics: great enthusiasm for their work, limited interest in making a profit, a propensity for knowledge sharing and a belief in the free circulation of information. [22]

In 2003, the Net Art group [epidemiC] engaged with this, activating a curious social short circuit. Invited to take part in the Ars Electronica festival, [epidemiC] created *Doubleblind Invitation*: a program that, if visualized in code form, looked like a beautiful piece of "obfuscated code", namely formatted like a calligram – a technical feat which holds great kudos in the hacking world, where there are competitions devoted to this particular art form. Yet if executed, [epidemiC]'s code sent out emails – seemingly on behalf of the curator Christiane Paul – to dozens of hackers, fans of obfuscated code, inviting them to take part in the

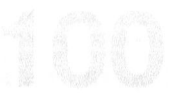

festival. The responses from the invitees, some embarrassed, some enthusiastic, show both the proximity of these two similar cultural niches, and the basic divergence between their two different approaches to programming.

This portrait of the New Media artist, albeit an abstract one, appears so far removed from the type of artist cultivated by the contemporary art world that we might be tempted to think that the difference between the two worlds is a question of anthropology rather than history. And while, as we have seen, the contemporary art world is permeable enough to occasionally accept anomalous figures entirely unconnected to the notion of the "career" artist, the appeal of an art world basically without any kind of market economy, devoted to developing knowledge and exploring the arena of digital media, remains strong.

Casey Reas is a case in point. Reas is an American artist whose work consists in defining processes and translating them into images. In other words, Reas writes programs that, when executed by a computer, generate animated images that can, if desired, be translated into videos or prints. Unsatisfied with the existing tools, in 2001 Reas, working with the artist and designer Benjamin Fry, created *Processing*, an open source programming language and freely downloadable program for the creation of images, animations and interactive installations. [23] *Processing* is now used by a slew of artists, designers and researchers, and obviously Reas himself, who utilizes it in his work. Although Reas works with galleries, he considers himself above all a programmer, designer and researcher: he writes books, holds conferences and coordinates the department of Design and Media Arts at UCLA; and while the resulting products (prints, videos and installations) are produced in limited series, his programs are released with an open source license. He earns his living mainly through teaching and holding workshops on *Processing* around the world.

It is not difficult to come across stories like these in the New

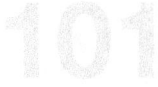

Media Art world, just as it is not difficult to meet artists who put their own talent and efforts at the service of temporary collaborative experiments, voluntarily sacrificing their own authorship.

New Media Art: the Confines

The New Media Art world is underpinned by an economy with a distribution system that does not involve an art market. This situation has significant repercussions on the way in which works of art destined to circulate in the New Media Art world are conceived and produced. A market based on the circulation of unique works, or limited series, demands fetish objects, items guaranteed to last over time, the reproducibility of which can be limited and the monetary value of which can be considerably higher than that of the materials used to make them.

Freed from these limitations, works of art can exist in immaterial, open form and can be forged out of the relationship between the work and the beholder. By rejecting the fetish object, and the aura that is both the cause and consequence of its financial worth, works of art lose the very characteristics that enable them to be distinguished from other kinds of artifacts. If we throw into the mix the fact that the New Media Art world has no objections to works with a functional value, but on the contrary is extremely well disposed towards works which elicit active engagement; that *techne*, in the New Media Art world, tends to prevail over content and that this very world has come together as a result of figures fleeing their respective "worlds" – various disciplines from visual arts to music, drama and dance – taking all these factors into account it is obvious that the typical work required by the New Media Art world is by nature a hybrid one, and that the confines of this world are anything but fixed.

While the contemporary art world has recently opened up to

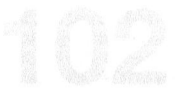

different disciplines, the New Media Art world is multidisciplinary by nature. Yet this "openness" takes two entirely different forms: while the contemporary art world, in a small number of cases and with precise conditions, takes upon itself to welcome works from different disciplines and bestow the status of "art" upon them, the New Media Art world is a "temporary holding center" for works that are so radical or marginal that no-one else will take them. The only passkey required to enter is a creative use of technology.

Having said that, the New Media Art world has no problems hosting – side by side – electronic music projects too radical to survive in the competitive world of commercial electronic music; works of experimental Game Design that do not fulfill, or only partially fulfill, the distributive needs of the multinational videogames companies; experimental architecture projects that will never turn into an actual building; and a lot more besides.

Some of these projects, once past their experimental stage, make their way in other circuits or abandon the definition of "art" to adopt more specific definitions, such as "indie games" or "computational design". The New Media Art world often remains the only real binding agent between practices so diversely inspired and intentioned. In any case, the confines of this world, if they actually exist, are open, fluid borders that are constantly crossed, most of the times without a passport.

New Media Art: the Value

The lack of an art market in the New Media Art world means that the processes for attributing value remain bound up with the systems for distribution and critical comment that belong to New Media Art. If we remove the fetishistic desire for objects, and the ambiguous, oscillating relationship between cultural value and financial value, the cultural value remains, directly linked to the presence of a given work in critical debate, its circulation in the distribution circuit of New Media Art, and, if applicable, its presence in prestigious museum collections. Being featured in an article in Leonardo (an academic journal founded in 1968 and published by the MIT Press), taking part in festivals like Ars Electronica and ISEA, and entering the collection of the ZKM in Karlsruhe, all represent breakthrough points in an artist's career.

Obviously the New Media Art world also has an economy, albeit a distinctive one. The production, distribution and criticism of art is made possible by public and private funding. Like in other arts, people usually have to pay to see the works. As for the artists, when they take part in an event this usually involves the organizer covering not only the cost of transporting and installing the work(s), and travel, board and lodging for the artist, but also some form of payment, which is unheard of in the contemporary art world but common in other art worlds more connected to performance and spectacle, like music and theater.

As for the rest, the same rule applies as in the contemporary art world: to pay the bills artists almost always have another job. In many cases this is directly connected to the artist's art, or at least based on the same technical skills. Many artists teach in the New Media departments of universities or art schools; many are also curators or academics; many work as web designers, software developers, system administrators or programmers, or have other jobs in the media or communications sector.

To consolidate their income, many artists approach the contemporary art world, translating their works into formats amenable to the art market: installations, prints or videos that are one-offs or limited series. Some sneak into other distribution systems, like the videogames market, the worlds of design, fashion or music, while others explore the option of applying distribution models similar to those of software, selling their works cheaply in unlimited runs, or simply asking for a donation.

Internet: a New Context for Art

The advent of the internet and consumer computing in the nineties completely transformed the panorama of the arts, and not just those in a technological vein. The arrival of the information society strongly influenced not only the social role of art, but also its distribution systems, the relationship between the work and the public, the settings for critical commentary, and market mechanisms. The rules of the global village apply in an even greater measure to art worlds: information circulates instantaneously, what happens in New York or Beijing has an immediate effect in Europe, and the time lapse between the advent of a new proposition and its normalization is now at a minimum.

What's more, all of this has literally swept away the strict divisions between the two worlds that I just described. In the first place, the new medium elicited growing interest among artists who did not belong to the New Media Art world, and had no connection to its history. Secondly, new generations of artists came onto the scene, artists who would see such a distinction between worlds as pointless, obscure and obsolete. Lastly the internet – not as a medium but as a social setting and public arena – offered itself up as the "art world" for a new "native" artistic practice that is produced, distributed and discussed there: Net Art. Despite its ups and downs, Net Art still represents the main challenge thrown down to the art market on one hand and to New Media Art on the other. If the New Media Art world is now facing a crisis, and increasing numbers of artists are trying to leave it for the contemporary art world, this is largely due to the new approach to new media introduced in the mid nineties by Net Art.

To better understand the reasons why, we can take a look at one of the first works of Net Art. It was 1995 when the site jodi.org appeared for the first time. It would later emerge that behind this name was a pair of artists: Joan Heemskerk, Dutch, and Dirk Paesmans, Belgian, but at the time jodi.org was just a weird site one might come across while surfing the net. It did not have a traditional access interface with artists' bios and a list of works, and the home page changed without warning as new works were added. One of the first was a black background with a progression of flashing green characters creating an unintelligible text of bars, brackets, punctuation marks, mathematical symbols and numbers. The first impression was that there was something wrong with the browser or some programming error in the code of the page. And if we stuck around and took a look at the HTML, we found something surprising: a picture of a bomb, done in ASCII characters, along with some other graphics.

What was going on was very simple, comprehensible to anyone familiar with the basics of HTML: the creators of the site had not instructed the browser to maintain the original format of the text in the code, which on the interface thus creates a compact block without any kind of linguistic or visual reference points. As Jodi were well aware: the aim was to subvert the traditional relationship between code and interface, getting the user to think about the fact that meaning can hide out where we least expect it, and ponder the layered languages that are a typical feature of all computing systems.

Moving around the site, we can observe many more things. By refusing to use web pages as an editorial platform, Jodi generates abstract pages where everything seems to be out of place, and where the basic functions of HTML are used for mainly figurative purposes. The aesthetic referenced is that of the old style text interface computers, teletext and early video games. There is no point of departure or arrival, and it is easy to get lost in a loop of indecipherable pages.

Like other works on the web in the same period, jodi.org succeeded in standing at the crossroads between two different ideas of art – contemporary art and New Media Art – and subverting both. The creators are not technicians, scientists or engineers, but artists who have got their hands on the languages of the net, not to explore their potential in a positive way, but to upend their basic rules and explore their margin of error. Whatever their level of knowledge of the language, they use it "badly", challenging the conceptual and functional premises it is based on. Their discourse focuses on the medium, but only to call it into question, criticize it and "reinvent" it, attacking the ideologies that have shaped it: while Nam June Paik attacked video as a medium for representing reality, Jodi attacks the web page as an editorial and advertising tool. There is no emphasis placed on *techne*, quite the opposite: anyone with a minimum of training could create a page like this. Lastly, the work lies outside of the tradition of technological arts, from early Computer Art onwards, tipping a wink at both the most radical provocations of contemporary art, from Dadaism to Fluxus to Situationism, and the technological subcultures of previous decades, from ASCII art to amateur telematics.

But if as in contemporary art the contents tend to take precedence over the medium, Jodi also challenges the notion of the artwork as a fetish object with financial value, and the traditional distribution systems of contemporary art. Jodi's work is on the net, accessible to all, not just a select few. Anyone can appropriate it, or rather, anyone who accesses the web page actually does appropriate it. Lastly, it is entirely devoid of any kind of frame to confer it the label of "art". On the contrary, the fact that it is not initially perceived as "art" undisputedly strengthens the subversive power of the work, because we come to it with our guard down.

To get a better understanding of this last point, here is another useful example. In 2000 a mysterious European dotcom called

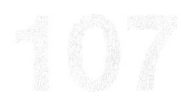

UBERMORGEN.COM set up a site purporting to sell the votes of American electors to the highest bidder. At first glance the site looks like a scandalous e-commerce platform that intends, as its logo states, to "bring capitalism and democracy closer together". Apparently, someone was trying to exploit the magic of the New Economy to interfere with the elections of the world's largest democracy. In October 2000, an article in *Wired* [24] stated that 21,000 votes were up for auction. Hans Bernhard, one of the founders of UBERMORGEN.COM, was described by *Wired* as an "investor" (while later on CNN described him as a "bizarre Austrian businessman"). In the months that followed, UBERMORGEN.COM managed to spike media attention without ever resolving the crux of the matter, the question that bothered both international public opinion and the FBI: satire or reality? Artistic provocation or actual possibility? It was only on 9 November, two days after the election, that the authors revealed the site to be a "hoax", and an "act for freedom of expression", in which no votes had ever actually exchanged hands. This came after hundreds of injunctions had been sent to their address, dozens of articles written and a program on CNN entirely devoted to the subject. By temporarily rejecting the "art" label, UBER-MORGEN.COM managed to take its critique of the American electoral system, in which the campaigns of the various parties are generously funded by multinational companies, to a vast audience, that the art world could never have reached, and above all to do so without the powerful message of the operation being undermined in the public eye as "just an artistic provocation".

To conclude, right from the very start Net Art stood proudly apart from the two worlds described above, despite having things in common with both. It established itself as a sort of caustic, irreverent end-of-millennium avant-garde, the "novelty" of which lay not in its use of a new medium, but in taking the implicit potential of the information era to extremes, like the avant-garde

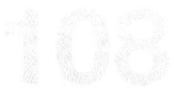

movements of the Twentieth century did with industrial capitalism. This period did not last long, but Net Art had significant consequences on the artistic use of digital media from then on.

It should therefore come as no surprise that Net Art was the first "media art" to arouse the interest of the art world, after the institutionalisation of video and a 40 year long rejection of the "art and new technologies" paradigm. Net Art went down well with those convinced that «excessive attention to the medium produces a dynamic that American artist Joseph Squier described as a "technophiliac infatuation with the tools" [...], and gives rise to self-referential art forms that play with the tool's potential and seemingly ignore art's ability to transfigure reality», in the words of the Italian critic Gianni Romano. [25]

But if this is true, why did it not spell the end of the era of "special interest shows", as hoped by the critics Inke Arns and Jacob Lillemose? [26] Why did the new approach to technology introduced by Net Art not succeed in doing away with, or at least redefining, the idea of art that the New Media Art world is based on? And lastly, why did it not manage to win over the contemporary art world?

We'll try to answer these questions in the next chapter, analyzing a series of contemporary art events organized from the mid 1990s to the present. It should also be noted that the ongoing challenge that Net Art laid down to the art market – together with some inevitable technological virtuosities that were lost on less tech-savvy critics – prevented its full integration into the contemporary art world, while neither the challenge to the market, or the technical virtuosities represented a problem for the New Media Art world, technologically aware and devoid of an art market. Moreover the great enthusiasm for Net Art shown by the art world in the second half of the 90s noticeably tapered off after the collapse of the New Economy and when the private funding that supported museum interest dried up. Lastly, the New Media

Art world, predominantly reliant on public funding, managed to set up a network of institutions, festivals, and small, dynamic online platforms that offered fertile terrain for developing this new approach to the digital media.

In this way the "new generation New Media Art" unwillingly adapted to a New Media Art world that continues, with few exceptions, to be rooted in obsolete ideological concepts. The current friction, however, proves that this arrangement was destined to be a temporary one. The freedom afforded to Net Art by the net, by its access to a global platform outside of any kind of niche discourse, and a context qualifying it as art, and its power to enter into contact with a wide, varied audience and compete with other types of cultural artifacts, still lends Net Art exceptional potential. The bomb hidden in the code of Jodi's homepage is still there, ready to go off.

Internet: the Artist

All of this becomes more comprehensible if we take a brief look at the figure of the artist, and the confines and systems of value attribution that belong to the internet, when examined as an art world.

As for the artists, it should be noted that, from the early days of the web, for many artists already using other media, the internet merely represented *a further opportunity*: a context in which to experiment with innovative modes of communication, interact with a diversified, international audience and find a way to get round censorship mechanisms. For many others the internet represented *the definitive opportunity*: to continue working outside of the art world, experiment with a new language, circumvent the marginal position that their work, social standing or geographical origins confined them to, or simply make creative use of the medium's extraordinary potential for communication, that few seemed to grasp. It was in the latter group of artists, mostly young and working in central and eastern Europe, that the term "net.art" began to circulate, between 1996 and 1997. This self-ironic label, which according to legend was spawned by a software glitch, catalyzed a dynamic, widespread scene, characterized by a series of elements which were as specific as they were radical: rejection of the mediation of the system and institutions; overcoming the work-as-object paradigm; eliminating the distinction between creator and beholder, challenging the very notion of authorship, and activating circuits – and short-circuits – of communication. The internet became the cabaret Voltaire for a new Dadaism. All of this makes it legitimate to talk about a movement, and at the same time lends "net.art" strong historic, geographic and cultural connotations.

This historic background shows that while there is no such thing as a "net artist", in view of the fact that the web is not chosen as an exclusive medium, and indeed is often used on an occasional basis, when artists decide to produce a project on the net they undoubtedly have to tackle a series of prerogatives which are not secondary to the nature of the project, and it is true that many artists, setting aside all reservations, embrace these unconditionally, seeing them as an opportunity to strike a mortal blow to some of the dogmas of the art system. In the first place, working on the web means abandoning the notion of authorship, or at least continually having to renegotiate it; working with others, and leaving the user, or software to perform part of the creative process. Identity itself can be simulated or constructed. While the romantic legend of the artistic genius could have survived in certain conditions, the net sounded its death knell. Net Art gathered and developed these elements in various directions – setting up collectives of artists and collaborative works, implementing platforms that elicited the creativity and active contributions of users, writing software that does most of the work.

The weakening of the notion of the author went hand in hand with that of the concept of artwork as fetish object. Digital data is replicable and always will be; information is by nature free. Any attempt to tackle this problem –limiting access to a given site, for example – can be worked around, and in any case goes against the very nature of the medium, given that browsers save local copies of pages as soon as users access them. What's more, the weakening of the concepts of author, unique work of art and originality not only change the artist's attitude to his or her own work, but also when it comes to "found" material. Working in a media arena flooded with a constant stream of information makes recycling and remixing practices the order of the day.

Lastly, the internet as a medium breaks down the art world's traditional distinctions between roles: community practices, art as communication and dialogue, the use of a medium that is at once means of production, distribution, promotion, dialogue, consumption and critique, rehashes the mediating role played by institutions, critics and curators, and redistributes these roles between the artists and the public.

All of this is not the exclusive preserve of Net Art, but it characterizes all present-day artistic practices. In *Postproduction*, Nicolas Bourriaud [27] develops some extremely interesting reflections on this theme, viewing art as postproduction and the artist as a multidisciplinary figure who selects cultural objects from reality and puts them into new settings. Yet Net Art undeniably presents an unprecedentedly radical take on this. As a consequence, the challenge that Net Art lays down to the art system is an unprecedented one. As Julian Stallabrass notes: «a radical art needs to do more than make politics its subject-matter; it must change the way it is made, distributed and seen», continuing:

«*One response is to step outside the conventional arena of gallery and museum display. From the mid-1990s, with the rise of the web browser, the dematerialization of the art work – especially its weightless distribution over digital networks – has threatened the protected system of the arts [...] In digital art, the use of the most up-to-date technological means to make and distribute work comes into conflict with the craft-based practice, patronage and elitism of the art world*». [28]

The fact of acting without a support system or market has consequences on artistic practice and the very figure of the artist. While on one hand independence from power structures favors anarchy, spontaneity, an irreverent spirit and a lack of responsibility, it also calls for a dedication that is unconnected to material and financial interests. At the same time, acting on a public platform where identity is a construct and the differences between roles blur enables artists to act at will as catalyst, institution or corporation, moving beyond institutional criticism to generate new, independent situations and new forms of activism.

Internet: the Confines

Rather than being a structured world with borders, for art the net is a border territory. It does not have confines, but rather represents a threshold: a point of encounter and exchange for different situations and cultures. Yet even the net has gradually developed its own filters and points of access, with a series of journals, portals and collections that lend authority to a work or an artist due to the simple fact of having produced it, linked to it or talked about it. There are numerous examples of this, such as *Neural*, a magazine set up in Italy in 1993 which garnered increasing international credibility through its website, the English version of the printed magazine (launched in 2001), and the networking of its founder, Alessandro Ludovico.

Another key player is undoubtedly *Turbulence*, which came about in 1996 as the online platform of New Radio and Performing Arts, Inc. (NRPA) of New York. [29] Since then, *Turbulence* has commissioned more than 150 Net Art projects, organized online exhibitions, promoted the work of the artists it works with and set up two important blogs. Then there is the story of *Rhizome*, set up in 1996 as a mailing list devoted to art on the net, which then developed into a non profit organization linked to the New Museum of Contemporary Art in New York, as of 2003. These small set-ups have managed to earn themselves the role of definitive points of reference, with a level of credibility that outside of the net would only be possible for a major institution.

Yet on the net, unlike in the two highly institutionalized worlds described previously, this credibility is a fragile thing, and there is always the opportunity of commanding the same level of attention as these sites offer (or more), but without going through them. The current dynamics of the Web 2.0, in particular, enable new players to enter rapidly into competition with more established situations. It only took a few months for the blog *We-Make-Money-Not-Art*, set up by a bored worker in the communications sector, to become a key point of reference for the worlds of New Media Art, innovative design, technology and contemporary art. Today the tags of Delicious – a popular "social bookmarking" service, which lets users publish and share their favorite links – or the notes on Tumblr – a micro-blogging platform – can rapidly determine the success (or lack thereof) of a site or a project, and a particularly well-tended account on Delicious, Tumblr, Twitter or Facebook can easily compete with any online magazine.

One reason for this is that the net lacks various "sanctioning" mechanisms that continue to play an important role in the so-called real world. In the real world attention is often governed and induced by factors that lie outside of the actual artwork; factors of a social, environmental and cultural nature. I don't always go to

MOMA because I get to see the best of contemporary art there. I go to MOMA because it makes me feel part of a certain cultural aristocracy. I go to MOMA because the selection of works that it offers enables me to see the best without traveling the world. I go to MOMA because *Artforum* published a favorable review of its latest show. I go to MOMA because it exhibits the work that Charles Saatchi paid a fortune for.

Vice versa, surfing the net is basically a private experience, and the socializing it offers is organized in a different way to real life. Reputations are never a given, but constantly have to be earned. On the web, the MOMA site, like that of the *New York Times* or any other traditional point of reference is just the same distance – one click away – as any other site, and there is nothing stopping me from visiting selections (of artworks, or information) offered by other sites, big names or not.

The net's lack of certain factors of social or environmental conditioning is one of the keys to understanding the failure of many "online galleries" of Net Art launched around the turn of the millennium by institutions of undisputed clout in the "real world". The fact of the matter is that online, these institutions find themselves competing on a par with other players that often have a more solid community behind them. And in an economy of attention like the internet, in an ocean of information where hierarchical filters only apply up to a certain point, the community element is a decisive one. Before concluding it is therefore worth taking a brief look at these two concepts, which have cropped up so often in this paragraph: community and the attention economy.

To understand its full potential, the first term should be seen in the context of "connective intelligence" put forward by Derrick De Kerchove towards the end of the 90s. On the net it is networking, with its open, rhizome-like dynamics, that creates communities, or, as De Kerchove puts it: «the network is the message of the medium Internet». [30] Now, in the Web 2.0 era, the social nature of the electronic media has become both a cliché and an opportunity explored by a growing number of people, but in the early days of the net it was seen as having extraordinary "artistic" and – before that – "political" potential.

The term "attention economy" became popular at the start of the millennium, when Thomas H. Davenport and John C. Beck used it as the title of their famous book, *The Attention Economy* [31] This theory is based on the idea that in the era of information overload, attention is the real rarity, and that as a consequence economic laws can be used to solve the various problems involved in managing information. This idea emerged as early as the 1970s, but began to make headway above all at the turn of the millennium, when the internet became a "fantastic market for attention". But attention is more than just the new objective of those who have already achieved financial success. It is also the goal of those who, competing in an immense cultural market, are desperately seeking an audience to talk to. The emerging artist, the outlying gallery and the young musician are all looking for attention, over and above money. Before the advent of the internet and the other cheap communications technologies (like email and mobile phones), what kind of public could be reached by an artist who did not manage to get picked by any well known galleries? Or a gallery unable to afford to advertise in the main trade rags, or buy a ticket to the main trade fairs? Or a musician who couldn't manage to secure an audition with any recording companies?

Today, clever use of alternative means of communication can, in certain conditions, achieve the same or a greater level of attention as that garnered by weighty marketing investments. This is something that Net Art has always been aware of, and exploited, as we have seen, to bypass the traditional filters that lie between an artist and his or her public. Little by little these filters have re-emerged, but there is still great scope for operating around them, and demanding and obtaining attention.

Internet: the Value

It follows that in the attention economy of the internet, value is not measured in financial terms, but in numbers of unique users, links and search engine results. Once results have been achieved in terms of quantity, the criteria of quality obviously reappears: the value of an online project thus also – and above all – depends on whether it is being talked about in contexts like *Rhizome, Neural* and *We-make-money-not-art*, whether it has attracted the attention of certain critics, and whether it has been exhibited in certain settings, online and off-line. The aura of the work of art, removed by the functional design of the screen we use to look at it, its infinite reproducibility without loss of quality, its accessibility and complete lack of financial value, re-emerges in the form of "tag clouds". This obviously applies to any "cultural artifact", inexorably influenced by the so-called "word of mouth on the web", but it applies particularly in the case of a form of art that does not generate any "real" economy. Obviously a work of Net Art can be commissioned, and therefore funded by a private individual or institution; during the last decade there have been various attempts to sell websites as works of art, and the idea of collecting sites is appreciated in certain circles. Some Net Art projects have even ended up "costing" considerable sums of money, not only in terms of their purchase price, but more due to their name. In 2000 Kenneth Aronson, the founder of Hell.com, a private web space that a community of artists had been using for years as a workshop in which to gather, comment on and perfect their works, put his domain up for auction for 8 million dollars. It didn't sell, but the starting price was anything but implausible for such a hot domain name. Towards the end of 1999, the online toystore eToys offered etoy 516,000 dollars for its domain, etoy.com. After the artists declined, eToys moved on to strong arm tactics, but found itself embroiled in a battle with activists, artists, journalists and other etoy supporters, who in the name of freedom of expression inflicted considerable financial damage on the company (the official figures for what went down in history as *Toywar* stand at 4.5 million dollars).

But an economy based purely on attention also has its weak points, the main one being its impermanence, something which does not suit works of art. Ultimately this is probably the reason why Net Art never developed into an independent art world, remaining mainly an extraordinary opportunity. The artists who debuted on the web in the late 90s have tried, without abandoning it, to transfer their works to more stable terrain, with systems of distribution and value attribution that are less open to manipulation, but more secure in the long term: the contemporary art world and that of New Media Art.

For the younger generations, in any case, it is no longer a question of "translating" works created on the web to suit traditional exhibition venues and the art market, but simply operating on all the available platforms. In these conditions, the very term Net Art is weakened. Rather than an art "specific to the net", today we are now looking at an art which is "post internet", to use a term coined by the American artist and critic Marisa Olson, or "internet aware", if we prefer the definition proposed by artist Guthrie Lonergan. [32]

Notes

[1] Cit. in Geert Lovink, "New Media Arts: In Search of the Cool Obscure. Explorations beyond the Official Discourse", in *Diagonal Thoughts*, 2007. Online at www.diagonalthoughts.com/?p=204 (last visit March 2013).

[2] Inke Arns & Jacob Lillemose, "'It's contemporary art, stupid'. Curating computer based art out of the ghetto", in Anke Buxmann, Frie Depraetere (eds.) *Argos Festival*, argoseditions, Brussels 2005. Online at http://uncopy.net/wp-content/uploads/2011/04/arnslillemose-contemporarystupid.pdf (last visit March 2013).

[3] Lev Manovich, "The Death of Computer Art", 1997. Online at www.manovich.net/TEXT/death.html (last visit March 2013).

[4] Lev Manovich, "Don't Call it Art: Ars Electronica 2003", in *Nettime*, September 22, 2003. Also available at http://manovich.net/DOCS/ars_03.doc (last visit March 2013).

[5] Cf. Arthur Danto, *The Abuse of Beauty. Aesthetics and the Concept of Art*, Open Court Publishing, Chicago 2003.

[6] Bonami 2007: pp. 3 – 18. Author's translation.

[7] See Joline Blais, Jon Ippolito, *At the Edge of Art*, Thames and Hudson, London 2006.

[8] Cf. also Alessandro Dal Lago, Serena Giordano, *Mercanti d'aura. Logiche dell'arte contemporanea*, Il Mulino, Bologna 2006. Author's translation.

[9] Mario Perniola, *L'arte e la sua ombra*, Giulio Einaudi Editore, Turin 2000, p. IX of the introduction.

[10] Rosalind Krauss, *A Voyage in the North Sea. Art in the Age of the Post-Medium Condition*, Thames & Hudson, London 1999, p. 19.

[11] Ibidem, p. 32.

[12] Rosalind Krauss, "Reinventing the Medium", in *Critical Inquiry*, Winter 1999, Vol 25, No 2, pp. 289 – 305.

[13] Tom McCarthy, *Remainder*, Vintage Books 2007, p. 237.

[14] Dal Lago, Giordano 2006, p. 225.

[15] Germano Celant, *Artmix. Flussi tra arte, architettura, cinema, design, moda, musica e televisione*, Feltrinelli, Milan 2008, p. 6. Author's translation.

[16] Paco Barragan, *The Art Fair Age*, Milan, Charta 2008.

[17] Julian Stallabrass, *Art Incorporated. The Story of Contemporary Art*, Oxford University Press 2004, p. 28.

[18] Edward A Shanken, "Historicizing Art and Technology: Forging a Method

and Firing a Canon", in Grau 2007: 43 – 70.
[19] Gerfried Stocker, "The Art of Tomorrow", in *a minima*, n° 15, 2006, pp. 6 – 19.
[20] In Geert Lovink, *Zero Comments...*, cit. From a post sent by the artist kanarinka to the mailing list [iDC] on August 13, 2006, available at https://lists.thing.net/pipermail/idc/2006-August/001755.html (last visit March 2013).
[21] Bruce Wands, *Art of the Digital Age*, Thames & Hudson, London – New York, 2006, pp. 12 – 14.
[22] Cf. Pekka Himanen, *The Hacker Ethic and the Spirit of the Information Age*, Random House 2001.
[23] Cf. Casey Reas, Ben Fry (eds.), *Processing: A Programming Handbook for Visual Designers and Artists*, MIT Press, 2007.
[24] Associated Press, "Vote-Auction Sidesteps Legalities", in *Wired*, 26 October 2000, online at www.wired.com/techbiz/media/news/2000/10/39753 (last visit March 2013).
[25] Gianni Romano, *Artscape. Panorama dell'arte in Rete*, Costa & Nolan, Ancona – Milan 2000. The phrase quoted is on pgs. 7 – 9. Author's translation.
[26] Arns & Lillemose 2005.
[27] Nicolas Bourriaud, *Post Production. La culture comme scénario: comment l'art reprogramme le monde contemporain*, Les Presses du réel, Paris 2004.
[28] Stallabrass 2004: 191 – 192.
[29] Cf. Domenico Quaranta, "Let's Get Loud! Interview with Helen Thorington, director of TURBULENCE.ORG", in *Cluster. On Innovation*, n. 5, 2005, pp. 12 – 17.
[30] Cf. Derrick De Kerchove, "Preface", in Bazzichelli 2008: 11.
[31] Thomas H. Davenport, John C. Beck, *The Attention Economy: Understanding the New Currency of Business*, Harvard Business School Press, 2001.
[32] Cf. Louis Doulas, "Within Post-Internet, Part One", in *Pool*, April 6, 2011, online at http://pooool.info/within-post-internet-part-i/ (last visit March 2013).

The Boho Dance. New Media Art and Contemporary Art

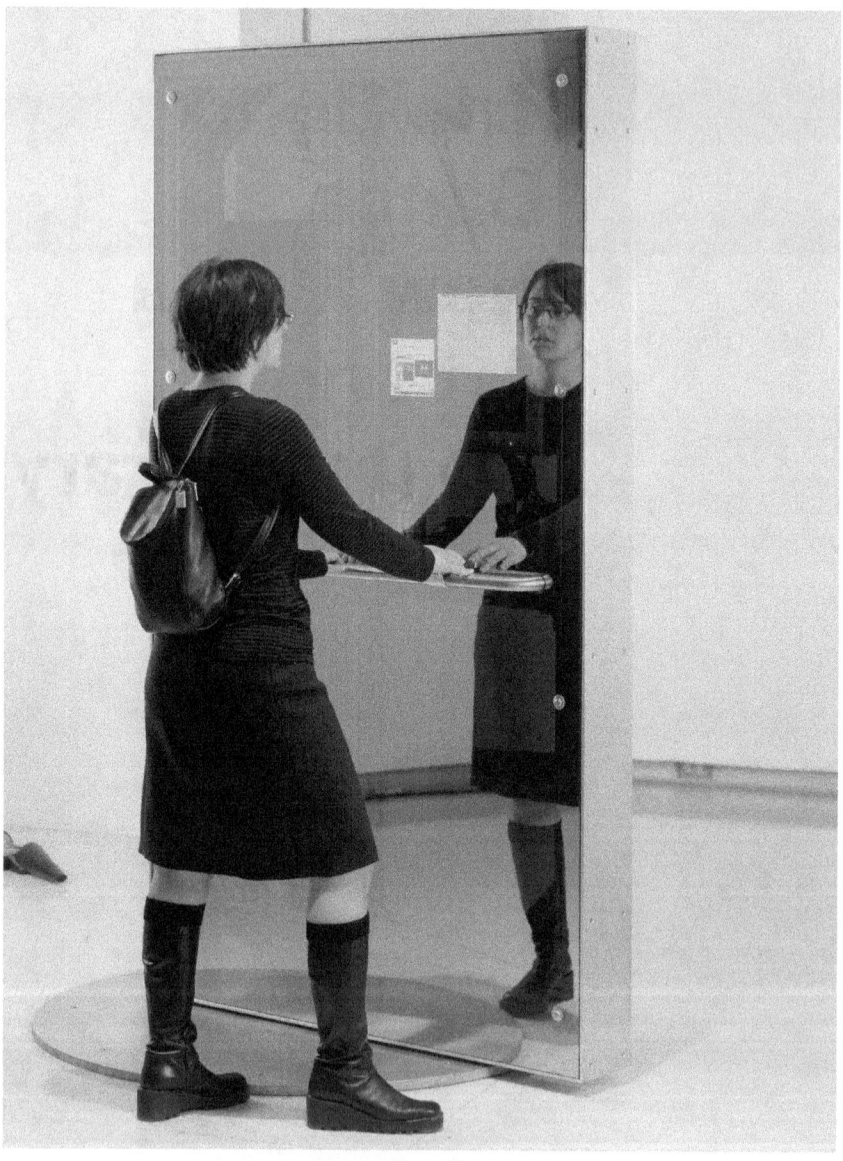

The portal designed by Antenna Design for Art Entertainment Network, Walker Art Center 2000. Courtesy Walker Art Center, Minneapolis.

In the previous chapters I have examined the notion of New Media Art. I have challenged its conceptual basis and highlighted its social role (if the term endures, it is because there is an art world that identifies with it); I have related the history of this world and described it in comparison to the contemporary art world. Lastly I have underlined how in recent years the New Media Art world has proved inadequate to the task of representing the complexity of the art that engages with the new technologies, and that has repeatedly attempted to make inroads into the world of contemporary art.

To understand the dynamics of this encounter, it is worth returning to *The Painted Word*, a successful pamphlet on the art world published in 1975 by the American satirical writer Tom Wolfe. In it, Wolfe ironically describes the relationship between avant-garde movements and the art establishment as a bizarre mating ritual, that takes place in two stages: the Boho dance, «in which the artist shows his stuff within the circles, coteries, movements, isms, of the home neighborhood, bohemia itself, as if he doesn't care about anything else»; and the Consummation, «in which culturati from that very same world, *le monde*, scout the various new movements and new artists of bohemia, select those who seem the most exciting, original, important, by whatever standards-and shower them with all the rewards of celebrity.». In the Boho dance, Wolfe explains, the artist behaves like the female in the Apache dances, mixing seduction and scorn, offer and refusal, before finally giving in:

«*The artist was like the female in the act, stamping her feet, yelling defiance one moment, feign- ing indifference the next, resisting the advances of her pursuer with absolute contempt... more thrashing about... more rake-a-cheek fury... more yelling and carrying on... until finally with one last mighty and marvelously ambiguous shriek – pain! ecstasy! – she submits... Paff paff paff paff paff... How you do it, my boy!... and the house lights rise and Everyone, tout le monde, applauds...*» [1]

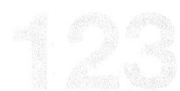

Despite the satirical tone and date of the piece, which renders it unsuited to deciphering some of the recent developments in contemporary art, *The Painted Word* still offers some keen insights into the dynamics of the art world, namely that contemporary art still continues to be a factor of social distinction, and the success of an artist still lies largely in the hands of a restricted elite of museum curators, gallerists, collectors and critics. For our purposes, however, the "Boho dance" model is a perfectly apt description of the way in which, over the last twenty years, New Media Art has approached the platform of contemporary art. Interpreted through the ritual described by Wolfe, this lengthy courtship could be described as an ongoing Boho dance enacted by two lovers who have never actually managed to consummate their relationship. The discourse of blowing hot and cold can still be witnessed today, for example in the book *New Media in the White Cube and Beyond* (2009), which gathers a series of essays regarding the curatorial issues that New Media Art raises for museums. [2] While on one hand Charlie Gere writes that museums and galleries must necessarily engage with New Media Art, because the art of the last few decades cannot be understood without taking it into account, on the other Steve Dietz and Patrick Lichty assert that New Media Art (and Net Art in particular) has no need of the institutions, given that it can exist perfectly well outside them.

There would be nothing wrong with this if New Media Art was a brand new avant-garde, ready to embark on its courtship ritual. The problem is that in our case, the Boho dance has been going on for almost twenty years, and while from time to time it might have seemed that Consummation was near, the applause never came. The result is that today this ritual looks like a pathetic tussle that has been dragging on for far too long. But why is this the case? What mistakes have been made? What expectations did the art world have of New Media Art? What strategies has the latter adopted to show itself in a good light on this platform? And is it still possible to remedy the errors of the past?

In this chapter we will try to answer these questions, in particular with regard to the exhibitions of the second half of the 90s and the debate on the presence of New Media Art on the contemporary art market.

Let the Dance Begin (1996 – 1998)

In the first chapter we saw the 1980s closing with three exceptional episodes of visibility for New Media Art on the contemporary art panorama: the exhibition *Les Immateriaux* (1985) at the Centre Pompidou in Paris, the Venice Biennale in 1986 and the ZKM in Karlsruhe being founded in 1989. These were, as we have said, episodes, which for a series of factors – their "institutional" nature, their geographic location and their detachment from financial interests – sank without leaving many traces on the artistic horizons of the period. The elements that spring to mind when considering the art of the 1980s was the recovery of the market, post modernism and the return of painting. Even Jeffrey Deitch's reflections on the post-human in the travelling exhibition *Post Human* (1992 – 1993) proved to be a losing horse for New Media Art, a ship that had already sailed. Though the curator's exploration was rooted in a keen awareness of the technological and scientific revolution that was under way, [3] he looked to artists like Charles Ray, Robert Gober, Jeff Koons, Wim Delvoye and Paul McCarthy to trace the aesthetic and cultural consequences of this revolution. With its invitation to reflect on the impact that information technologies, media and biotech are having on our lives, Deitch's study of the post-human dimension remains a precious and all too often overlooked indication for the curators of today.

As for New Media Art, it was once more by insisting on the use of "technology as a tool" that it reappeared on the contemporary art panorama towards the mid 90s. Strangely enough, this occurred thanks to Thomas Krens, the dynamic director of the Solomon R. Guggenheim Foundation from 1988 to 2008. During his long reign, Krens became the living symbol of the museum's entry into the era of globalization and spectacle, transforming his institution into a global brand, and, with the opening in 1997 of the Guggenheim Bilbao, turning the museum building into a landmark, a container with more appeal than its contents. His third, less notorious battle, got under way quietly in 1993 when the museum's SoHo venue hosted the exhibition *Virtual Reality: An Emerging Medium*.

Curated by Jon Ippolito, the show presented "virtual reality", at the time seemingly destined for future glory, in various installations by artists. Despite its brief duration (around ten days), the exhibition attracted a great number of visitors, and gave Krens the idea of transforming the SoHo Guggenheim, initially established to give the foundation's collection of modern art an airing, into the museum's "new media" division. In March 1996, the project was presented to the press. The first step was the staging of a major exhibition – in collaboration with the ZKM – scheduled for the June of that year, entitled *Mediascape*. The exhibition relied on funding from Deutsche Telekom and the Italian electricity company ENEL, which had already sponsored the Guggenheim on previous projects. Both ENEL and Deutsche Telekom committed to future projects; in specific terms, Deutsche Telekom forked out something like 2.5 million dollars a year for the Guggenheim, and covered the cost of producing a giant videowall, connected to a similar system in Germany, for which artists would be invited to create new works, while ENEL undertook to create an "electronic library" for the viewing of CD-ROMs and other digital material, and produce CD-ROMs of the shows hosted by the museum. Krens also announced his intention to expand the museum's collection of "multimedia art". [4]

In this context *Mediascape*, curated by Jon Ippolito and John Hanhardt, played a dual role: on one hand it underlined the bright newness of the art that works with the new technologies, while on the other it highlighted how this was rooted in the recent history of contemporary art, by placing it alongside works by well-known, established artists. On the first floor visitors encountered a colossal video installation by Nam June Paik, *Megatron* (1995), followed by an interactive installation by Toshio Iwai, *Piano-As Image Media* (1995) and a text generator by Bill Seaman, *Passage Sets* (1994).

The interactive installations were rounded off by Jeffrey Shaw's work *The Legible City* (1991): a virtual reality installation which enabled the viewer, sitting on a bicycle, to navigate around various urban spaces where the buildings had been replaced by 3-D letters forming a description of the city. *Mediascape* combined these works with the video installations of Ingo Gunther, Marie-Jo Lafontaine, Bruce Nauman, Bill Viola, Steina and Woody Vasulka, and a piece by Jenny Holzer displaying her famous "truisms" in LED lights.

All the works on show, except for those by Paik, Holzer, Nauman and the Vasulkas, came from the ZKM collection, which at the time boasted more than a thousand works of New Media Art without a permanent home. And Deutsche Telekom and ENEL were anything but reluctant to show off their own contributions. As Roberta Smith commented ironically in the *New York Times*:

«the Guggenheim SoHo now includes the first galleries in a major New York museum dedicated to corporate sponsors. [...] Although small, these galleries represent a Faustian low point in museum design: each has a completely superfluous floor-to-ceiling decor of shiny metal, fancy hardware, black rubber and kinky chairs [...] In these trendy, overwrought rooms, it's hard to know whether to dust off your Luke Skywalker costume, get *out the exercise equipment or just sit tight until young Dr. Frankenstein arrives». [5]*

As for the exhibition, Roberta Smith described *The Legible City* (one of the icons of New Media Art) «one of the worst works in the show», concluding:

«Too often Mediascape operates in the gap between art and entertainment without quite being either [...] It's fun, it's exhilarating, but it's mostly technique. No matter which century you're in, from the Egyptians and the Greeks onward, technique or, now, technology has never guaranteed lasting aesthetic power».

With regard to *Afterimage*, Lucy Bowditch underlined the playful superficiality of the interactive pieces, which paradoxically proved less engaging than other, more reflective pieces, like those of Holzer and Nauman: «ZKM appears to have many toys, and at this point random distraction is the greater part of the game». [6] Lastly, John Haber explains that «to the detriment of some interesting artists and puzzling artistic trends, this show is about technology», the curators' mistake lay in insisting on what computers can do, rather than what is new about them, an approach that the critic found «surprisingly old-fashioned». [7] All three agreed that the idea of placing the "multimedia art" from the ZKM alongside various classic examples of "media-based" contemporary art in order to lend it legitimacy actually had the effect of trouncing it: it professed to be new but came across as "old-fashioned"; it set out to be interactive but in the end was merely game-like, all tech and no content. The dichotomies analysed in the previous chapter which produced the scission between the two worlds re-emerge intact in this first encounter.

At its debut ball in New York society, New Media Art came across as a gaudy, tacky newcomer, a green hillbilly on the payroll

of the hi tech companies. *Mediascape* was New Media Art's misstep in its Boho dance with the art world, a false move that it repeated at almost all the leading events in the years to come. The underlying error was one of perspective: New Media Art made its appearance on the contemporary art platform attempting to sell the idea that first occasioned its exclusion, in other words insisting on technology and "research on the medium" rather than its cultural potential. Technology, its uses and celebrating its topicality became the "theme" of the show, its conceptual nucleus: New Media Art made its opening moves in the dance dressed in shabby old clothes.

The second mistake was the choice of partner: New Media Art was promoted with the support of the hi-tech sector, which naturally had a vested interest in celebrating and lending legitimacy to its achievements. Obviously the latter conditions the former: if there is a hi-tech sponsor footing most of the bill, the exhibition is bound to be a celebration of technology. Anything else – and, even more so, any critical notions – will inevitably be in second place. Moreover, not having developed any other "partnerships" (in terms of critics, or the market), when this support is removed, New Media Art will appear to have suddenly fallen out of favor.

Its third mistake was one of selection. In *Mediascape*, New Media Art introduced itself to the contemporary art platform with works not suited to representing it in that arena: "contraptions" like *The Legible City*, culturally too weak to fulfil the idea of art that the contemporary art world supports. Even when exhibitions began to feature works which were more solid in terms of contents, the feeling of looking at something alien did not go away. And here we are back to square one: for as long as these works are promoted with the aim of celebrating technology, as Haber says, this very perspective will defeat any valid works and interesting trends. As we will see in the next chapter, the only way for New

Media Art to be taken seriously by the contemporary art world is to rid itself of this perspective and the term that embodies it once and for all.

Another problem that emerged with *Mediascape* was that the exhibition took place in a sort of "vacuum", in which the enmeshed interests of the museum and the technological sponsor did not appear to be supported by other sectors of the art world. While official criticism appeared sceptical about the formal characteristics of New Media Art, its playful, technophile approach, there was no such thing as "militant" criticism around in the art world that was able to fight its corner. What was on show at the Guggenheim SoHo had never put in an appearance in any small, hip and happening institutions, not to mention private galleries. There was no market, no group of collectors buying into this kind of art.

It was in this very period that a number of "pioneers" set about preparing the terrain in this regard, but while the love affair between New Media Art and the major museums proceeded apace, between 1996 and 2001, thanks to the complicity and financial backing of the companies of the New Economy, preparing the terrain was a slower business. In terms of private venues, the first to move in this direction was undoubtedly the Postmasters Gallery in New York. Established in the East Village in 1984 by Magdalena Sawon and Tamas Banovich, the gallery moved to SoHo in 1989, and Chelsea in 1998. In 1996, in its SoHo venue, Postmasters presented two interesting group exhibitions: *Can You Digit?* and *Password: ferdydurke*, both curated by Tamas Banovich. These were followed in 1997 by *MacClassics*. The three exhibitions clearly responded to a need to explore this area and raise awareness of the issues raised by the new technologies. The first show presented forty works by artists and designers mostly working in Silicon Valley. *Password: ferdydurke* took its name from a Polish novel that was a favorite of the gallerists', and focussed on the dematerialisation of the image. Meanwhile *MacClassics* drew on the appeal of the computer as an object, the cult status of old Macs and the nostalgic attitude implied. This art was a reaction to the breakneck speed of technological progress. For the exhibition, the curator got hold of a number of old computers and asked the featured artists to use them as they wished. Well ahead of its time, *MacClassics* shifted the focus from celebrating technology or some particular aspect of it, an aspect which still featured in *Can You Digit?*, to exploring the impact that the media, in this case personal computers, are having on our culture and tastes. Moreover, side-stepping any "New Media" rhetoric, *MacClassics* sought an artistic retrieval of "new" technology that was already obsolete, pushed out of the picture by the new models, and focussed on the element of nostalgia in this look back to the recent past. Last but not least, *MacClassics* solved the issue of the alleged "immateriality" of digital art in one fell swoop, asking the artists to produce something for the exhibition venue and use the computers not just as a medium or vehicle for the work, but an integral part of it.

At the time this latter element was anything but a given. Heated debate was incurred, in particular, by the Net Art section of documenta X (1997), curated by Catherine David. Simon Lamunière, also responsible for the documenta X website, was appointed to take care of this section. Catherine David's documenta was to go down in history as the edition that reawakened critical and political consciences, resumed the stances of the neo avant garde movements of the 60s and rejected the "domestication" of art. [8] This major initiative was more than an exhibition, representing a platform of events, debates and screenings, in which the works expressly rejected the institutions, many taking up position in public areas. Painting was strictly left out of the picture, while the event traced a connection between the generation of the 60s and the critical, radical art of the 90s, between the end of the Cold War, the victory of capitalism and the looming advent of globalization. In this context the website played a key role. As David explains, documenta X took place in different "spaces": the five exhibition venues, but also the book / catalog, the program of debates and above all the website:

«Of the concentric circles which constitute the cultural event documenta X, the website is so to speak the outermost ring. It allows participation in the event in Kassel in the combination that distinguishes internet: within a framework both intimate and global, in one's own living room and in the most varied corners of our world». [9]

As well as providing practical information about the event, the site presented a series of projects for the web, some of which were commissioned by documenta X, and offered a list of resources documenting the nascent art scenes and activism on the net. The list included some historic Net Art projects, from Jodi to *Metronet* by Martin Kippenberger, from *Visitors Guide to London* by Heath Bunting to *On Translation* by Antoni Muntadas to *Makrolab* by the Slovenian artist Marko Peljhan.

The projects among these which also had an installation element, like *Metronet* and *Makrolab*, were distributed among the various venues of the event. Those which only existed online were made accessible on a series of computers grouped in single area of the documenta-Halle, near the bookshop and café. It was this decision that sparked debate, debate that can still be followed on the site's forum. The "Websites" section of documenta X was a closed space, surrounded by a blue wall that some interpreted as a crude tribute to one of the sponsors, IBM. The computers were set up on desks, which introduced another association that proved unpopular with the artists: the link between computers and the workplace. Lastly, the computers were not hooked up to the net, meaning that the works were basically cut off from their setting.

The idea of grouping a dozen or so works in a space that would usually host a single work undoubtedly did not help to add value in the eyes of the public, as well as creating, as Jodi observes on the forum, [10] a false association between artists whose only common characteristic is that they use the net. In his response Simon Lamunière [11] showed that he was aware of all this, but at the time ghettoization appeared to be the only alternative to not existing at all.

Aside from this debate, however, it is interesting to see David's take on the "new media" question:

«*New technologies are nothing other than new means to an end. Alone they are of significance; it always depends upon how they are applied. I am against naive faith in progress, glorification of the possibilities of technological developments. Much of what today's artists produce with New Media is very boring. But I am just as opposed to the denunciation of technology. For me technology in itself is not a category according to which I judge works. This type of categorization is just as outmoded as division into classical art genres (painting, sculpture...). I am interested in the idea of a project; ideally the means of realizing the project should arise from the idea itself.*». [12]

David's decision to ask Lamunière to select a number of net projects for Documenta X should be seen in this sense: there is something going on there that goes beyond the traditional New Media paradigm, shifting the focus from the medium to the content. If David's message had been understood then, the history of the last fifteen years would have been very different.

In actual fact, the same period saw a similar attempt to stage an exhibition of New Media Art that avoided celebrating technology and steered clear of "New Media" rhetoric, focusing on works with that had something to say: the show *Serious Games: Art*

Interaction Technology (1996 – 1997) curated by Beryl Graham – on firstly at the Laing Art Gallery in Newcastle, and then at the Barbican Art Gallery in London. The aim of the show was evident from the slogan that accompanied it: "Not a show about new technology; a show about interaction", with interaction referring not just to the naturally interactive nature of the digital medium, but the relational dynamics generated by the works on display. As the curator explained: «Having a background in photography had convinced me that the tiresome "is it art?" debate about any technological art forms, recurring since at least the 1840s, was probably best addressed by showing good work until somebody announced a decision». [13] The "good work" gathered by Graham were interactive installations that involved an element of play, or at least user involvement, in the work, but also raised "serious" issues. *Rehearsal of Memory* (1995), by the English artist Harwood, is a navigable hypertext that gathers texts and images provided by the inmates of a psychiatric hospital. *Indigestion* (1996), by Diller+Scofidio, is an interactive table in which a lunch becomes an opportunity to unfold a vaguely noir narrative, and explore crucial issues related to class and gender.

By the late 90s, these major events no longer appeared isolated, but the base of a pyramid under construction. In 1993, at the School of Visual Arts in New York, Bruce Wands established the New York Digital Salon, an annual exhibition of "digital art". The first few editions of the Salon focussed on computer graphics and it took some time to cast off this approach and start exhibiting something more than insignificant pieces that at best showcased a given technology. [14] Yet the existence of the Salon demonstrated the growing interest in digital technologies in the academic world. In the years that followed the American university museums were to be the driving force behind pioneering exhibitions of New Media Art.

The same period saw various no-profit initiatives, often linked to the web. In 1997, at the MIT List Visual Arts Center, Massachusetts, Robbin Murphy and Remo Campopiano organized the show *PORT: Navigating Digital Culture* (25 January – 29 March 1997), one of the first exhibitions devoted to the net as a workplace for artists. [15] Murphy and Campopiano are the founders of Artnetweb, set up as a BBS in 1993 and launched on the web in 1995: a network of artists, intellectuals and curators that produces events, projects and an online magazine. Other similar initiatives came into being at this time: The Thing, set up in New York in 1991 by the artist Wolfgang Staehle as a BBS and launched on the web in 1995; äda'web, launched – also in New York – by the curator Benjamin Weil in 1994 as a platform for producing online projects commissioned from artists supported by a production team; Stadium, founded in 1995 and bought in 1999 by the DIA Center for the Arts in New York, and Rhizome, founded in Berlin by the American artist Mark Tribe in 1995. The work of these institutions – some of which, like Rhizome and The Thing, are still going – proved crucial in various ways: they promoted networking and debate, produced online works, organized exhibitions and forged contacts and partnerships with leading institutions. [16]

In the meantime, some of the latter were starting to take on curators specialized in New Media Art. In 1996 the Walker Art Center in Minneapolis appointed Steve Dietz as "founding director" of New Media Initiatives. In 1998, Dietz curated *Beyond Interface: net art and Art on the Net* (1998), a group show which came about as a contribution to *Museum & The Web*, an annual conference held since 1997 in Toronto. *Beyond Interface* aimed to show museum professionals that there was such a thing as artistic practice on the net, and raised various issues regarding the way in which contemporary art museums could engage with this new form of art. Over the years Dietz gave rise to a whirlwind of activity, including exhibitions and discussion platforms, developing a collection, and commissioning projects.

The Next Big Thing (1999 – 2001)

Initiatives like *Museum & The Web* testify to the growing need felt by museums to get on the digital train and enter into the information society: digitalizing their resources, experimenting with new ways of engaging with the public and taking up the challenge laid down by other less institutional, but more tech savvy players. In a period in which Le WebLouvre (now Web Museum), an amateur site launched in 1994 by the French curator Nicolas Pioch, appeared richer in information and more accessible than most museum websites, museums realized they had to get their act together. If we combine this with the exponential growth of the New Economy, with the advent of dozens of corporate structures in search of something to lend them legitimacy, including in cultural terms, and the media hype over the new technologies, which imposed their own narrative and fired up the collective imagination (just think of the how the terms "virus" and "hacker" were bandied around, and the hysteria surrounding the so-called Millennium Bug), and lastly the genuine interest aroused by certain artistic practices linked to the new media like Net Art, it is easy to understand the proliferation of institutional exhibitions devoted to the theme of "art and the new technologies" around the turn of the millennium.

However in the late 90s the net, and the technologically more advanced and culturally more aware New Media institutions, led the way, coming up with the most significant initiatives. Tokyo's NTT InterCommunication Center (ICC), which finally gained a permanent venue in the Tokyo Opera City Tower of Nishi-Shinjuku in 1997, was very active with exhibitions, seminars and conferences. In the same year the Karlsruhe seat of the ZKM opened, staging a decidedly ambitious show of "global" scope and form in 1999. Coordinated by Peter Weibel, *Net_Condition* boasted a pool of curators and was presented simultaneously in different four venues: the ZKM Center for Art and Media in Karlsruhe; the Steirischer Herbst in Graz, Austria (curated by Peter Weibel); the MECAD (Media Center d'Art i Disseny) in Barcelona, Spain (curated by Claudia Giannetti), and the NTT InterCommunication Center in Tokyo, Japan (curated by Toshiharu Ito). The main venue was that of Karlsruhe, where the show, coordinated by Jeffrey Shaw, featured almost seventy artists and seven curators, all, with the exception of Benjamin Weil, connected to the ZKM. After äda'web closed (1998), the American curator was taken on by the ICA (Institute of Contemporary Art) in London, and it was in the role of New Media Curator at the ICA that he took part in *Net_Condition*. In 2001 he appeared at the San Francisco Museum of Modern Art (SFMoMA), contributing to the organisation of *010101: Art in Technological Times*.

Net_Condition was about "the artist's look at the way society and technology interact with each other, are each other's 'condition'", and explored the question of how to organize an exhibition of art on the net in a series of physical venues. Yet at the same time *Net_Condition* was not intended as a show of Net Art, rather as a reflection «on the social conditions that created the Net and what the conditions are that the Net imposes on the other arts». [17]

In line with this, much of the venue was devoted to physical installations which also had a net-based dimension. One representative example of this is the hypertrophic structure entitled $|H|U|M|B|O|T|$ (1999 – 2004), a collaborative project on the theme of travel and navigation, as both practice and metaphor, which involved artists, hackers, writers and the group of Italian architects A12. In the ZKM venue their work took the Babelian form of an installation that featured pallets, scientific instruments, books, maps, computers, lamps and old pieces of furniture.

But despite this, the key question tackled by critical debate was whether it was indeed possible to reconcile institutions and the anti-institutional art par excellence (namely the art that chooses the net as a means to engage directly with the viewer), and the ways this could be achieved. *Net_Condition* attempted to formulate various different responses to this question, all of which were problematic. Firstly there was the Lounge (curated by Walter van der Cruijsen), which sought to recreate the internet's atmosphere of "social connection": it contained a series of vintage work stations where people could surf the net, chat and follow the artists' conferences. Some works were shown on computers connected to the net, while others were projected. Then there was the section *Plain.html*, curated by Benjamin Weil and devoted to a series of historic projects, not developed for the exhibition but forming a sort of "history of net art", which featured a hi-tech browser called *The Net.Art Browser* designed by the artist and co-curator Jeffrey Shaw. And this was where the first problems emerged. The installation was a sort of "physical navigator", a flat screen attached to the wall on runners and controlled by the viewer using a wireless keyboard. By moving the screen right or left the visitor could link up to the selected sites. According to the critic Josephine Berry, who reviewed the event for *Telepolis*, «one can only hope that the *Net.Art Browser* […] is meant as some kind of a joke», given that its only effect was that of «denaturating […] the browsing experience into one of public and inept performance, as opposed to a private and habitual practice». [18] And Berry was not alone in this view: Jodi refused to exhibit their work in this setting and Vuk Ćosić, after accepting the invitation, turned up on the day of the opening with a bunch of flowers that he laid pityingly at the entrance to the museum. And it has to be said that while the desire to remedy the errors of documenta X is appreciable – rejecting the office metaphor and refusing to tie Net Art to its common means of access – the computer screen – it is also true that the display that Shaw and Weil came up with presented various problems. The sense of ghettoization remains: all 32 works are gathered in the one container, which moreover is the work of an individual artist who inevitably ends up imposing his own vision on the others. Add the fact that Net Art's distinctive approach to technology is as about as far as you can get from Shaw's vision, and the rest is history.

The year 2000 saw a significant increase in the number and quality of events, with new players joining the field. Under the aegis of Steve Dietz, the Walker Art Center started the year with a new online project, *Art Entertainment Network*, the online arm of a major exhibition that took over the entire museum, entitled *Let's Entertain*. Inside the physical venue of the museum, the exhibition – which featured more than 40 artists – was presented in a special installation designed by Masamichi Udagawa and Sigi Moeslinger from Antenna Design New York Inc.: a black, monolithic "portal" bearing a computer screen. The different works could be accessed simply by rotating the portal on its axis, turning online navigation into a physical movement. This gateway functioned as an interface between the "real" exhibition and the "online" exhibition, implicitly asserting that the net is the ideal place for experiencing Net Art. This show of humility meant Dietz avoided the slew of criticism directed at Jeffrey Shaw's *Net.art Browser*, but temporarily shelved, rather than actually solving, the problem of how to exhibit Net Art in a physical space.

In April of that year, the Beachwood Center for the Arts, Beachwood (Ohio) staged the exhibition *Through the Looking Glass*, curated by Patrick Lichty. The show featured more than 200 works and an online exhibition that ran alongside the "physical" event. This show set out to ponder the impact of technology on the artistic object, exploring the New Media Art arena – for the first time – in all its territorial and geographical complexity. In fall, while the Iris and B. Gerald Cantor Center for the Visual Arts at Stanford University analyzed the artistic potential of the screensaver in an online exhibition (*Refresh: The Art of the Screen Saver*, curated by James Buckhouse and Merrill Falkenberg) another university museum (the Beall Center for Art & Technology at the University of California, Irvine School of the Arts) ran *SHIFT-CTRL – Computers, Games & Art*, the first institutional exhibition devoted to the relationship between art and videogames. Curated by Antoinette LaFarge and Robert Nideffer, one interesting thing about this show was that it involved the San Francisco MoMA (which loaned the Beall its newly appointed New Media Curator, Benjamin Weil), and the Walker Art Center, which loaned it Antenna Design, appointed to design the layout. Technical sponsorship came from Apple Computer. [19]

In the meantime, in Europe, the prestigious Kiasma Museum of Contemporary Art in Helsinki also got in on the act, presenting the exhibition *Alien Intelligence*, curated by Erkki Huhtamo, in February 2000. Footing the bill for this weighty New Media Art show – that featured works by artists like David Rokeby, Toshio Iwai, Christa Sommerer and Laurent Mignonneau, Perry Hoberman and Ken Feingold – was Nokia, leader of the telecoms industry and nascent mobile telephony sector. In the words of the curator, «media artists are curious about new technologies, and big companies, such as Nokia can really benefit from this type of outlook, too. Not surprisingly, many technology companies have established programmes and laboratories for visiting artists during recent years». [20]

These events further confirm the favourable conditions for New Media Art at the turn of the millennium, in which the museums' desire to get with the times, and the support of the hi-tech sector, which sought the kudos of culture, gave rise to new curatorial figures who worked to support the art of the new technologies in the museums, or on a freelance basis, moving from one museum to another.

The results of this joint effort were seen in 2001, but even in 2000 this process, and its lacunae, manifested themselves in the millennium edition of the Whitney Biennial, one of the events traditionally credited with sketching out the art of the immediate future. With 55 artists, 29 of whom were born outside the States, the 2000 Whitney Biennial was one of the biggest and most international in the history of the event. Coordinated by the then director of the museum Maxwell L. Anderson, in collaboration with six external curators, the Biennial also featured a section devoted to "Internet Art" (curated by Lawrence Rinder), that presented the work of nine artists (in a single screen). This section, funded by France Telecom, was amply publicized and became one of the event's highlights. But despite this the novelty did not make much of an impact in the press, for the most part critical towards a Biennial that Jerry Saltz described as «a train wreck with survivors». [21]

Now we come to 2001. A simple list of the events on in that year suffices to show how much was going on:

010101: Art in Technological Times. SFMoMA, San Francisco, 3 March – 8 July 2001. Curated by John S. Weber, Aaron Betsky, Benjamin Weil, Janet Bishop, Kathleen Forde, Davit Toop, Adrienne Gagnon and Erik Davis, the show presented 35 artists and designers, and was produced by Intel Corporation.

Art Now: Art and Money Online. Tate Britain, London, 6 March – 3 June 2001. Curated by Julian Stallabrass, it presented three installations. The main sponsor was Reuters.

BitStreams. Whitney Museum, New York, 22 March – 10 June 2001. Curated by Lawrence Rinder and Debra Singer, and featuring 49 artists. The main sponsor was Philip Morris Companies Inc.

Data Dynamics. Whitney Museum, New York, 22 March – 10 June 2001. Curated by Christiane Paul, featuring five installations. The main sponsor was France Telecom North America.

Telematic Connections: The Virtual Embrace. Walker Art Center, Minneapolis, 7 February – 24 March 2001. Organized by Independent Curators International (ICI), New York and curated by Steve Dietz, it toured six other venues in 2001. The event was partially sponsored by the Rockefeller Foundation.

Dystopia + Identity in the Age of Global Communications. Tribes Gallery, New York. 2 December 2000 – 13 January 2001. Curated by Cristine Wang and featuring more than fifty artists.

Net.art per Me. Venice, Santa Maria del Soccorso / Venice Biennale, 6 June – 27 June 2001. Curated by the artist Vuk Ćosić, this show was an extension of the Slovenian pavilion at the Venice Biennale, which in that year hosted Vuk Ćosić, 0100101110101101.ORG and Tadej Pogačar.

Game Show. MASS MoCA, North Adams, Massachusetts, 27 May 2001 – March 2002. The show presented "art games" created in the previous decade and also had an online section, curated by Mark Tribe and Alex Galloway from Rhizome.

The first aspect of note is obviously the number of high profile events in that year, in terms of the number of artists, the venue, the investments made and their cultural standard. We can easily reflect on how this interest is bound up with the media hype surrounding the new technologies and the financial interests behind that, but this does not detract from the topicality and caliber of some of the proposals. Take two events which have little in common with the "major institution / major sponsor / major exhibition" model: *Dystopia* and the exhibition organised on occasion of the Venice Biennale. *Dystopia* was presented at the Tribes Gallery, a non-profit organization, by Cristine Wang, curator at the Alternative Museum in New York. This venue is known for the quality of its shows, but, compared to the major museums, remains a niche player. The exhibition did not have any big sponsors, and – starting from the title – avoided channelling the media hype, choosing to focus on the theme of identity in the era of global communications. The success of *Dystopia* – which went down extremely well with both public and critics – appears to be linked less to the selection of works it presented and more to the design of the exhibition, which marked it out as "alternative", and succeeded in bringing together video, digital prints, but also paintings and sculptures, big names (like Mike Bidlo and Jonas Mekas) and lesser known artists, new media and old media. In other words, works were not chosen according to their medium, but in terms of what they had to say about the theme of the exhibition.

Neither does the presence of Net Art at the Venice Biennale reflect this criteria. In his introduction in the catalogue, Vuk Ćosić hints at the fact that the opening of the Slovenian pavilion occasioned a minor political incident. Given that neither of the opposing factions managed to impose their chosen candidate, the decision to invite two relatively marginal figures (Vuk Ćosić and Tadej Pogačar) and a duo of Italian artists (01001011101-01101.ORG) turned out to be a diplomatic solution, which also drew attention to the Slovenian contribution to a movement that was getting a lot of press in that period. This strategy was also praised by the curator of the Biennale, Harald Szeemann, who asserted that the virus circulated by 0100101110101101.ORG was the most innovative work in the whole event, and garnered an enthusiastic response from the public. As well as exhibiting his work in the Slovenian Pavilion, Vuk Ćosić decided to curate a group show that rejected the New Media paradigm outright, presenting works that dusted off obsolete technologies. Ćosić came up with the term "New Low Tech Media", explaining: «With this slogan, I'm trying to identify artists that are reacting to the dumb way in which the art system and the society at large are non-reacting to the technological development». [22]

But despite their rejection of "New Media" rhetoric, both these events managed to give the impression that what they were presenting, together with the other events listed, was "the next big thing" in art. The involvement of three major museums, like the Whitney Museum, the SFMoMA and the Tate Britain, alongside the ongoing efforts of the Walker Art Center and the newly launched MassMOCA, necessarily added to this impression.

Rather than looking at these events in detail, at this point it is useful to explore the circumstances which led to their existence, and how they were received. *010101: Art in Technological Times* came about thanks to David A. Ross, the museum's dynamic, visionary director. It was Ross who appointed Benjamin Weil as "new media curator" in February 2000. However *010101* was not an exhibition of New Media Art, but an event devoted to the impact of the new technologies on our daily lives. [23] In this way it did not fall into the trap of ghettoizing New Media Art in yet another 'dedicated' exhibition, but rather created a platform in which old and media could be compared. The theme of the exhibition was however presented in celebratory and promotional tones which did not admit criticism. «These pioneering artists are demonstrating that digital technology, like photography and video before it, offers a new and vital means of creative expression and communication», wrote Pam Pollace, vice-president of marketing for Intel, in the catalog. [24] The design of the exhibition, a high-tech setting with white curtains and plasma screens scrolling aphorisms by visionaries like Arthur C. Clarke and Marshall McLuhan, also showed that *010101* was not entirely over its infatuation with the medium. Presented as SFMoMA's most ambitious event, the exhibition opened its doors in March, and expectations were further heightened on January 1, 2001, by the online section, curated by Benjamin Weil. This section was set up to host the online projects in the exhibition, which would not be on show in the physical venue. Weil had obviously clocked the failure of *Net.Art Browser*, the interface created to access the online projects featured in *Net_Condition*. The launch of the online section of *010101* represented the end point of a process initiated the previous year, when the SFMoMA, in collaboration with the Webby Awards, announced the launch of a digital art award, and the founding of e-space, its very own online Net Art gallery. [25]

All of these factors meant that, while the exhibition attempted to shift attention from technology as a medium to technology as an issue, the former aspect continued to occupy most of the critical discourse. Yet ten years on *010101* remains an ambitious, visionary and intelligent project, and much can be learned from both its strengths and weaknesses. [26]

The fact that *010101* clashed with the two shows on at the Whitney certainly did it no favors. *Bitsteams* and *Data Dynamics* were sister exhibitions that filled the Whitney's schedule from March to June. The former was a major collective of almost 50 artists, while the second featured only five installations. Although complementary, the two initiatives should be viewed as separate; while *Bitstreams* was a major overview of the artistic use of the new technologies, as both tool and medium, *Data Dynamics* [27] was a smaller scale event but with big ambitions: to give online art a presence in physical space, even just in the banal sense of "occupying space". Moving beyond the approach of big screen and projections adopted by the previous Whitney Biennial, and the idea of uniting all the works in a single installation designed by the curator, Christiane Paul worked with the artists to create an installation-style presentation of the five works. Some of them started life as installations or sculptures, while others, like *Apartment* (2001), by Marek Walczak and Martin Wattenberg – were accessible on the net and translated into installation form for the museum venue; some predated the exhibition while others were commissioned for it.

To go back to *Bitstreams*, the approach adopted is evident from the opening lines of the catalogue text by Larry Rinder, one of the curators: «Nothing since the invention of photography has had a greater impact on artistic practice than the emergence of digital technology». [28] This celebratory tone did not escape the critics. In *Art in America*, Barbara Pollack dedicated a long article to the exhibition, which she called a «irony-free digital extravaganza» which does no more than show that «artists, like everyone else, use computers». In Pollack's view, the exhibition revealed «studied superficiality», and the artists appeared to have been selected to represent specific technological gizmos. Pollack continues with a critique that is more circumstantial, but no less valid: the absence of the human dimension, in any form; the predilection for abstract languages, the almost total exclusion of female artists, reinforcing the stereotype of technology as the preserve of young males, and the total absence, in its general celebratory tone, of the dark side of technology, and the artists whose work sets out to subvert it.

Pollack's article is interesting because it is based on a good knowledge and appreciation of New Media Art, while challenging its existence as a category. She writes: «Digital art [...] is a messy category that turns formalism on its ear by simulating art forms such as painting, sculpture, photography, film and installation, and by subverting the once sacred distinctions between these categories». This critique is shared by Stefanie Syman, in *Feed*:

«Being digital or made with digital tools doesn't really say much about the art itself [...] digital art is a category of convenience that should be retired». [29]

The End of the Dance (2002 – 2010)

Little by little the museums' passion was cooling, however. There were various reasons for this: financiers with a vested interest were bowing out; critics were questioning the utility of a medium-based definition, as reflected by the refusal of some key institutions to set up a dedicated department, and there was a growing perception, highlighted by Stefanie Syman in the aforementioned article, that the new media were in any case entering the studios of all artists, making this already debatable category even more meaningless.

It should be said that at the time, Syman was one of the few to understand that New Media Art was beginning to wane. The enthusiasm of Rinder and Ross was contagious, and the resistance of conservative critics appeared to be the natural consequence of a hands-down victory. The doubts over the contextualization of digital art did not go away, but were small fry respect to this aggressive, alpha campaign, in terms of both museums and the market. If I was directing a movie in the style of Hollywood's golden age, I could present 2001 by filming the jubilant newspaper headlines of the day: «Digital goes critical. Now that digital art has been brought inside the museum, will the artworld take it seriously?» (*Arts Journal*); «Now that they have seen the glowing blue light, no one in the museum world wants to be caught missing the Next Big Thing» (*Nymag.com*); «The commitment of these museums to new media has prompted debates on the issues of collecting and conserving digital media» (*The Art Newspaper*); «The new new-media blitz. Digital art – in all its forms – is gaining prominence among artists, curators, and audiences» (*Art News*). We could continue in this vein, but the situation appeared clear-cut: skeptics and converts alike appeared to think that the boho dance was over and it was finally time to consummate the relationship. Yet none of the big museums ever returned to the enthusiasm demonstrated in 2001. In subsequent years some of them quietly disposed of their "new media curators" (the Walker Art Center, the SFMoMA and the Guggenheim), while others, like the Whitney Museum and the Tate Gallery, effectively sidelined them, continuing to work on this arena but with a much more cautious approach, limited to producing online projects. And the market, which had appeared ready to snap up these tasty new morsels, turned sluggish too.

But to return to the exhibitions, the events from 2002 to 2009 that involved a New Media Art component essentially appear to follow three different models. The first could be dubbed the "ivory tower" approach: basically, albeit a few years on, taking up the model of the major exhibition exploring the artistic use of the new technologies. Like in *Bitstreams*, the theme, if there is one, is purely incidental: wrapping paper to dress up a recycled gift. In actual fact the model had not changed since the period of *Mediascape*: presenting a mixed bag of artworks with little in common apart from the increasingly ambiguous label of New Media Art, or digital art. Replicating this model could lead to exhibitions of interest, well curated and even useful from an educational point of view. The problem is that whatever you do to dress it up, the concept basically boils down to Pollack's laconic observation: these days artists, like everyone else, use computers. And while the aspiration was to achieve institutional legitimacy, the inevitable effect was basically confining it to a ghetto; a golden prison, but a prison nonetheless.

The second model could be couched in terms of the oft-debated "workplace quotas". Despite the ironic description, this is a basically positive model: New Media Art starting to appear, in small doses, in themed contemporary art shows. This is the approach that was attempted in *010101*, but without the technophile superstructure. In 2003, for example, the Künstlerhaus Wien in Vienna staged a show entitled *Abstraction Now* (curated by Norbert Pfaffenbichler and Sandro Droschl). As the title says, this was a major overview of the state of abstract art, and it featured a good number of artists who work with software and the web, from Jodi to Marius Watz, Golan Levin and Casey Reas.

The third model, that of the "discreet guest", is the one adopted

by most of the shows staged between 2002 and 2010. In this case New Media Art makes its entrance on the contemporary art stage by means of well curated, conceptually solid, medium-sized events, often held in small institutions or private galleries. The themes are normally borrowed from the arena of digital culture, and the works belong to New Media Art, though this is rarely emphasized. New Media Art understands that, when operating in areas that are not its own, it is better to operate discreetly. For this reason, statements like "this is the art of the technological era, the definitive contemporary art" are carefully avoided. The aim, obviously, is to show that this arena is capable of producing interesting works that perfectly capture a particular aspect of the *zeitgeist*: contemporary art at its best. Events of this kind play a very important role in terms of mediation, comparable to that of the previous category: they offer the contemporary art public the opportunity to get a handle on topical issues that are often treated superficially in the media and overlooked in the mainstream art world, and familiarize themselves with a certain type of works, and they show that New Media Art is not just an exploration of the medium and a celebration of technology, but also an inquiry into some key aspects of our age: video surveillance, the post-human world, the end of privacy, the invasive nature of communications and possible ways of subverting them, and so on. Without the aggressively assertive approach that characterized the initiatives of 2001, these events elicit a different mood among visitors, and the fact that no-one is insisting that these works belong to a certain category avoids the annoyance and prejudice that the term usually arouses in the art world.

Its Specific Form of Contemporaneity

Although with various positive aspects, the "workplace quota"

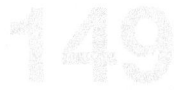

and "discreet guest" models also highlight some critical areas. The former shows, positively, that it is possible to insert New Media Art into other systems of discourse, not necessarily linked to the media, technology and the digital arena, but negatively reveals the contemporary art world's resistance to a key question of the present period: the advent of the information society and its consequences on life, society and identity. In other words the issues that shows like *Posthuman* (1993) and *010101* (2001) – albeit with a basically flawed approach – endeavored to raise. It is difficult to find a reason for this resistance beyond a lack of "media awareness" among contemporary art curators. Figures like Deitch and Ross are needed, figures able to reconcile being involved in both "media culture" and contemporary art.

Figures of this kind have already appeared on the scene, and are probably destined to increase in number, if for no other reason than purely generational factors. In May 2008 at the Stedelijk Museum in Amsterdam, Andreas Broeckmann, director of the Transmediale festival in Berlin, curated a show entitled *Deep Screen. Art in Digital Culture*. In this show Broeckmann, "new media curator" by training, attempted to move beyond the New Media paradigm, gathering works that, independently of their medium, reflected the new aesthetics and cultures of the information society: Jasmijn Visser's large format drawings on paper, genuine catalogues of icons and images from the world of communication; the abstract paintings of Roland Schimmel, explosions of light drawn from digital animations, or the small modular sculptures by Driessens & Verstappen, generated by software programs and produced using large 3D printers. [30] *Deep Screen* addressed both of our worlds, attempting to send a different message to each. It told the New Media Art world that the New Media paradigm no longer had any reason to exist, and it told the contemporary art world that that paradigm had deprived it of artists and works essential in terms of providing a convincing picture of contemporary reality.

Another curator doing a lot of work, with various means, in this direction, is the German Inke Arns, artistic director of the Hartware MedienKunstVerein in Dortmund, Germany, since 2005. According to Arns,

«What defines Media Art today is not its range of media, but rather its specific form of contemporaneity, its content-related examination of our present, which is to a high degree typified by media. [...] Which media are used becomes progressively more irrelevant. In other words: Media Art is no longer the formal category or formal genre it was considered to be, above all in the 1990s [...] Rather it defines itself through an intensive content-related examination of the world surrounding us, one increasingly medialised and based upon new technologies. At the same time this examination does not necessary entail the use of the new technologies, but rather makes use of (almost) all media and technologies. It frees itself from the compulsion to utilize the latest technology, discards the conceptual support afforded by the newness of the medium and faces the challenge of art. It is (finally) growing up.». [31]

This belief translates into curatorial practices that, albeit developed in a small media center at the edge of the empire, are producing some very interesting results. Arns selects culturally strong projects for her venue, and talks with the artists about the best way to convey their energies in an exhibition. In many cases this can mean "producing" the works from scratch, above all in the case of Net Art. In this process, wherever possible, Arns avoids using high tech devices to present the works. *The Wonderful World of irational.org. Techniques, Tools, and Events 1996 – 2006* (2006), for example, set out to document the work of irational.org, an online community of artists and activists founded in Great Britain in 1996 and still up and running. Irational.org is a server, a catalyst of projects, a list of personal pages, collective projects and mailing lists. So how on earth to go about presenting something so connected to the web, to horizontal collaborations and communications in a public venue? In Dortmund they did it with a very pared-down use of the classic computer hooked up to the net, along with videos, projections, printed logos and slogans on the walls, documents, posters and "ephemera" generated during ten years of activity. The exhibition transferred irational.org into a physical space, and introduced us to its "magical world". Any visitors particularly taken with it could get to know it better by checking it out on the web. The event was a success, and ended up being hosted in various other venues: something made possible by its ability to cut straight to the chase, presenting the crux of the project without imposing a "technological frame" that would have had little to do with irational.org (to date the site still sports a resolutely low-tech aesthetic).

Both the issue of the "materialization of New Media Art" and that of the current unsustainability of this conceptual category can be found in a show staged in April 2009 at the iMAL Center for Digital Cultures and Technology, curated jointly by myself and the director of the center, Yves Bernard. Born out of the doubts and reflections that emerged while writing this book, it turned out to be the perfect benchtest for it. Framing my questions as provocative statements and putting them into the public arena helped me find a lot of answers.

Like *Deep Screen*, *Holy Fire. Art of the Digital Age* also had a two-pronged approach. Staged by a Media Center, the show was part of the external program of one of Europe's most important contemporary art fairs, Art Brussels. Thanks to this connection, *Holy Fire* was like a pebble that skimmed two adjacent but not communicating ponds, bouncing ideas off both. The curatorial concept echoed the rationale behind the organizational process, namely staging a New Media Art show using works exclusively from private collections and commercial galleries. This practice, entirely run of the mill in the contemporary art world, was by no means a given for a New Media Art show. The project, starting from the title, ironically referenced the rhetoric of the major exhibitions that had embraced the new technologies so enthusiastically, subverting this approach from the inside, as it were. It showed visitors to Art Brussels that so-called New Media Art really was art, was collectable and that its finest outcomes were already available on the market. It showed New Media Art circles that the New Media paradigm had had its day, by boldly presenting a wide variety of works with basically nothing in common "apart from the medium". And in many cases not even that. One of the most interesting things about exploring the collections and the galleries was observing that artists and works usually associated with the New Media Art arena often choose stable, object-based forms, and entirely traditional media – drawing, sculpture, prints and video – to present their work in the contemporary art world. This is the case not only because, as is often insinuated, a print is easier to sell than a piece of software, but also and above all because, in an exhibition venue, a print works better than a piece of software, conveying the content of the work more effectively; and lastly because, as Inke Arns writes, "New Media Art" (the quotation marks are now mandatory) has "finally grown up", and gotten over its initial reverence for the medium.

Holy Fire also set out to elicit internal discussion, by publishing in its catalog a circular interview with artists, curators, critics and gallerists; but above all it sparked heated debate, generating around a hundred articles and comments that mostly focussed on whether it was opportune to be talking about the market. [32] Yet collecting was just one of the issues addressed by the show. As Régine Debatty wrote: [33]

«To be honest, i needed such exhibition. Last Summer I

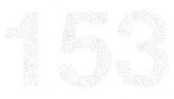

realized that I was getting a much more fruitful and satisfying art experience at the Venice Biennale than at Ars Electronica. Media art often suffers from faddism and from a series of misunderstandings. For example, i can't count the number of times i heard someone (or seen an exhibition) confuse "something weird done with technology" with media art.».

Collecting and the Market

However boring or interesting, necessary or uncomfortable it turned out to be, *Holy Fire* proved at least one thing: that raising the question of the relationship between the market and New Media Art is the equivalent to heading into a fireworks store with a lit match. Otherwise this issue – one of the many raised by the exhibition, and not the main one – would not have been in pole position in the public debate, a position it has yet to relinquish. It should come as no surprise, however. As we have seen, the sale of works is not a traditional part of the distinctive economy of New Media Art. The "financial fetishization of art" plays a key role in the world of contemporary art, which as Yves Michaud pointed out, quoting Leo Castelli, is made up of «a limited number of rich people who want to get their hands on certain works before they become unaffordable». [34] It is fairly obvious that this macroscopic difference is a focal point of the war between the two worlds. In any case the advent of a form of collecting that supports a given trend, language or movement still represents one of the tipping points of the Boho dance. Many things have changed in the art world since Wolfe wrote the piece, and perhaps his observation that "the public is not invited (and never has been)", having no role in the victory (or defeat) of a trend, needs to be revisited. But it remains indisputably true that the dealer-collector node continues to be one of the factors that most influences the fate of art.

The New Media Art world is evidently intuiting that if the art market manages to get hold of its practices, the latter could succeed where 15 years of museum exhibitions failed, enabling New Media Art to join the ranks of contemporary art. For some, the show reawakened fears that insisting so pointedly on this issue could in some way compromise this delicate process, while others hoped this would give it a helping hand. Naturally *Holy Fire* did not have the power to do either of these things. Moreover, as we will see in the next chapter, the New Media Art world has too many good reasons to exist in order to be torn to pieces when the Boho dance climaxes. In any case, lest that worry anyone, that stage is still some way off. *Holy Fire* attempted to raise the profile of the enthusiastic work of a limited number of galleries and private collectors, but there is still much work to be done. While museums have repeatedly attempted to ride the digital art wave, it is also true that other key areas of the contemporary art world have taken things much more slowly. And the sluggishness of critics, curators, galleries and collectors is what has occasioned the failure of all attempts to lend legitimacy to work using the new media in the contemporary art world.

Together with the other players mentioned, the market and the collectors therefore have the power to reverse this trend. In the next few pages we will take a brief look at the steps that have been taken in this direction.

As we have seen, the first gallery to take an interest in the New Media field was the Postmasters Gallery of New York, in 1996. For a long time, it was also the only one. In February 2008 its founders stated:

«We have always sought art that is reflective of our time: idea driven, forward looking work that could not have been done before. While this, of course, is not dependent on the medium – it seemed that new media artists were the infusion of fresh blood [...] New media art is a terrific expansion of available tools and the cultural playing field – an addition, not a

replacement. Our goal is to actually strip the "New Media Artists" of the New Media part and deliver them to a larger pool where they are known simply as Artists». [35]

As we can see, Postmasters insists that it is not a specialized gallery, even though its pioneering work earned it that reputation for a long time. In 2001, magazines published the news of Postmasters' sale of a digital work by Camille Utterback and Romy Achituv (*Text Rain*, 2000) for 15,000 dollars. In subsequent years, Postmasters continued to pour its energies into this type of work, representing artists like etoy.corporation, Natalie Jeremijenko, John Klima, Eva and Franco Mattes (aka 0100101110101101.org), Jennifer and Kevin McCoy, Wolfgang Staehle, Eddo Stern and Maciej Wisniewski, exploring, together with some of these, alternative strategies for financial support.

Now, however, Postmasters is no longer alone. In 2001, an article in *Forbes* mentioned the name Sandra Gering alongside it. Founded in 1991, the Sandra Gering Gallery (now Gering & Lopez) moved to Chelsea in 2000, and began to include a few "New Media" artists in its pool: names like John F. Simon, Jane Simpson, Xavier Veilhan, Vincent Szarek, David Tremlett and Karim Rashid. Susan Delson, who wrote the article, explains that Simon's works take the form of sculptures that incorporate a monitor with a software animation, produced in limited edition runs, and relates that «one collector, New Jersey physician John Burger, who's bought all five editions to date, never even owned a personal computer. For him, Simon's works are abstract art – "so intelligent, so creative, so unlike anything I'd ever seen" and the digital aspect is almost beside the point». [36] Another private individual interested in the work of Simon – thanks to efforts of the curator Mario Diacono – was the fashion designer Max Mara, who made it public knowledge in 2009 by staging a show in his foundation featuring the works purchased or commissioned from the artist during the previous decade (from the historic *CPU*, 1999, to the recent *Visions*, 2009). Diacono's text in the catalog [37] hints at motivations similar to those of Burger: Simon's "software art" acquires value in the eyes of the critic – and the collector – in so far as it unexpectedly picks up the legacy of twentieth century abstract art.

Forbes also mentions the Julia Friedman Gallery, which opened in Chicago in 2001, and closed in 2006 only a year after moving to New York. In 2001 this gallery presented *Genesis*, a complex installation by Eduardo Kac that blended digital technologies and biotechnologies. For obvious chronological reasons, *Forbes* does not mention the Bitforms Gallery, which opened in Chelsea a few months later (November 2001) with an ambitious program: that of supporting «emerging and established artists who embrace new media and contemporary art practice – resulting in new languages and artistic experiences». Bitforms was the first, and for some time the only gallery specialized in New Media Art. Its founder, Steven Sacks, was getting over a bad experience in the dot.com sector, when in 2001, he saw *Bitstreams* and *010101*: «He saw a maket opportunity: there weren't any galleries exclusively devoted to new media», he told *Wired* in 2005. [38] At that time the gallery appeared to be going great guns. The article was published on occasion of the opening of Bitforms Seoul, its first branch outside of the States. This was the outcome of an agreement with Chung Jae-Bong, one of South Korea's richest businessmen. Chung had seen a work by Daniel Rozin installed in the W Seoul Walkerhill Hotel and immediately contacted Rozin's gallery, Bitforms. The result was the opening of a branch of Bitforms in the MUE Store, one of Chung's fashion stores. Bitforms was just back from ARCO, the Madrid fair: «"it was a huge success; we sold a lot of work," he says [...] "I brought Danny Rozin's *Wooden Mirror* – it was like the Mona Lisa. I had to hire a person to manage the crowd. To me, there was just this huge evolutionary moment in the way people were looking at art"». Two editions of the work were sold to Spanish institutions for 120,000 dollars. The business of educating collectors was obviously going well, at least on certain fronts. Daniel Rozin creates "interactive mirrors" in which the technology disappears completely behind pieces of wood, metal discs, mosaic tiles of reflective glass or trash collected on the street. The creations are controlled by an invisible system that detects the form of those standing in front of the work and shapes the materials that make up the mirror in such a way that they "reflect" the shape and colour of the person looking into it. These works rely heavily on the magic of technology, but translate it into entirely captivating objects.

Yet it continues to be trickier, even for Bitforms, to sell software works. A talking point in 2002 [39] was the sale of *The Waiting Room*, a "networked installation" by Mark Napier, for 1,000 dollars per "share". The work was a single piece "shared" by its collectors: an interactive online environment animated by the actions of the visitors / collectors with abstract shapes and sounds. By April Bitforms had only sold three shares out of the fifty made available. Three years later, according to the article in *Wired*, they were all sold. As one of the owners relates: «One night, at 2 am – someone in LA must have come home and started partying – there was this incredible racket [...] I'm listening to this sound – it isn't the television, it isn't a truck. I thought, "Oh, I left the art on." I turned it off and went to sleep».

Another of Sacks' projects was Software Art Space, a website that sells big runs of reasonably priced artist software. The idea was to create something that lay between the software available free of charge on the web and works of art in the form of installations, prints or videos in limited editions and often too pricey for most. The vision that Software Art Space [40] is based revolves around the increasing accessibility, and quality, of the technologies available for viewing animated images, like LCD screens and touch pads. In this situation, software art could become the painting of the future: animated, possibly interactive, displayed on a flat screen on the living room wall, above the sofa.

Despite its Yankee pragmatism, however, the idea is struggling to take off, and the core business of Bitforms continues to be the sale of installations, prints and videos in limited editions: in other words, objects. And it has to be said that New Media Art's increasing willingness to engage with the world of objects is what has guaranteed it a bigger presence in galleries. 2002 saw the opening in New York of the Bryce Wolkovitz Gallery, with a mission statement stating its interest in «moving image, new media, sculpture, photography and the limitless interplay between these mediums». [41] In 2003 in Berlin, Wolf Lieser, former director of the DAM Digital Art Museum, an online digital art museum, founded the DAM Gallery, another specialized gallery. In 2005, the Fabio Paris Art Gallery in Brescia, Italy, organized the first solo show of Eva and Franco Mattes (0100101110-101101.ORG), key figures in the Net Art world. The growing interest in an art capable of responding to the challenges of the information era has led to the gallery working with artists like UBERMORGEN.COM, Eddo Stern, Jon Rafman and Gazira Babeli. [42]

There are (and have been) numerous private galleries making considerable investments in this direction. A no doubt incomplete list should include: And/Or gallery, Dallas; artMovingProjects, New York; VertexList, New York; Stadium, New York; Numeriscausa, Paris; Future Gallery, Berlin. And / Or Gallery operated in Dallas from 2006 to 2009, and was run by artist and musician Paul Slocum together with some collaborators. Thanks to the owner's sensibility toward technology and to a high level of dialogue with the artists, the gallery pioneered new methods of archiving and displaying new media artwork and websites, materializing digital works in a way that was not primarily market-driven. [43] ArtMovingProjects and VertexList were two artist-run spaces founded in Williamsburg, respectively, by Aron Namenwirth and Marcin Ramocki, that played an equally important rule in introducing new media to New York and educating collectors and audiences. While VertexList stopped operating in 2011, ArtMovingProjects is still active, but mainly as an online platform and no-profit venture. [44] Stadium was founded in New York in 2011, and since then it has organized solo and group shows focused on an emerging new generation of "post internet" artists, often very active online but operating in the white cube with traditional media such as painting, installation and sculpture, but with a strong sensibility to the issues raised by the information age. [45] A similar approach is displayed by the Berlin-based Future Gallery, which opened in 2011 with a show by Jaakko Pallasvuo; [46] while Numeriscausa, which opened in 2007 and closed a few years later, mainly represented a group of French new media artists of different generations, including Samuel Bianchini, Grégory Chatonsky, Miguel Chevalier, Joseph Nechvatal and Antoine Schmitt.

But it is above all the "occasional" presence of this kind of works in non-specialized galleries that can give us a measure of how far the genre has penetrated the contemporary art world. There are numerous examples of this, some at a very high level. In December 2005, the New York gallery Pace Wildenstein staged a group show entitled *Breaking & Entering: Art and the Video Game*. In the essay in the catalog, its curator Patricia Hughes has this to say about the featured artists:

«*These artists, conditioned by video games to act upon their environments, find ways to reassert the self in this new world […] Products of a generation whose cultural habits and memory have been very much formed by interactive experience, they construct their own reality out of the detritus of imagination*». [47]

Unfortunately, however, the gallery did not continue to work with any of them. Cory Arcangel, on the other hand, following a joint show with Paper Rad at Deitch Projects (2005), joined New York's respected Team Gallery. In 2007, the work of the Mexican artist Raphael Lozano-Hemmer, represented by Bitforms, was presented in the new Mexican pavilion at the Venice Biennale. Since then he has worked with various galleries, including London's Haunch of Venison. Commercial galleries that work or have worked with New Media artists include Cosmic Galerie, Paris; Seventeen, London; Carroll / Fletcher, London; Skuc Gallery, Ljubljana; Lia Rumma, Milan; Gloriamaria Gallery, Milan; ARC Projects, Bucharest, Vadehra Art Gallery, New Dehli; Analix Forever, Geneva; Gentili Apri, Berlin; Virgil de Voldere, New York; Foxy Productions, New York; American Medium, New York; Ernst Hilger, Vienna.

This increasing interest in New Media Art from private galleries has also given rise to another interesting phenomenon: that of dedicated fairs or specialized sections in general art fairs. Naturally we could object that both phenomena merely reinforce the ghettoization of New Media Art, which, to some extent, is true. Yet at the same time, in a period like the present one, the pioneering, passionate work done by a number of galleries indisputably deserves to be safeguarded and promoted. Moreover, specialized art fairs or sections help the galleries network, support each other and lobby. In this direction ARCO, the Madrid art fair, did some groundbreaking work. Arco has had a special section for New Media Art from 1998 to 2010, a section that has changed name and mission several times: in 1998 it started life as Arco Electronico, becoming Netspace@Arco in 2000. In 2002 it took a break, coming back in 2004 in the form of a prize sponsored by the Ministry of Science and Technology. In 2005 the prize went back to being a section, this time dubbed Black Box, with the involvement of prestigious external curators. In 2008 it had another name change, becoming Expanded Box, and staying that way through 2009 and 2010, when the fair also added a separate section for video. In spite of all this chopping and changing and the criticism it received over the years, [48] this special section had the undisputable historic merit of having presented New Media Art in an international market context, boosting the interactions between galleries and public and private collectors. The fair's "New Media" program also included the Arco Beep Award, a purchase award devoted to the new technologies, and the presentation of the winners of the Vida Competition, launched in 1999 by Fundación Telefónica. Two corporate initiatives, the first devoted to building a collection, the second aiming to fund major projects that explore issues pertaining to artificial life and biotechnologies. In 2011 the fair had a major revamp but these two initiatives survived, and the fair's commitment to new media produced in 2013 the "ARCO Bloggers" forum, a panel discussion moderated by Roberta Bosco and Stefano Caldana, curators and art critics for *El Pais*. [49]

2003 saw the launch of a small specialized fair, DiVA (Digital and Video Art Fair), which in 2005 became a travelling fair, with events in New York, Brussels, Cologne and Paris (2005), Miami Beach (2006), New York and Paris again, (2007 and 2008), and Basel (2009). As the director Thierry Alet explained in an interview:

«DiVA is a very distinctive event: it targets curators, collectors and young buyers, but is not your usual art fair. The accent is on information, giving people direct access and helping them get a better understanding of the works on show». [50]

The fair stopped any activity after 2009. In February 2009 London hosted the first Kinetica Art Fair, an even more specialized no-profit event featuring public and private exhibitors. Its 2012 edition hosted the work of over 45 galleries and art organisations,

with representatives from 18 countries, collectively showing over 400 works of art. [51]

So it looks like a turning point is on the cards at the end of the decade opened by *010101*. Markets and galleries are waking up, taking up the challenge thrown down by the institutions at the start of the decade. In the words of Wolf Lieser, director of the DAM Gallery in Berlin:

«*The market is growing, and there is increasing interest in this form of expression [...] I don't think digital art will ever overtake painting or sculpture, but I'm sure that in the future the combination of sculpture and software art, interactive or otherwise, will be very popular [...] The prices are always much lower than those of traditional art, meaning that you can buy masterpieces at reasonable prices*». [52]

But a market can only exist if, on the other side, there is someone looking to buy and collect. Unfortunately, among the various kinds of people interested in New Media Art, collectors have always been something of a rare breed. Numerous reasons for this have been posited, with three in particular coming around like a tired old refrain: the ephemeral, performative and time-based nature of New Media Art; the trouble with conserving it, due to its dependency on rapidly obsolete technologies and languages, and its duplicability, viewed as a threat to the supposedly unique nature of the artistic object. [53]

Yet these seem to be excuses rather than genuine reasons. The art market has already got to grips with the ephemeral nature of contemporary artworks. For our purposes it matters little whether these solutions are compromises, or in some cases, not terribly functional. The "Black Box" came about with the aim of offering a safe haven for the temporal nature of video, enabling it to be experienced over time; performance and conceptual art have learned to use methods of documentation (photography, video) and in some cases, certification. Even rapidly obsolete media have found a protocol: old film reels or VHS videos have migrated onto digital media, possibly also being restored in the process. Organic materials can be replaced, as can neon tubes. Sometimes it can be impossible to replace the original material: this was the case for Dan Flavin, who used a particular shade of red in his neon installations which has been withdrawn from the market due to toxicity. It was a fairly predictable outcome, but did not overly trouble his collectors. Hirst knows his sharks' days are numbered but the artist's popularity is not suffering as a result. Or it might be suffering, but for different reasons.

The issue of the "technical reproducibility" of works of art has also found a solution: photographs and videos sold in limited editions. Not even the digitalization of the image has challenged this convention, as absurd as this might seem.

The fact of the matter is that those who collect works of art, be they museums or private individuals, do not let things like this stand in their way – unless they are convinced of the low cultural or financial value of the work in question. In other words, if New Media Art is struggling in market terms, this is not due to the aforementioned issues, but because there are still doubts over its value as art. Once again, it comes down to a question of appeal, a question that is influenced both by the technology and generation gap, the difficulties faced by traditional criticism and resistance to the New Media paradigm. If I have to choose between two things I have my doubts over, I will go for the one that offers more guarantees in terms of conservation and uniqueness. Such as a painting, for example.

The most solid proof for what we are saying is the behavior of the very museums who set about showing the public the appeal of New Media Art around the turn of the millennium. Compared with their exhibition programs, their collecting agenda is at best rather disappointing. While staging exhibitions like *Mediascape*, *Bitstreams* and *010101*, that insisted on the cultural importance of the new technologies, museums like the Guggenheim, Whitney and SFMoMA were spending trifling amounts on acquisitions and commissions. In 1995 the Whitney Museum purchased the work *The World's First Collaborative Sentence* by Douglas Davis, [54] which it archived on floppy-disk. The piece consisted in an online collaborative writing experiment, where the artist provided the first sentence, inviting the public to continue ad infinitum. This purchase was actually the result of a donation from the collectors Barbara and Eugene M. Schwartz, who had bought it that same year. Around 2000 the museum got itself an "adjunct curator of New Media Art", in the shape of Christiane Paul. As well as arranging temporary initiatives, Paul set up the platform *Artport*, which between 2001 and 2006 commissioned and hosted a number of works. Since 2006 the curator has suspended the online commissioning program in order to rationalize the limited budget the museum gives her and to work on more ambitious projects for the institution's bricks and mortar space (which included, in 2011, a huge retrospective of the work of Cory Arcangel). Only in 2010, the Whitney Museum started a new online commissions program, and launched a preservation initiative to conserve and integrate the digital artworks featured in Artport, of which we still have to see the results. [55]

Artport is not an isolated case: at the turn of the millennium a number of museums equipped themselves with an online gallery to gather net based projects they commissioned. The DIA Center for the Arts in New York did so in 1995, creating a commissions program that is still up and running. Curated by Sarah Tucker and Lynne Cooke, the section has slowly but surely commissioned a series of net based projects from artists in various sectors and disciplines (from music to dance, video and performance), providing a tech support team to help them. The DIA's Web

Projects" are also the only online gallery that can be accessed directly from the museum's main site. According to the researcher Karen Verschooren, this program is backed by the New York State Council on the Arts, with annual funding of between 7,000 and 9,000 dollars. [56]

From 1996 to 2003, when Steve Dietz was fired and the New Media Initiatives shut down, the Walker Art Center put together an impressive collection of online works, which can still be accessed from the museum's website, albeit not directly from the homepage, entitled *Gallery 9*. [57] The initiative gathered donations (like äda'web), the sites of the exhibitions curated by Dietz and a number of commissioned projects, like *Life Sharing* (2001) by the duo 0100101110101101.org. The Walker should be credited for always having promoted this section of its collection, and for having invested, in its day, considerable sums in commissioning online works (10,000 dollars was allocated to the aforementioned project, for example).

The SFMoMA launched its *e-space* shortly before *010101*, but the project was short-lived, given that no new commissions were added after David Ross left as director in the same year. The new director was not interested in Net Art, and Benjamin Weil left two years later, in 2003. Here too, the section has survived various revamps of the website, but it is not easy to track down. [58] In 2006, the SFMoMA appointed Rudolf Frieling, who was formerly working at the ZKM in Karlsruhe, as "Curator of Media Arts". After that, Frieling worked for the museum on a number of exhibitions, including the monumental survey *The Art of Participation: 1950 to Now* (2008), and on improving and preserving the collection, but did not launch any more online initiatives. [59]

The attention devoted to collecting online art by the Tate Gallery was more substantial, with the launch of an online Net Art gallery in 2000. Captained by various curators, with the rate of

commissions suffering slightly as a result, the section was active until 2008, when it was relabeled "Intermedia Art". This program ran until 2010, and featured not only online projects, but also broadcasts and public art projects. The last featured project dates back to 2011. [60]

But the most shocking case, in terms of expectations raised and then not fulfilled, is that of the Guggenheim Museum. In 2001 the Guggenheim, under the guidance of Jon Ippolito, launched the Variable Media Initiative, [61] the aim of which was to develop a protocol for conserving Net Art. In 2002, in the context of this project, the Guggenheim commissioned two works of Net Art, *net.flag* by Mark Napier and *Unfolding Object* by John F. Simon Jr. In the same year, when the long-standing relationship between Ippolito and the Guggenheim came to an end, the acquisitions program was terminated too. The two works remained accessible from the museum website for a few years, but have since been removed.

As can be seen, for the most part museum acquisitions and commissions have focused on art on the net, which in some ways presents more problems, but is usually cheaper than other kinds of New Media Art. Some of these purchases were the joint outcome of the hype described above and the efforts of a number of passionate, visionary figures, and did not outlive either (namely the collapse of the New Economy and the firing of the curators). In other cases it was a question of giving due support to a marginal, much maligned form of art: easy on the pocket but boosting the image of the museum.

Some smaller, more marginal concerns displayed more mettle: a case in point is that of MEIAC (Museo Extremeño e Ibero-americano de Arte Contemporáneo) in Badajoz, Spain. As of 2000, thanks to the curator Antonio Cerveira Pinto, the museum purchased various works of New Media Art, collecting international players like Alexei Shulgin, Olia Lialina, Peter

Luining, Vuk Ćosić, Young-hae Cheng Heavy Industries and 0100101110101101.ORG, along with several local artists. [62]

Spain is also witnessing the creation of a number of interesting corporate collections, such as that linked to the Arco Beep Prize, adding to the collection owned by BEEP, one of the country's main IT retailers, and the Vida Competition, organized by Foundación Telefonica: hi tech companies that, in contrast with what went on a few years ago, have decided to invest their money not in sponsoring temporary events but actually building a collection.

This is made possible by the fact that, as we have seen, the art market has made considerable progress since the distant days of 2001. A clear sign that something is changing lies in the fact that in 2004 and 2006 respectively, the Metropolitan Museum of New York – one of the most solid, conservative institutions in the United States – purchased works by Jim Campbell and Wolfgang Staehle. Jim Campbell uses a LED display panel, rather than a normal screen, to play video images, working with the magnetic allure of light and the low resolution offered by this technology. Staehle, on the other hand, has been working with webcams for a number of years now, placing them in front of an urban or natural landscape and broadcasting the results in the gallery for the duration of the exhibition. The installation captures one frame every five seconds, and the resulting archive of images is saved on a hard disk. The work becomes a kind of landscape in movement, mid way between the landscape tradition and Andy Warhol's *Empire*, with the added feature of real time screening.

In 2009 the Whitney Museum bought a work by Cory Arcangel, *Super Mario Clouds* (2003). This piece consists in a modified cartridge for the game *Super Mario* for Nintendo Entertainment System (NES), in which all the elements of game play have been removed to show only blue sky and white clouds moving horizontally from left to right. The work was purchased with funds

from the Painting and Sculpture Committee. With these acquisitions the two museums were not interested in possessing a generic work of New Media Art, but that particular work by that particular artist, which was held to reflect, better than others, a specific aspect of the contemporary period.

It is more difficult to take stock of private collecting. Collectors often wish to preserve their anonymity, and do not make the contents of their collections public. A significant part of the works exhibited in *Holy Fire* came from a Belgian collector who preferred to remain anonymous. In recent years he has added works of New Media Art to his collection, buying not only from galleries, but also from artists who are not represented on the market, in the belief that this art offers a logical contemporary progression from the issues and styles of the 1970s and 1980s, conceptual art first and foremost.

In June 2006, Carly Berwick interviewed a number of collectors for *Art & Auction*, trying to get a snapshot of the market for New Media Art. [63] Berwick underlined that the collectors buying software works and interactive installations mostly belonged to the forty-something age group – a generation used to life with computers. At the same time, however, these collectors are looking for immediate works that can be placed in a recognizable tradition. For them, buying these works means investing in the future, both financially – at decidedly affordable prices – and culturally. «In finance, I see things change dramatically due to the use of computers. The art we will remember in 20 or 30 years will be linked to the changes of today», says Alain Servais, a Belgian banker who began by collecting photography. His collection now includes numerous videos, but also works by Mark Napier, Manfred Mohr, and Jennifer and Kevin McCoy.

This growing interest in New Media Art among collectors is obviously linked to its increasing collectability. In *Artinfo*, Robert

Ayers [64] explains that on one hand artists are finally coming to terms with the idea of work of art as object, while on the other technological progress is also giving a helping hand:

«The computerization of hardware, the advances in software, rapid advances in screen technology, the continuous miniaturization of components, and decreasing costs for all of this mean that artworks that were unimaginable even five years ago can be made, exhibited, and collected today».

This does not detract from the fact that collecting New Media Art almost always involves a healthy dose of uncertainty, which in some ways adds to its appeal:

«The difference between owning new media art and older forms is not unlike the difference between keeping pets and plants. "Things can go wrong," says Sacks. "And depending on the complexity of the work, many things can go wrong. But the magic of the piece doesn't exist without that."»

All things considered, it looks as if the Consummation is finally drawing near. The final embrace might be less passionate than the fanfares of 2001 led us to hope, but at least there is to be an embrace. That is, if artists, collectors, museums and galleries are not left alone to support this work in the contemporary art arena. In the light of what has been discussed so far, it appears to be the critics and curators who are lagging behind. In the forthcoming chapter I will dwell briefly on the critical strategies that can be developed to accompany New Media Art along this challenging but intriguing path.

Notes

[1] Tom Wolfe, *The Painted Word*, New York 1975, p. 15

[2] Christiane Paul (ed), *New Media in the White Cube and Beyond. Curatorial Models for Digital Art*, University of California Press, Berkeley 2008.

[3] Cf. Jeffrey Deitch (ed), *Post Human*, cat., Cantz / Deste Foundation for Contemporary Art, 1992.

[4] Cf. Lee Rosenbaum, "guggenheim soho to go high-tech", in *Artnet*, 29 March 1996, online at www.artnet.com/magazine_pre2000/news/rosenbaum/rosenbaum3-29-96.asp (last visit March 2013).

[5] Cf. Roberta Smith, "A Museum's Metamorphosis: The Virtual Arcade", in *New York Times*, 18 June 1996.

[6] Cf. Lucy Bowditch, "Driven to distraction – multimedia art exhibition by the Guggenheim Museum Soho", in *Afterimage*, January – February 1997.

[7] Cf. John Haber, "Medium Rare", 1996, online at www.haberarts.com/tvscape.htm (last visit March 2013).

[8] Cf. Jonathon Nichols, "Documenta X", October 1997, online at www.artdes.monash.edu.au/globe/issue7/doctxt.html (last visit March 2013).

[9] Catherine David, "dx and new media", 20 June 1997, online at www.documenta12.de/archiv/dx/lists/debate/0001.html (last visit March 2013).

[10] Jodi, "dx webprojects", 9 July 1997, online at www.documenta12.de/archiv/dx/lists/debate/0010.html (last visit March 2013).

[11] Simon Lamunière, "dx webprojects", 10 July 1997, online at www.documenta12.de/archiv/dx/lists/debate/0014.html (last visit March 2013).

[12] Catherine David, "dx and new media", 20 June 1997, cit.

[13] Beryl Graham, "Serious Games", in Christiane Paul (ed), *New Media in the White Cube and Beyond*, cit., p. 191.

[14] Documentation regarding the various New York Digital Salons from 1993 onwards can be consulted at www.nydigitalsalon.org (last visit March 2013).

[15] Artnetweb has not been accessible online since 2008.

[16] Cf. Domenico Quaranta, *Net art 1994-1998. La vicenda di Ada'web*, Vita e Pensiero, Milan 2004.

[17] Matthew Mirapaul, "Museum Puts Internet Art on the Wall", in *The New York Times*, 16 September 1999, online at http://theater.nytimes.com/library/tech/99/09/cyber/artsatlarge/16artsatlarge.html (last visit March 2013).

[18] Josephine Berry, "The Unbearable Connectedness of Everything", in *Telepolis*, 28 September 1999, online at www.heise.de/tp/artikel/3/3433/1.html (last visit March 2013).

[19] Cfr. Robert F. Nideffer, "SHIFT-CTRL. Mediating the process of academic exhibitionism", 2000, online at www.nideffer.net/classes/135-09-W/readings/nideffer.html (last visit March 2013).

[20] In Perttu Rastas, "Alien Intelligence", 2000, in *Kiasma Magazine*, 5 -99.

[21] Jerry Saltz, "My Sixth Sense", in *The Village Voice*, 2000.

[22] In Vuk Ćosić (ed), *Net.art Per Me*, exh. cat., Venice, Santa Maria del Soccorso, June 2001. MGLC 2001, p. 14.

[23] Cf. Ross's declarations to *Wired*, in Jason Spingarn-Koff, "010101: Art for Our Times", in *Wired*, 28 February 2001, online at www.wired.com/culture/lifestyle/news/2001/02/41972 (last visit March 2013).

[24] In AA.VV., *010101: Art in Technological Times*, cat., SFMoMA, San Francisco 2001, p. 7.

[25] Cf. Joyce Slaton, "Museum Offers Webby Art Award", in *Wired*, 18 February 2000, available online at www.wired.com/culture/lifestyle/news/2000/02/34414 (last visit March 2013). The project was suspended in January 2002.

[26] Cf. Beryl Graham, *Curating New Media Art: SFMoMA and 010101*, University of Sunderland 2001.

[27] Cf. Sarah Cook, "An interview with Christiane Paul", in *Crumbweb*, 28 March 2001, available online at http://crumbweb.org/getInterviewDetail.php?id=10&ts=1241707558&op=3&sublink=9 (last visit March 2013).

[28] Lawrence Rinder, "Art in the Digital Age", in Lawrence Rinder, Debra Singer (eds), *Bitstreams*, cat., Whitney Museum of American Art, New York 2001.

[29] Stefanie Syman, "Bell Curves and Bitstreams. Stefanie Syman on the beginning of the end of digital art", in *Feed*, 27 March 2001.

[30] Cf. the exhibition catalog, Andreas Broeckmann (ed), *Deep Screen...*, cit.

[31] Cf. Inke Arns, in "Media Art Undone", conference panel at transmediale07, Berlin, February 3, 2007. Full transcript of the presentations is available here: www.mikro.in-berlin.de/wiki/tiki-index.php?page=MAU (last visit March 2013).

[32] One of the venues for the debate was the Rhizome site, where the announcement of the exhibition gave rise to a discussion featuring more than 70 contributions. The debate is archived online at http://rhizome.org/editorial/2008/apr/1/the-rematerialization-of-art/ (last visit March 2013). In parallel, an

article on the French site Fluctuat.net garnered an equally substantial response, archived at www.fluctuat.net/blog/9941-Holy-Fire-le-net-art-est-il-soluble-dans-le-capitalisme-. Articles and reviews were published in *Art Fag City*, *We-make-money-not-art*, *El Pais*, *Poptronics*, *ABC* and other online and paper magazines.

[33] Regine Débatty, "Holy Fire, art of the digital age", in *We-make-money-not-art*, 22 April 2008, online at http://www.we-make-money-not-art.com/archives/2008/04/holy-fire.php (last visit March 2013).

[34] In Yves Michaud, *L'artiste et les commissaires*, Hachette Pluriel Reference 2007.

[35] In Domenico Quaranta, Yves Bernard (ed), *Holy Fire...*, cit., p. 125.

[36] Susan Delson, "If Picasso Were A Programmer", in *Forbes*, Best of The Web, 25 June 2001, pp. 44-47.

[37] Mario Diacono (ed), *John F. Simon, Jr. Outside In. Ten Years of Software Art*, cat., Collezione Maramotti, Reggio Emilia 2009. Gli Ori, Pistoia 2009.

[38] Tom Vanderbilt, "The King of Digital Art", in *Wired*, issue 13.9, September 2005, online at www.wired.com/wired/archive/13.09/sacks.html (last visit March 2013).

[39] Matthew Mirapaul, "Selling and Collecting the Intangible, at $1,000 a Share", in *The New York Times*, 29 April 2002, online at www.nytimes.com/2002/04/29/arts/arts-online-selling-and-collecting-the-intangible-at-1000-a-share.html (last visit March 2013).

[40] Cf. Domenico Quaranta, "We Are All Ready for a Change. Interview with Steven Sacks", in *Rhizome*, 28 June 2007, online at http://rhizome.org/discuss/view/26364#48892 (last visit March 2013).

[41] From the original gallery statement. The current statement is even more explicit: «Re-composing the moving image since its founding in 2002, the Bryce Wolkowitz Gallery has made a major commitment to representing artists who are exploring the intersection of art and technology. The gallery's roster has made significant contributions to the genre of video and new media and have profoundly influenced future generations of moving image makers». Cf. http://brycewolkowitz.com/h/gallery.php (last visit March 2013).

[42] The gallery closed in September 2012, when Fabio Paris decided to concentrate his efforts on the Link Center for the Arts of the Information Age, the no-profit organization he co-founded in 2011. Cf. www.fabioparisart-gallery.com/ (last visit March 2013).

[43] The gallery's archive is still online at www.andorgallery.com (last visit March 2013).

[44] Cf. the gallery's blog, online at http://artmovingprojects.blogspot.it/ (last visit March 2013). Cf. also Paddy Johnson, "Interview with Aron Namenwirth of artMovingProjects", in *Rhizome*, April 9, 2008, online at http://rhizome.org/editorial/2008/apr/9/interview-with-aron-namenwirth-of-artmovingproject/ (last visit March 2013).

[45] Cf. http://stadiumnyc.com/ (last visit March 2013).

[46] Cf. http://thefuturegallery.org/ (last visit March 2013).

[47] Patricia K. Hughes, *Breaking and Entering: A User's Guide*, Pace Wildenstein, New York 2005.

[48] Cf. José Luis de Vicente, "Una historia del arte y la tecnología en ARCO", in *El Cultural*, February 2008. Available online in *Elastico*, at http://elastico.net/archives/2008/02/post_59.html (last visit March 2013).

[49] Cf. http://arcobloggers.com/ (last visit March 2013).

[50] Monica Ponzini, "DiVA Digital Video Art Fair", in *Digimag 33*, April 2008, available online at www.digicult.it/digimag/article.asp?id=1125 (last visit March 2013).

[51] Cf. www.kinetica-artfair.com/?about_us/art-fair.html (last visit March 2013).

[52] In Margherita Laera, "Arte Digitale: Collezionisti, fatevi avanti!", in *Wired.it*, 22 April 2009, available online at http://daily.wired.it/news/cultura/arte-digitale-collezionisti-fatevi-avanti.html (last visit March 2013).

[53] Cf. at least Steve Dietz, "Collecting New Media Art: Just Like Everything Else, Only Different", in Bruce Altshuler (ed), *Collecting the New*, Princeton University Press, Princeton (New Jersey) and Oxford 2005.

[54] Davis' work is available online through the museum website, at http://artport.whitney.org/collection/davis/ (last visit March 2013).

[55] Artport's current interface can be visited at http://whitney.org/Exhibitions/Artport (last visit March 2013). The new commissions program includes, so far, eight works, by artists like Jodi, Jonah Brucker-Cohen, Ecoarttech and UBERMORGEN.COM. *Cory Arcangel: Pro Tools* ran from May 26 to September 11, 2011: a lot of information about the show is still available on the dedicated web page: http://whitney.org/Exhibitions/CoryArcangel (last visit March 2013).

[56] In Karen A. Verschooren, *.art. Situating Internet Art in the Traditional Institution for Contemporary Art*, 2007. Master of Science in Comparative Media Studies, Massachusetts Institute of Technology, online at http://cms.mit.edu/research/theses/KarenVerschooren2007.pdf, p. 47.

[57] Available online at http://gallery9.walkerart.org/ (last visit March 2013).

[58] The e-space is currently archived here: www.sfmoma.org/exhib_events/exhibitions/espace (last visit March 2013).

[59] The SFMoMA has a consistent collection of media art, mainly including video installations. Interestingly enough, the e-space is not listed as part of this collection. Cf. www.sfmoma.org/explore/collection/media_arts (last visit March 2013).

[60] The "Intermedia Art" section of the Tate Gallery website is archived here: http://www.tate.org.uk/intermediaart/ (last visit March 2013).

[61] The material produced by the initiative can be accessed at http://variablemedia.net/ (last visit March 2013).

[62] For more information, cf. www.meiac.es (last visit March 2013).

[63] Carly Berwick, "New Media Moguls", in Art & Auction, June 2006, pp. 138 – 143.

[64] Robert Ayers, "Code in a Box", in Artinfo, 3 August 2007, online at www.artinfo.com/news/story/25445/code-in-a-box/ (last visit March 2013).

The
Postmedia
Perspective

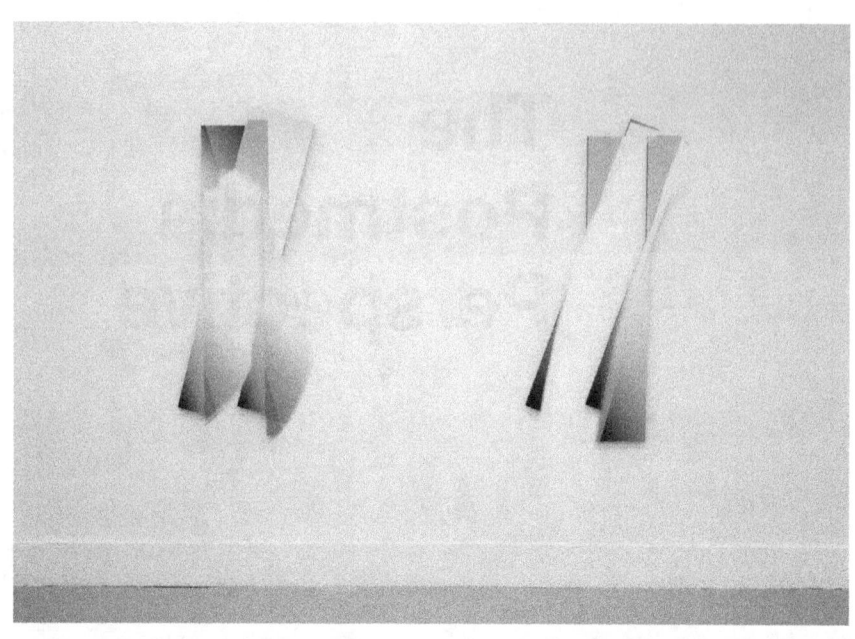

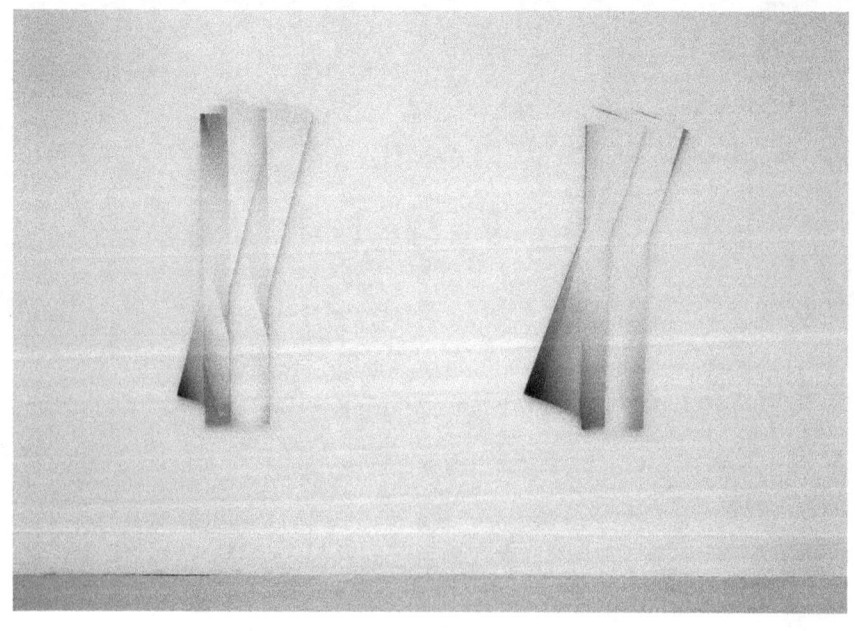

Artie Vierkant, *Image Objects*, 2011 – ongoing. Digital prints on CNC-routed MDF, image alteration (Image Objects shown installed at Reference Gallery, Richmond VA). Images courtesy the artist.

> «At one time, the new media of photography both changed the aesthetic understanding of painting and participated in the creation of a cultural understanding of (fixed) time and representation. At another time, the new media of video changed the aesthetic understanding of film while participating with television in the creation of a cultural understanding of (real) time and distance. The art most recently known as "new media" changes our understanding of the behaviors of contemporary art precisely because of its participation in the creation of a cultural understanding of computational interactivity and networked participation. In other words, art is different after new media because of new media – not because new media is "next", but because its behaviors are the behaviors of our technological times». Steve Dietz [1]

At the end of this trip, three questions remain unanswered. If the art formerly known as New Media is moving from its native world to the contemporary art world, is there a future for the New Media Art world? If the conceptual paradigm of creative research on the medium has proven to be weak, obsolete and inadequate in promoting the art formerly known as New Media on the contemporary art platform, is there another approach that can help us call attention to its specificity and topicality? And finally: is it really necessary to insist on this specificity?

The specter of the responsibility of critics and curators haunts all these questions, and this will be our starting point.

A Few Notes On Curating

There's no two ways about it: critics and curators have to take a lot of the responsibility for the bad rap that the art formerly known as New Media Art has in the contemporary art world. On one hand, specialized critics have made the mistake of trying to impose the value criteria applied to works of art in the New Media Art world to the contemporary art world too, and develop a "sectorial" (or even "sectarian") discourse, attempting to present an entirely heterogeneous situation as a unitary phenomenon. On the other hand, with very few exceptions, contemporary art criticism has proved incapable of bridging the technological divide and tackling these works with their own tools of criticism. Or falling into the "unitary phenomenon" trap and merely writing the whole lot off. «The art form lacks the depth and cultural urgency to justify the ICA's continued and significant investment in a Live & Media Arts department», stated Ekow Eshun, artistic director of the ICA in London in 2008, justifying the closure of its Live & Media Arts department. [2]

And there's more. The debate over the care and conservation of New Media Art, which is the final arena in which a medium-based definition still appears to make sense, is constantly used to convey this definition to the contemporary art world. In the last decade this debate has been carried on in articles, publications, seminars, mailing lists, and more recently, blogs and online resources, and has focused on defining the role of the "New Media Curator" and the main issues he or she has to tackle.

Emblematic in this regard is the work of CRUMB (the Curatorial Resource for Upstart Media Bliss), an English initiative led by the curators Beryl Graham and Sarah Cook, which manages a mailing list and has produced a number of publications. These, together with the aforementioned *New Media in the White Cube and Beyond* edited by Christiane Paul, offer excellent insight into the current state of play in this debate. [3] In parallel, when museums started making their first purchases, and coming up against new stumbling blocks, the question of how to conserve new media also began to be explored. [4]

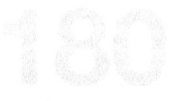

Great progress has undoubtedly been made in the last decade, and some of the resulting developments will be outstanding tools for curators of the present and future for a long time to come. Yet I believe that it is important to challenge a number of the assumptions and idiosyncrasies involved, and come up with a few curatorial strategies that spring directly from the ideas discussed here.

In particular there are two misconceptions that have become something of a mantra: that curating New Media Art raises specific issues that can only be tackled by a specific "media art curator"; and that New Media Art raises some pretty insurmountable challenges for those interested in collecting and conserving it. As can be seen, both of these ideas are based on the assumption that New Media Art is one homogeneous mass with the same curatorial and conservation issues; issues that can ultimately be linked to the medium used. Yet the so-called "new media" are about as complex and varied as you can imagine, and the variety of forms that it can take means that a single strategy (and term) is entirely inadequate.

But this approach is rooted in an even more perverse equation: namely that which identifies New Media Art with the technology it uses. When people talk about curatorial issues, the expression "new media curating" invariably comes to mean "bringing the new technologies into the physical space of a gallery or museum". New Media Art is reduced to being the art that uses digital technologies as a medium. We have already challenged this point of view. But what are the consequences when this misconception is used as the basis for curatorial practice?

In the introductory essay [5] to the book she edited, Christiane Paul analyzes the issues that in her view a "new media curator" has to tackle to get New Media Art into the white cube: issues of a purely technological nature. The curator's reflections hinge on technology rather than art. But reducing things down to the equation New Media Art = technological art means losing sight of the real substance of the curator's work. As Inke Arns and Jacob Lillemose write:

«[...] there is no such specific thing as curating computer based art. There is just curating art. Of course, computer based art involves new formats and offers new possibilities for curating but we believe that the discursive role of the curator nevertheless remains the same: To make a statement that explores the art in question and finds new ways of thinking about it and the context it refers to by putting it is a larger cultural or theoretical context». [6]

If, on rare occasions, this work maintains something specific, it is not to do with technology, but the cultural context in question. But this, when all is said and done, is still part of the curator's traditional role: to act as a mediator between work of art and exhibition setting, work and public, work and the different settings it can inhabit.

When dealing with an artistic practice that is entitled to exist in various different worlds and different exhibition settings, this mediation has to be strengthened: more often than not the work needs to be redesigned – in agreement with the artist – according to the setting, depending on whether it is hosted in a private or institutional space, a New Media Art festival or contemporary art museum, a physical setting or online. This applies above all to works without a tangible component, that use the net as a distribution platform or that are usually experienced through a computer screen. In these cases the work has to be "translated" to come across effectively in a setting that differs from its original one.

This "translation" work is one of the most complex and fascinating aspects undertaken by the curator looking to import works born elsewhere into the world of contemporary art. Translating means taking account of the morphology and syntax of both languages. Often comprehension is only possible if both sides make hefty compromises (the way things sound, the nuances of meaning): it is up to a good translator to get those compromises to work for the text being translated. The good translator has to take account of his or her own limits, the culture (or lack thereof) of his or her readers and their ideological stances. If the translator is translating for the first time, he or she will choose an easy text; if the translation is from an almost unknown culture into his or her native language, he or she will choose a culturally simpler text before moving onto something more complex, or if translating from a culture that some people have reservations about, the translator will try to use the translation to render it more acceptable.

Metaphors aside, proposing the art formerly known as New Media Art in the contemporary art context means above all choosing a work of art not overly bound up with the predominant "idea of art" of the New Media Art world, and if possible lend it a stable form, avoiding the unnecessary use of computers and complex technologies.

It would be easy to criticize this approach as erring on the side of excessive caution. If we cop out when it comes to taking technology into the exhibition venue, when will we get the chance to change the rules of the game? If we tone down the revolutionary energy of New Media Art to make it more acceptable, don't we risk eliminating its very *raison d'être*? The weak point of these objections lies, once more, in the fact that they consider the medium and its specific characteristics to be the strong point, the most revolutionary thing, about New Media Art. In the previous chapters we showed that this approach has repeatedly failed. The uniqueness of New Media Art in the cultural arena does not lie in the media it uses, but in its familiarity with the cultural consequences of the advent of these media.

Moreover, "translating" New Media Art into forms that enable it to interface with the contemporary art audience does not mean

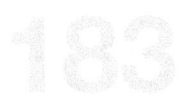

completely giving up on technology: it means choosing, on a case by case basis, the form most suited to initiating this dialogue.

A good curator should try to avoid the main errors that can trap a bad translator: barbarisms and metaphrasis. A barbarism is a failed act of translation, where the translator throws in the towel and merely imports a foreign word into the translation, with barbaric sounding results. Metaphrasis is literal translation: the grammar and vocabulary might be correct, but the translation fails to take the culture of the destination language into account. Try using an automatic translator and you will get your fill of literal translations.

In our arena, installing a computer in an exhibition venue to exhibit a website or software work cannot be seen as an act of translation. Perhaps in the past – in the days of documenta X, for example – this could still be seen as a foreignism, or necessary barbarism. Now, it is a genuine barbarism. This is the case because computers, not as objects that are part of a work of art, but as a display device – look out of place in exhibition venues. At an exhibition, visitors do not want to sit in front of a computer and click on links. We cannot just blithely dump a tool designed for private use in a public setting. Not to mention the fact that artists have long been studying translation strategies that render foreignisms unnecessary.

A recent example of a barbarism is the installation of an online work by Rosa Barba in the exhibition *21x21* (2010), curated by Francesco Bonami for the Fondazione Sandretto Re Rebaudengo in Turin. Commissioned by the Dia Art Foundation of New York, *Vertiginous Mapping* (2008) is a hypertext that gathers images, texts and videos produced by the artist during a residency in Sweden. It takes the viewer on a tour of a town that is imaginary but based on the artist's actual experience: an entire city that has to be moved to a different location due to the instability of the terrain, after intense mining in the area. In the exhibition the site was projected onto the wall and the hypertext could be navigated using a mouse. Viewers sat down, clicked randomly on a few links and then got up again, irritated. This reaction could have been avoided by translating the work into an installation that rendered the hypertextual nature of the online narrative by distributing texts, videos, maps and photographs around the exhibition venue. In this case the barbarism was the easiest, cheapest solution, as well as being pseudo-innovative (it was interesting to see the rhetorical use of the term "interactive" in the caption written for the work, entirely inappropriate for a website). It was also symptomatic of the lack of familiarity of the curator and museum with works of this kind, and the artist's reluctance to translate the work into a form more suited to the venue.

Metaphrasis, on the other hand, is based on the assumption that translation is a simple transition between different states: from bits to atoms, process to object, the intangible world of the media to the tangible sphere of life. Adapting a digital work to a "physical" setting does not just mean turning it into an object or installation: it means adapting it to the aesthetic, cultural and formal demands of an audience that is not its habitual one. It means being aware of the setting, grammar, conventions and idioms of the destination language. Not taking these things into account, out of ignorance, arrogance or an erroneous notion of consistency, means an unsuccessful, and therefore basically unfaithful translation.

An example of metaphrasis can be seen in *Data Dynamics*, the exhibition curated by Christiane Paul for the Whitney Museum in 2001. The exhibition contained five works, two of which were translated into installations for the first time on that occasion. The theme of the exhibition (the relationships between physical space and the social space of the web) was fairly obscure and self-referencing; the works were technologically sophisticated and made a show of being hi-tech, and they required the viewer to interact with them. While raising issues of space (the spaces of life and those of communication), they did so in a cold, clinical, distant way. *Apartment*, an online application where words inserted by users structured the various parts of a 3D apartment, was projected onto the wall, with interaction mediated by a specially designed work station. While on one hand this got round the need to have a normal PC in the exhibition venue (a barbarism), on the other it evoked technology in ways that might work well at Ars Electronica, but not at the Whitney Museum (metaphrasis). In other words, Paul had no consideration of visitors' cultural horizons and their ideas of art: using the self-same terminology she merely "teleported" New Media Art from its ghetto to a broader audience. An audience that looked on bemused and slightly hostile, as if confronted with an alien.

So how does a good translation come about? It is basically about identifying the essence of a work and trying to translate that into another language. In general, in the contemporary art world, if the technological interface, connectivity, processual nature, accessibility, openness and non-uniqueness of an artwork are not essential, it is a good idea to set them aside. If these characteristics are essential, it is better to keep them: the art world is mature enough to accept open, replicable, processual pieces if this is an essential part of the work, and if their value can be transferred onto something else. Tino Sehgal's performances are a good example of this. The main thing is that the translator has to be not just bilingual but bicultural.

That said, translations must be crafted on a case by case basis, by the artist or curator (if possible, in constant contact with the artist). In some cases the work can be related or documented using remnants of the production process or documentary elements produced ad hoc, exactly as was done in the past for performance art. Documentation inevitably entails making a "diminished" translation of the original, but this is accepted as a necessary evil by both the translator and the audience.

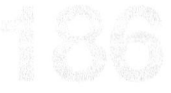

Translation in the proper sense takes place when the curator selects a work and sets about adapting it to a setting, if possible together with the artist. The result aims not to be a "diminished" presentation of the piece, but another version of it. If you like, another interface for the same contents: an option made possible by the inherent variability of new media.

The works that arise as a result of this process are not "*the work*" but other artefacts that recall – wholly or in part – the conceptual nucleus of the piece, which transfer its semantic value onto tangible talismans that unlike the former (but thanks to it), are capable of acquiring economic value. In the New Media Art world it is fashionable to dismiss these derivative works, often created using traditional media (prints, video, sculpture), as simple "concessions to the market". While this is true – they are *also* concessions to the market – they are above all translation strategies developed for a context, that of art, in which the translatability of cultural value into economic value is key to the success, circulation and museification of the work.

By way of example, let's look at a particularly emblematic case: the 2001 work *Biennale.py*, which sprang from a collaboration between [epidemiC] and Eva and Franco Mattes (010010111010-1101.ORG). The original work was a virus in Pyton which was unleashed on the web when the two collectives took part in the 49th Venice Biennale. The work existed in two forms right from the start: language and performance. The performance consisted in spreading the virus by email but also in the form of t-shirts distributed at the Slovenian Pavilion of the Biennale, and the fact of being recognised by some of the main antivirus systems in circulation. On the level of language, the code of the virus could be read as such by a computer, or read by a human reader as a "love poem". As a performance, *Biennale.py* could only be restaged if the artists decided to organise a re-enactment of it – assuming that it would make sense to remove it from its "here and now" of 2001, when the whole notion of a virus was much more potent than it is today. The most natural strategy is therefore that of documentation. Both [epidemiC] and the Mattes widely documented the operation for the web, on their respective sites. In a concrete venue, "documenting" the work would mean exhibiting the t-shirts, videos or photos of the virus "spreading" around the Biennale, the programming code, the press response, and a diagram of how it circulated on the net. In the past [epidemiC] also exhibited a print-out of the virus with autographed notes, an authentic conceptual fetish item, while the Mattes enshrined a limited edition of golden cd-roms containing the virus in plexiglas display cases.

Lastly, two years after the fact, the Mattes produced a series of sculptures: "derivative works" in which a computer, taken to pieces and put back together and presented in a plexiglas case, displays its circuits engaged in an endless cycle of infection and disinfection. These machines do more than just document *Biennale.py*, they also take reflections on the virus that created the previous work to a new level: they take a virus, about the most intangible thing that exists, into an exhibition venue; and they conserve it for the benefit of history.

This story invalidates many of the claims that it is impossible to "conserve the digital". If the work is documented or translated into physical artefacts, "conserving" New Media Art entails the exact same problems as the rest of contemporary art. Documentation and derivative works are known strategies for conserving the ephemeral.

Naturally the problem of how to preserve technology remains. How, for example, are we to store Eva and Franco Mattes' self-disinfecting machines? What can be done when a power outage, some other accident or merely the passing of time, irremediably damages the computers these pieces contain? We do not have the space here to enter into the current debate. Various solutions have

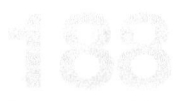

been examined, from conserving obsolete hardware and software to creating software emulators that simulate old operating systems and programs on new machines.

The Variable Media Initiative, the New York Guggenheim's platform for the conservation of variable media, has the outstanding merit of having cleared up three key points. In the first place, it asserted that the problems raised by the digital media apply to all variable media used in art, from Dan Flavin's neon tubes to Mario Merz's twigs. Secondly, it underlined the fact that it is impossible to develop a common protocol: every work is a case in point. Lastly, it argued that the final say on the conservation of variable media had to be had – if we are still in time – by the artists; and it formulated a questionnaire that enables the artists to give instructions about how they would like their works to be "restored" in the event that the media used are no longer available.

When I asked Eva and Franco Mattes how to conserve their first online works, the answer was: "Write a novel!" Yet this is not as provocative an answer as it might sound. Once we have got rid of the medium-based definition of New Media Art, we have to acknowledge that technological ways of conserving works might not necessarily be the best tactic.

Net Art once more represents the most significant example of this. Seeing as net art lives on the net, it would be reasonable to think that conserving Net Art means conserving websites. To do so we could adopt the usual strategies deployed in these cases: conserving hardware and storing the original software (operating systems, browsers, etc.); emulation (creating emulators capable of simulating the operating systems, browsers, screen resolution, bandwidth used by the artist when the work was created), or migration (rewriting the code of the page to give the same result on new platforms).

Each of these strategies is debatable, but for some pieces they might even work. Let's take two very different works: *My*

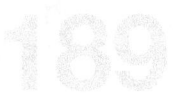

Boyfriend Came Back From the War (1996), a narrative hypertext by the Russian artist Olia Lialina; and the aforementioned *Vote-Auction* (2000), by the Austrian duo UBERMORGEN.COM. Fourteen years on the former is still online in its original form (the only "posthumous" addition is the Google advertising bar on the homepage). Yet the work relies heavily on frames, a technique used to create a grid in which various web pages are loaded in a single framework. Popular in the 90s, frames are an archaeological relic of the old web that the browsers of the future might decide not to read at some point, making this work inaccessible.

But are we sure that the work has actually been "conserved" up to the present? In an interview she gave to *Neural* a few years back, [7] Lialina observed that even if the work is still accessible, everything around it has changed. Connections are now much faster than a 1996 modem, the sluggish pace of which lent a feeling of suspense when navigating the site; the site was designed for the sober, minimalist interface of the early browsers, which offered a completely different frame to those currently in use; the images were conceived for a 800x600 screen resolution, and their original quality is seriously compromised when viewed on today's screens.

In other words, the original version of *My Boyfriend Came Back From the War* is irretrievably lost. Nothing in its code has changed, but everything around it has. Yet any act of restoration would be a betrayal. Even just a slight tweak to give the images back their original look would in any case involve changing the original materials. A museum could decide to make it accessible through an old Mac OS, using the 1996 version of the Netscape browser, artificially reducing band-width to slow down navigation, but this would have the glaringly erroneous consequence of making it look like a resuscitated corpse, while the work itself is very much alive. A result of this kind would in any case just be an interpretation of the original.

For the time being Lialina has settled for making the work accessible through an interface called the *Last Real Net Art Museum*, which gathers all the tributes, parodies and remixes that other artists have devoted to her famous piece over the years. The museum tells a story – that of the life of a work of art on the net. Perhaps for the moment this remains the best conservation strategy. At least for this work.

At this point let's take a look at *Vote-Auction* (2000). *Vote-Auction* started life as a site that auctioned the votes of American voters for the presidential elections. The site caused a stir which erupted into a media storm and led to the artists being spied on and hit with a flurry of law suits. The media frenzy was ably managed by the artists, who put out a succession of ambiguous statements and updates, moved the site around and so on. In actual fact *Vote-Auction* can be described as a complex performance involving the media, the net, American voters and dozens of other extras. Conserving the original site of *Vote-Auction*, and guaranteeing its original look and accessibility would not mean conserving the work: the site is just a part of the work, which also includes the articles published, the injunctions, the TV shows and user feedback. In this case reducing the work to a website and trying to preserve that site in its original form would be like looking after the case of a VHS cassette without worrying about the actual tape.

To exhibit *Vote-Auction*, the artists produced a print on canvas of the logo of the project, a paper installation comprising the legal injunctions they received and a video that appropriates the program CNN made about the project: three "derivative" works that are a good way of documenting and preserving the piece. Yet, as with many performances, the best way of conserving *Vote-Auction* remains that of telling its story. This is behind the provocative stance of 0100101110101101.ORG: ok, so we can keep the data, but we won't be turning it into untouchable fetish items, and above all we're not going to kid ourselves that we have conserved the actual work itself, which is first and foremost a story. If we overestimate the power of technology all we will be left with is a fistful of pixels.

What Future for the New Media Art World?

«But if New Media becomes a theme in Contemporary Art and dissolves there, this would be a real loss». Olia Lialina [8]

The reasoning developed in the preceding chapters appears to converge on a single conclusion: that today New Media Art no longer needs that specific "art world" which formed beginning in the 1960s to respond to the challenges introduced by media not compatible with the contemporary art world. Does this mean that this world is destined for oblivion?

In actual fact, the question is much more complex, as much of what has been said so far shows. In the first place, not all New Media Art appears ready to take that quantum leap into a parallel universe, towards a more open discursive system, and production and distribution structures entirely different from those it developed in. In 2005 at Ars Electronica the Dutch artist Dirk Eijsbouts presented the installation *Interface #4 / TFT tennis V180.* [9] The work enabled the user to play a virtual game of tennis in which the screen the ball was visualized on was also the racket used to hit it. The two rackets / screens were fixed to a mechanical arm that revolved around a central arm: when the player moved the screen it not only directed the trajectory of the ball but also changed the game visually. This installation deployed a considerably complex form of interactivity, which would be difficult to apply to a commercial gaming platform; and it introduced an interesting reflection on the relationship between simulation and reality. At the same time, however, it was also a fun game, in some aspects a precursor to the modalities of play subsequently made popular by the Nintendo Wii, based on physical movement. Industrial prototype or work of art? Toy or generator of meaning? Undecided between these two natures, *TFT Tennis* is a typical artefact of the world of New Media Art. Outside of that world, it would not have much of a chance: the contemporary art world would disparage it as a vacuous celebration of technology, while the videogames industry would file it away under unsustainable ideas. The New Media Art world gives it a context in which it can be produced, exhibited and discussed. The importance of this should not be underestimated: even if the piece never fulfils the idea of art that other arenas have, it will have heralded a new development in knowledge that can be brought to fruition elsewhere. We can look down on the "toys" of Ars Electronica as much as we like, but we must not forget that without them the history of media would have progressed more slowly, and New Media Art would never have surpassed itself and arrived at the point of challenging its very identity.

On the other hand, it is not just a question of "maturity." While it is true that consumer IT is now a deeply rooted part of our everyday existence, it is also true that some technologies and languages remain inaccessible to the common artist, due to the costs involved and usage difficulties. While it is true that much New Media Art is capable of taking on the market, it is also true that this path remains unsustainable for many currents and projects even now. And while it is true that much New Media Art can be tackled critically without particular knowledge of the new technologies, it is also true that many works cannot be properly understood without an in-depth knowledge of the medium and its dynamics, and therefore continues to require a specialized critical approach.

Let's take an example. Although there is a form of "amateur biotech" that some artists have worked with, as yet it is not easy

for biotechnology research to exist outside of universities and laboratories. At the same time, we have to acknowledge that, as Jeffrey Deitch noted at the beginning of the 1990s, biotechnologies represent one of the most interesting drivers of change in our era. Tackling biotech as an issue in the form of content is undoubtedly interesting, but it would be a shame if artists did not have the opportunity to gain more in-depth knowledge of this field, and use it as a potential artistic medium.

From this starting point, in 2000 the artist Oron Catts founded Symbiotica, an art research lab hosted by the School of Anatomy & Human Biology of the University of Western Australia (UWA) in Perth. Since then, Symbiotica has offered residencies to artists from all over the world, providing a well-equipped biotech research laboratory and the experience of scientists and researchers. This represents an exceptional opportunity, taken up by the Australian performer Stelarc, among others, who created the third ear he now proudly displays on his forearm at the lab. Thanks to the opportunities offered by Symbiotica, Catts – who, together with two other artists, has been working as the Tissue Culture & Art Project since 1996 – has succeeded in creating fascinating installations that explore the potential and problems involved in tissue engineering. *Victimless Leather* (2004), for example, is a miniature leather jacket that "lives" inside a bioreactor. The work is a reaction to the barbarous use of animal skins to make clothing, something that tissue engineering could offer an alternative to. The artists grafted cells from a living animal (a mouse) onto a structure of polymers in the shape of a jacket, the idea being that the cells will stay alive and multiply in a protected environment. The work also has an ironic side, because in order to save "living" beings, the Tissue Culture & Art Project had created a "semi-living" being, the existence and exploitation of which raises ethical issues similar to those they were attempting to get around. When the project was exhibited at MoMA in New York in 2008, in the show *Design and the Elastic Mind* (curated by Paola Antonelli), it elicited heated reactions when the curator was forced to "kill" the semi-living jacket by cutting off its supply of nutrients, as the cells were growing out of control. "Museum Kills Live Exhibit" ran the *New York Times* headline. [10]

Despite this exceptional appearance at MoMA (and more recently at the Mori Art Museum in Tokyo), the exhibition career of *Victimless Leather*, like most of the works by the Tissue Culture & Art Project, remains firmly within the New Media Art world. Outside of it, it is no simple matter to find the technological expertise and intellectual courage required to exhibit a work of this kind. Its very production would have been unthinkable outside a context that fosters research not directed at the immediate creation of an artefact. The installation in itself is inaccessible to the art market, though the highly performative and relational nature of this piece could occasion its circulation in documentary form, as prints and videos. These elements also foster an interpretation of the world that goes beyond the traditional "art and (bio)technologies" paradigm. Paola Antonelli's killing of the "semi-living" being was a "funeral rite" that Tissue Culture & Art Project has orchestrated on other occasions, in forms familiar to relational art. The project *Disembodied Cuisine* (2003), for example, entailed the creation of tiny "frog steaks", produced by implanting on polymers cells taken from a biopsy on a living frog. The "meat" was cultured and kept alive in a laboratory accessible to the public for the duration of the exhibition the project was conceived for. At the end of the event, the Tissue Culture & Art Project cooked up its "victimless" meat and served it to the public.

The work of the Tissue Culture and Art Project appears to demonstrate that the existence of another system of production and distribution is both necessary and instrumental to the growth and evolution of contemporary art. As Joline Blais and Jon Ippolito assert, the art that comes into being "at the edge of art" is an irreplaceable source of dynamism, a force that evolves the very idea of art at the root of the contemporary art world. But to survive, the New Media Art world must first of all formulate a clear idea of its identity, and to do this it must go back to the phenomena that generated it.

As we have seen, the New Media Art world came about as a multidisciplinary arena of research, a reaction to the rigid conventions of a whole series of other worlds: that of contemporary art, but also the performing arts, music, design and industrial research. Its "borderline" status and dynamism should not only be acknowledged but also cultivated, and if possible, reinforced. Historically the New Media Art world filled the gaps between one creative arena and another, between arts and science, arts and technology. This was its mission, its destiny. Reducing it – or as is often the case seeing it reduce itself – to a niche in the contemporary art world, is not only unjust but also historically unfounded, and the same goes for considering it – or seeing it consider itself – an incubator for industrial research. Yet the conceptual model introduced by the term "incubator" is an apt one: like a business incubator, the New Media Art world has to act as an incubator for the other, more solid art worlds, creating the ideal situation for the development of advanced, risky, financially unsustainable or aesthetically challenging work, and subsequently enriching those arenas that, not out of conservatism but due to their very characteristics, would have nipped it in the bud. The New Media Art world can potentially generate the energy that powers the other art worlds, giving their respective "ideas of art" a radical evolution. While for Shigeko Kubota video was a holiday for art, New Media Art can be the childhood of art, or its spring.

Obviously, for this to happen the New Media Art world must stop considering itself in competition with the other worlds, and cast off its own ineradicable inferiority complex (which often manifests itself as an undue affirmation of superiority, clearly visible in the perspective introduced by Gerfried Stocker [11] in chapter three). It needs to cultivate hybridization between different arenas and figures. It needs to recognize and proudly accept the entrance of some of the fruits of its labours into the contemporary art world, and not condemn this as a deplorable surrender to market pressures. It needs to recognize the cultural necessity of the practices it cultivates. And, like every other art world, it needs to take a look outside of itself, because only an unprejudiced dialogue with contemporary art can stop it from becoming fossilized as an ingenuous "exaltation of the medium," as has happened all too often in recent years.

All of this is not only possible, but already taking place. As we have seen, the New Media Art world is complex, and cannot be reduced to the paradigm sustained by situations like ZKM or Ars Electronica. One example of a virtuous approach comes from Slovenia. There, like other areas of culture, the "Intermedia" sector, as it is described in the administrative setting – receives public funding. In the last fifteen years this has enabled numerous small institutions and organizations led by artists to thrive, producing and exhibiting works that would be unlikely to see the light of day elsewhere. While in the "Contemporary Art" sector the weak market and the presence of public funding has led to a degree of stagnation and a lack of quality work, it has proved quite the opposite in the Intermedia sector. The result is that the most interesting contemporary art in Slovenia is the outcome of long-term projects developed in the Intermedia sector. Artists and collectives like Marko Peljhan, Janez Janša, BridA (Tom Kerševan, Jurij Pavlica and Sendi Mango) and Polona Tratnik, and a setting like the Kapelica Gallery in Ljubljana, are the real drivers behind contemporary art in Slovenia, and have garnered increasing institutional acknowledgement. At Ars Electronica in 2008, *Ecology of Techno Mind*, the exhibition curated by the artistic director of Kapelica Jurij Krpan at the Lentos Museum of Linz, turned out to be the most interesting event of the whole festival. A year later, Krpan was back with *Arzenal Depo 2K9*, an ambitious exhibition project organised in the Slovenian capital. Marko Peljhan presented the project *INSULAR Technologies*, in progress since 1999, which is centered on developing an open, decentralized, global, independent radio communications system to offer stable, permanent links to charities, NGOs, individuals and groups of activists operating in remote areas where official communication systems are anything but stable. The system is independent from commercial and state-run communications networks, and thus lends itself to becoming an emblem of resistance to global control, the dark side of the telecoms networks. *INSULAR Technologies* is one of the offshoots of the project *Makrolab*, which was launched in 1994 and presented at documenta X in 1997, and involves the creation of an independent unit in which people can live, do research and communicate in extreme locations such as the Antarctic. In spite of its name, *INSULAR Technologies* has little in common with the *cultural insularity* that characterizes much of New Media Art, raising crucial issues such as surveillance, climate change and the construction of islands of resistance. It is an imaginative undertaking, and like Klüver's projects in the 1960s, would appear absurd to an engineer, but without the skills of the engineers and hackers who were involved in developing it, it would have remained just another interesting piece of arty science fiction. Now it has succeeded in combining the futuristic projects of Antonio Sant'Elia and Archigram with today's technology, fusing imagination and reality. It is unlikely that the production system of the contemporary art world would have been able to back the production of such an ambitious and long-term undertaking, yet it is on the conceptual horizon of contemporary art that all the implications of a project of this kind can be fully understood.

The Postmedia Condition

In the Fourth chapter of this book (*The Boho Dance*), I tried to develop an in-depth analysis of those events that, beginning in 1996, promoted New Media Art in the contemporary art arena. That analysis shows that any attempt to import on the contemporary art platform the idea of art and the system of values on which the New Media Art world is grounded (that is, New Media Art as a category based on the use – and, often, the celebration – of technology) has failed miserably, garnering criticism both about the suitability of basing an artistic category on the use of a medium, and on the cultural value of celebrating technologies. While, on the other hand, events that focused on the impact of the current techno-social delevopment on art, without introducing any distinction of medium, as well as events that researched the way a specific, not technology-related topic (ie, abstraction) was developed in both new media and old media art, proved to be quite well accepted. In the contemporary art arena New Media Art is only allowed to exist if it abandons its techno-centric outlook and the very term that identifies it. Or, to sum up the issue with the help of an early statement by Catherine David:

«*New technologies are nothing other than new means to an end. Alone they are of significance; it always depends upon how they are applied. I am against naive faith in progress, glorification of the possibilities of technological developments. Much of what today's artists produce with New Media is very boring. But I am just as opposed to the denunciation of technology. For me technology in itself is not a category according to which I judge works. This type of categorization is just as outmoded as division into classical art genres (painting, sculpture...). I am interested in the idea of a project; ideally the means of realizing the project should arise from the idea itself*». [12]

Having taken this on board, how, then, can we underline New Media Art's "specific form of contemporaneity" (Inke Arns) without violating these taboos?

The concept of postmedia, in a broader, more inclusive sense than Rosalind Krauss introduced, does the job nicely. As previously mentioned, the term has a complex history that influences its meanings. Before Krauss, the expression "post-media era" appeared for the first time [13] in some of Félix Guattari's later writings, published in *Soft Subversions* (1996). As Michael Goddard [14] observes, Guattari's references to the post-media era are often hermetic; and while they were greeted by many as an anticipation of the advent of the internet (Guattari was a keen supporter of the French Minitel system), the term seems to be a front for a more complex theory, that starts with a reflection on the independent media and free radios of the 1970s to posit, at the end of the consensual era of mass-media, a post-media era in which the media would be a tool of dissent, revising the relationship between producer and consumer.

In this "political" sense the term was adopted in 2002 [15] by the Spanish academic José Luis Brea, who used it to map out the network communities and networking practices deployed by the new "media producers." In this way, the term therefore implies the decline of the mass media used by the powers that be to maintain consensus, in favor of a grass-roots use of the media as a tool for activists and political and cultural movements.

When Rosalind Krauss wrote *A Voyage in the North Sea. Art in the Age of the Post-Medium Condition* [16] in 1999, she used the term "post-medium" rather than "post-media", reflecting on the decline of the Greenberghian concept of medium-specificity. This term is normally used in contemporary art criticism, while the New Media Art world prefers "post-media," but with a different meaning from that posited by Guattari. According to Peter Weibel, who in 2005 organized a show entitled *Postmedia Condition,* [17]

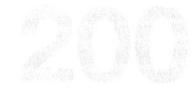

postmedia art is the art that comes after the affirmation of the media; and given that the impact of the media is universal and computers can now simulate all other media, all contemporary art is postmedia, as he explains:

«This media experience has become the norm for all aesthetic experience. Hence in art there is no longer anything beyond the media. No-one can escape from the media. There is no longer any painting outside and beyond the media experience. There is no longer any sculpture outside and beyond the media experience. There is no longer any photography outside and beyond the media experience». [18]

According to Weibel, the postmedia condition was arrived at in two stages. The first stage saw all media achieving equivalent status and the same dignity as artistic media. The second stage saw the various media intermingling, losing their separate identities and living off one another.

Lev Manovich also uses the expression "post-media." [19] Unlike Weibel, Manovich succeeds in combining a reflection on the crisis of the concept of artistic medium and medium-specificity (Krauss) with the idea that the immense impact of the media has completely altered the destiny of art (or rather, aesthetics). According to Manovich, the concept of medium was challenged first by the development of new artistic languages (assemblage, happening, installation, etc.); then by the advent of media (such as photography, film and video) which clashed with the normal definition of artistic medium, and above all with the usual methods for circulating and distributing art.

The third attack on the classic notion of artistic medium came from the digital revolution. In the first place, the computer appropriated all media, and imposed its own operative approach on them. Copy and paste, morphing, interpolation, etc., are operations that can be applied, regardless of the medium, to photographs and synthetic images, sounds and moving images. The distinction between photography and painting, film and animation, falls away. The web establishes a standard for multimedia documents that combines text, images and sound. Lastly, different versions of every "artistic object" can exist, including in terms of medium: a Flash animation can be put online or burned onto a DVD, generative software can be transformed into a video or a print, a website can be exhibited as an interactive installation.

«These are just some examples of how the traditional concept of medium does not work in relation to post-digital, post-net culture. And yet, despite the obvious inadequacy of the concept of medium to describe contemporary cultural and artistic reality, it persists. It persists through sheer inertia – and also because to put in place a better, more adequate conceptual system is easier said than done». [20]

A concept of postmedia that takes all these strata into account would prove a useful key to the art of the present. Obviously I'm not suggesting we use the term "postmedia" to describe the art of the present. This term has its own flaws, firstly because the prefix "post" has been abused in art criticism, and secondly because, as used by Rosalind Krauss, it is predominantly associated with the art of the twentieth century, and not up to the challenge of describing the art of the information age. Recognizing that we are living in a postmedia age is not a point of arrival, but a point of departure. It means recognizing that the digital revolution completely changed the conditions for the production and circulation of art, and that it is slowly but inevitably changing the ways in which art is experienced, discussed and owned. In these circumstances, art is becoming something completely different from what we were used to – and art worlds have to change accordingly, developing new values, new economies, new structures. This is already happening, and if we haven't caught on yet, it is because this kind of change doesn't happen overnight, but takes time, mediation and slow adaptations.

Under different names, this point of view is already making its way into art criticism. It is significant to mention, for instance, how Nicolas Bourriaud identifies the socio-cultural impact of the new technologies as one of the points of departure for analysing contemporary art. In *Relational Aesthetics* (1998) he noted how «The main effects of the computer revolution are visible today among artists who do not use computers», [21] and how in the 1990s, with the exponential development of interactive technologies, artists explored «the arcane mysteries of sociability and interaction». Bourriaud's then condemnation of the art that uses computers (described as the representation of an «alienation of methods dictated by production needs») only demonstrates how much these practices have changed since then, and it should not divert our attention from the close relationship that Bourriaud traces between the "interactivity of the media" and "relational art." In his subsequent work *Postproduction* (2002), the French critic further develops this reflection on the impact of digital media on artistic means of production. According to Bourriaud, the contemporary artist works like a DJ or programmer, cherry-picking cultural objects from the «proliferating chaos of global culture in the information age» [22] and incorporating them into new contexts.

«The contemporary work of art does not position itself as the termination point of the "creative process" (a "finished product" to be contemplated) but as a site of navigation, a portal, a generator of activities». [23]

In the era of post-production the artist appropriates various operative paradigms introduced by the media, from sampling to copy-and-paste, and various related ideologies such as sharing and copyleft, to produce works starting from secondary materials, which exist not as isolated objects but nodes in a network of meanings. Lastly, in his recent "Altermodern Manifesto" (2009)

Bourriaud introduces the concept of "altermodernity" in a socio-cultural context characterized by globalization, travel and increasing opportunities for communication. [24] And he concludes:

«*Altermodern art is thus read as a hypertext; artists translate and transcode information from one format to another, and wander in geography as well as in history. [...] Our universe becomes a territory all dimensions of which may be travelled both in time and space*».

This acknowledgement of the impact of the media on life and art is however entirely free from media determinism, as Bourriaud reiterates in *The Radicant* (2009):

«*Radicant art implies the end of the medium-specific, the abandonment of any tendency to exclude certain fields from the realm of art [...] Nothing could be more alien to it than a mode of thought based on disciplines, on the specificity of the medium – a sedentary notion if ever there was one, and one that amounts to cultivating one's field*». [25]

And while Krauss appears to envisage in the "reinvention of the medium" a way to avoid postmedia being transformed into a "new academia", Bourriaud boldly declares:

«*Today, one must struggle, not – as Greenberg did – for the preservation of an avant-garde that is self sufficient and focused on the specificities of its means, but rather for the indeterminacy of art's source code, its dispersion and dissemination, so that it remains impossible to pin down – in opposition to the hyperformatting that, paradoxically, distinguishes kitsch*». [26]

The idea of *Radicant*, if interpreted correctly, not only enables us to rescue New Media Art from its position on the margins, but even translates the postmedia perspective, still bound to a century of "post" phenomena, into a valuable indication for 21st century art. Cultivating «the indeterminacy of art's source code» also means giving up on the contextual definition of art that was the glib pretext of the last century, as Blais and Ippolito hoped; it also means, at least on the critical level, breaking down the barriers that still separate contemporary art from film, architecture and design to arrive at a new, open vision of the visual realm; lastly, it means replacing these barriers with a new, definitive dividing line between art, defined by the indeterminacy and dissemination of its source code, and media, the land of kitsch and medium-specificity.

In other words, a set of vertical barriers (between media and different distribution circuits) is replaced by a horizontal divider. Art and media can use the same means, be identical in formal terms and travel on the same distribution circuits, because it is their deep-seated nature that distinguishes them, not incidental elements.

From this perspective, independently of the medium it uses to express itself, the art that is most aware of the cultural, social and political consequences of the new media is in line for a position of key importance and unexpectedly reacquires a social function: to combat the flattening of culture with complexity, numbness with sensation and standardization with critical thought.

Among the examples that Bourriaud offers of rejection of the «monoculture of the medium», that of Paul Chan fits very well into the discourse we are developing. Chan studied film, video and new media at Bard College in New York. An artist and political activist, since 2000 he has been running the site national-philistine.com as an online container for his work. Both Chan's works and writing reveal a lucid awareness of the socio-cultural impact of new technologies. The artist has adopted the ethic of sharing on the web, making a large part of his work available on the site: essays and publications, but also video and audio archives, such as *My Own Private Alexandria* (2006), a personal selection of essays that form a sort of self-portrait in library form, released in MP3 format and free to download. National Philistine also enables users to enjoy Chan's most famous digital animations, like the series *Sade Before Sade* (2006 – 2009), and to download and install the various alternative fonts that the artist is constantly working on. «I could still write. But I wanted more», he explains on the site, «I wanted language to work for me and no one else». In 2008, Chan exhibited the series *The 7 Lights*, which he started working on in 2005, at the New Museum in New York. The show, curated by Massimiliano Gioni, combined seven video installations with a series of charcoal preparatory drawings. The projections were distributed in space like outlines of light cast through a window or backlit door. Shadows moved across the bright, coloured light: silhouettes of men, animals, plants and objects that flow past at an increasing pace, converting the initial atmosphere of tranquillity into the sinister mood of a nightmare. The animations contained multiple references to history and current affairs, from Greek mythology and the Bible to the war in Iraq, which intersected in an allusive, non-linear narrative, while in linguistic terms the clear reference was to Chinese shadow theatre.

In agreement with the museum, Chan published an online version of the show, [27] which combined the video documentation of the installations with the drawings and an audio archive featuring a selection of essays from *My Own Private Alexandria*: texts by Anna Freud, Henri Michaux, Theodor Adorno and Chris Marker, an ideal soundtrack for the exhibition. Here too, the essays were freely downloadable, as were the source files (in Flash) for all the animations.

As well as adopting the free software ethic, Chan often draws inspiration from it for his works and his exploration of our technological present. In the essay "The Unthinkable Community," for instance, Chan reveals how one of the points of departure for *Waiting For Godot* (2007), his revisitation of Samuel Beckett's

play for the streets of New Orleans, was a reflection on the meaning of words like solitude and community in an age in which the explosion of technologies – from mobile phones to social networks – that facilitate communication, have actually increased the individual's sense of alienation and solitude, rather than reducing it.

«*Time deepens connections, whereas technology economizes communication. This is why, despite the growing number of ways for people to be seen and heard, tele-technologies have ironically made it harder for people to comprehend one another*». [28]

As we can see, Paul Chan uses the new media and develops a critique of the new technologies without ever falling prey to the pitfalls of New Media Art. His work is devoid of any kind of self-referencing, and focuses on issues such as history, war, religion, sex and power; and, as Bourriaud writes, [29] it

«*reflects our civilization of overproduction, in which the degree of spatial (and imaginary) clutter is such that the slightest gap in its chain produces a visual effect; but it also points to the experience of homo viator, moving through formats and circuits, far from that monoculture of the medium to which certain critics would like to see contemporary art restricted*».

After Art

Of course, Nicolas Bourriaud is not alone in this recognition of the impact of the digital revolution on art creation and dissemination. Rosalind Krauss herself, in her recent book *Under Blue Cup*, seems to ground her "reactionary" interest in medium specificity and in the "knights of the medium" (in her own words, artists who «appropriated a technical support and used it to "invent" a medium») in the realization that the digital age has turned the "post-medium condition" from a conscious choice into a generalized condition of production which we should resist by going back to the medium "as a form of remembering":

«For all media theory these nested Chinese boxes cancel the very idea of a separation between mediums. Kittler's cancellation turns on the numerical streams into which all information – visual, auditory, oral – will be quantified. Once the digitization happens, any medium can be translated into any other. A total media link un a digital base will erase the very concept of medium». [30]

While Krauss addresses the changes introduced by the digital shift in art production, other theorists focus on the dramatic change produced by new means of circulating art among audiences. This comes as no surprise. Throughout the twentieth century, its delivery site has often been the primary means of distinction between what was art and what wasn't. Art was art because it happened in the white cube of the museum and gallery. Furthermore, contemporary art has often been the result of a dialogical relationship with its primary place of delivery: even when art criticized the white cube, escaped it, defied it, brought ordinary life in it, the white cube was the "other" in a one-to-one relationship. Finally, it is in the white cube, and thanks to it, that art distinguishes itself from its documentation, and that art documentation sometimes is converted into art.

In the digital age, the distinction between copies and originals has become blurred and artificial, and the advent of new platforms for distributing cultural content undermines the traditional role of old platforms, from museums to libraries to music stores. In *Art Power*, Boris Groys writes:

«Digitalization would seem to allow the image to become independent of any kind of exhibition practice. Digital images

have, that is, an ability to originate, to multiply, and to distribute themselves through the open fields of contemporary means of communication, such as the Internet or cell-phone networks, immediately and anonymously, without any curatorial control. In this respect we can speak of the digital images as genuinely strong images – as images that are able to show themselves according to their own nature, depending solely on their own vitality and strength». [31]

Actually, Groys goes on re-affirming the role of the museum, the only place where the digital image – which is not an original, but the staging of an "invisible original" (the image file) – can be re-created, find its own identity, become an "original":

«[...] the contemporary, postdigital curatorial practice can do something that the traditional exhibition could do only metaphorically: exhibit the Invisible». [32]

But if the digital may enforce the curatorial and institutional role in terms of "re-creation of the lost aura", it is also generating habits that seem to go in the opposite direction. We have got used to mediation to the point that we no longer see any difference between primary and second hand experience, and sometimes we prefer the latter to the former. As artist Seth Price wrote in his influential essay *Dispersion*:

«Does one have an obligation to view the work first-hand? What happens when a more intimate, thoughtful, and enduring understanding comes from mediated discussions of an exhibition, rather than from a direct experience of the work? Is it incumbent upon the consumer to bear witness, or can one's art experience derive from magazines, the Internet, books, and conversation?» [33]

In *Dispersion*, Price discusses the possibility of disseminating art in the public environment through media as a new form of public art, which is challenging the art world and its structures:

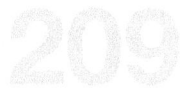

«Publicness today has as much to do with sites of production and reproduction as it does with any supposed physical commons, so a popular album could be regarded as a more successful instance of public art than a monument tucked away in an urban plaza [...] Perhaps an art distributed to the broadest possible public closes the circle, becoming a private art, as in the days of commissioned portraits. The analogy will only become more apt as digital distribution techniques allow for increasing customization to individual consumers». [34]

Another artist who focuses on the digital circulation of art on public online platforms is Hito Steyerl. In the essay "In Defense of the Poor Image", Steyerl analyses the cultural and socio-political implications of the online circulation of low resolution versions of different cultural artifact, from self-produced media to avant-garde movies. She explains how they mirror a culture of access, speed, resistance against privatization and copyright, distributed authorship, social relationships based on the creation, manipulation and experience of cultural content. And she concludes:

«The poor image is no longer about the real thing – the originary original. Instead, it is about its own real conditions of existence: about swarm circulation, digital dispersion, fractured and flexible temporalities. It is about defiance and appropriation just as it is about conformism and exploitation. In short: it is about reality». [35]

For the generation of artists who have grown up in this media environment, the online circulation of the artwork, with all its implications, is more often than not the primary means of distributing their art and interfacing with an audience; and the presentation in the white cube, if it takes place, is just a step in an ongoing process that further develops online. In the essay "The Image Object Post-Internet", artist Artie Vierkant writes:

«In the Post-Internet climate, it is assumed that the work of art lies equally in the version of the object one would encounter at

a gallery or museum, the images and other representations disseminated through the Internet and print publications, bootleg images of the object or its representations, and variations on any of these as edited and recontextualized by any other author». [36]

This, of course, doesn't mean that the new distribution platform will prevail over the old ones, but only that it is reconfiguring the relationship between artists and audience, and with the art world; and that it's forcing the latter to reconfigure itself. If it's true that «with today's burgeoning potential for digital mass viewership, transmission becomes as important as creation», [37] the art world has to face the fact that it is no longer the the primary medium for transmitting art, and adapt accordingly.

A recent attempt to analyze the conditions of this reconfiguration is *After Art*, by David Ioselit. As he explains in the Preface, *After Art* is interested in «what images *do* once they enter circulation in heterogeneous networks». [38] This interest comes from the realization that «the scale at which images proliferate and the speed with which they travel have never been greater. Under these conditions, images appear to be free, but they carry a price». [39] According to Ioselit, this economic value (art as a currency) is strictly related to art's ability to circulate in information networks at an high speed. [40] But in order to understand this concept, we first

«[...] must discard the concept of medium (along with its mirror image, postmedium), which has been fundamental to art history and criticism for generations. This category privileges discrete objects – even objects that are attenuated, mute, distributed, or "dematerialized." One of the goals of After Art is to expand the definition of art to embrace heterogeneous configurations of relationships or links – what the French artist Pierre Huyghe has called "a dynamic chain that passes through different formats."» [41]

The link between this shift (from objects to relationships) and the digital shift is emphasized a few pages later:

«*Images might become forms of currency that do not conform to the monetary (like many forms of communication). Because they emerge in an "information era" where documentation is virtually inherent in the production of art, contemporary artworks typically belong to the category of documented objects*». [42]

To conclude, if recognizing that we are living in a postmedia era is just a starting point, the integration of the art formerly known as New Media Art into the contemporary art world is, again, only the preliminary phase of a broader reconfiguration of art worlds. The continental drift has begun. When it will be over, we will be probably able to understand what the word "art" will mean in the new millennium.

Digital Natives

To return to the present, we can say that, clawed back from the contemporary art world, the art formerly known as New Media Art does not lose its specificity, and can actually become one of the most effective incarnations of our postmedia world. A world in which it no longer makes sense to distinguish, as Bourriaud did in 1998, [43] and as the paradigm implicit in the term New Media Art does, between art which uses computers and art which doesn't; a world in which on the other hand it increasingly makes sense to distinguish between art that acknowledges the advent of the information society and art that retreats to positions typical of the industrial era we are moving out of. It is according to this distinction that in a few decades' time we will be able to identify the academia and avant-garde of the present day.

This approach is particularly apt when it comes to interpreting the art of "digital natives," namely that generation of artists who have never experienced life without computers. For this generation, daily use of the internet is the norm, to the point that there is not much sense distinguishing between online and offline. The latter state is simply dying out: they are always online. Computers and mobile technologies have profoundly impacted their social lives and the ways in which they handle their lives, their relationships with others and a constantly mediated reality. In their lives, the dividing line between public and private is being irremediably redefined. Constant tweets render the web privy to all their comings and goings, holiday snaps are immediately posted on Facebook or other sites, and relationships are managed via messages and videocalls and often reported on online for their duration. [44]

The artists of this generation are experiencing the creation of the vernacular imagery of the internet from the inside: the ever-expanding mass of amateur photography and low-res videos, but also postcards, greetings cards, little animations and artifacts of all kinds produced from an ingenuous use of the standard tools and effects of the multimedia production studio that is the resource at our fingertips. Today's artists often contribute to this, seeking approval from those communities before branching out into the art world. «I absorb, then I translate and lastly I create», declares Ryan Trecartin, a young American artist who has been eliciting increasing attention in the art world for the last two years, but who was already well-known on YouTube. In his video works, young, heavily made-up exhibitionists are portrayed in domestic settings, enacting snippets of everyday life, while they inundate the viewer with details of their private lives. They are an expression of what Trecartin calls "transumerism", the encounter between posthuman and postmedia: our way of life in the information era. They speak to the web of the web, where they continue to be accessible even now that they are a solid presence on the art market.

His productivity notwithstanding, Trecartin's work is but a miniscule contribution to the 24 videos that every minute are uploaded to YouTube, the platform that has helped make video, as the artist Tom Sherman wrote, «the vernacular form of the era [...] the common and everyday way that people communicate». [45] Among the artists who, like Trecartin, take YouTube very seriously, many have been part of the so-called "pro surfer" scene, that since 2006 has grown up around a number of collectively-managed blogs such as Nasty Nets and Supercentral, in which the participants establish a remote dialogue based on exchanging, manipulating and commenting on media materials – images, videos and texts – found on the net. [46] This collective practice, which is a background to participants' solo work, encourages them on one hand to focus on practices such as montage, postproduction, copying and remixing, and on the other hand to attribute considerable importance to a double dialogue: the internal one between members of the "surfing club" and the external one with the wider, variegated community of internet users, or users of a particular service such as YouTube.

Petra Cortright's video work is a shining example of this, perfectly camouflaged as one of the most common genres of vernacular video, namely "ego clips": narcissistic self-representations in which users pose, dance, sing and play sports in front of the camera. Cortright capitalises on her own attractiveness and teen style to do the same, before applying a few simple postproduction tricks to convey her individuality with respect to the culture that she nonetheless strives to be a part of. She incorporates animations, clips and "glitter" effects into her videos, or uses standard filters, as in *Das Hell(e) Modell* (2009), where a lighting effect suffices to transform a girl dancing into an eerie and evocative presence.

Produced for YouTube or other platforms, these videos are both a conforming response to and a note in the margin of the culture that these platforms have given rise to. They might be in line to become the next "viral video" but they are also a comment and a critique of the presumed democracy of the "vote for this video" culture and the low level of individual attention devoted to such a vast mass of material. Cory Arcangel developed this critique, appropriating one of the *topoi* of "digital folklore," the cat. [47] On December 22 2005, a cat called Pajamas starred in the first ever video posted on YouTube. In a sophisticated remix, Arcangel used hundreds of its successors to create *Drei Klavierstücke op. 11* (2009): a series of three videos in which the artist plays this difficult piece by Arnold Schoenberg utilizing found footage of cats walking across the keys of a piano. In the work, vernacular and avant-garde – *Op. 11* is considered to be Schoenberg's first "atonal" piece of music – mingle irresistibly, garnering more than 160,000 viewings on YouTube.

This dialogue with the online vernacular is just one of the many possible manifestations of the work of those artists who have been variously labeled "post internet", or "internet aware". The two terms emerged around 2008 to label art that addresses «the impact of the internet on culture at large» without necessarily happening online or using digital media, [48] and at least had the merit of emphasizing not the use of a specific medium, but the awareness of its consequences on culture and society. Vierkant rephrases it this way in his essay:

«*Specifically within the context of this PDF, Post-Internet is defined as a result of the contemporary moment: inherently informed by ubiquitous authorship, the development of attention as currency, the collapse of physical space in networked culture, and the infinite reproducibility and mutability of digital materials*». [49]

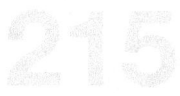

Only a few years later, these labels may sound somehow unnecessary: how can you be "contemporary" without fitting this definition? At the same time, however, we may still need them, in order to underline that this level of awareness is far from being equally distributed around the art world population. Although it doesn't belong to a specific generation (digital natives) or to a specific group (former net artists), it's still quite difficult to find it outside of these circles: artists such as Thomas Ruff, Seth Price, Maurizio Cattelan are the exception that confirm the rule.

Within the context of our argument, what's important to note is that post internet art practices are already operating beyond the New Media Art / contemporary art dichotomy, in a fully postmedia perspective.

Other Critical Approaches

But once we have acknowledged these changes, it should also be noted that the art formerly known as New Media Art has a strong need of other points of view, other critical approaches, other associations. It is time to cast off the old prejudice, reiterated by Christiane Paul, according to whom

«[...] new media could never be understood from a strictly art-historical perspective: the history of technology and media sciences plays an equally important role in this art's formation and reception. New media art requires media literacy». [50]

This is only true to the extent that it is true of all other artistic practices, on two levels. Firstly, I will have a better understanding of the painting of John Currin if I am familiar with his medium (painting), in terms of both its history and its purely instrumental elements. Secondly, I will have a better understanding of the painting of John Currin if I am familiar with today's media, and the ways that images circulate in the current information landscape. The American painter looks to figurative painting traditions from the fifteenth century onwards, but takes his subjects from magazines like *Cosmopolitan* and *Playboy*, and observes the amateur pornography that does the rounds on the net.

In other words, all contemporary art needs to be media literate. For its part, New Media Art needs above all to be conversant with art history, and to have a working knowledge of contemporary art. Let's take an example that verges on the extreme. Gazira Babeli is an artist who has been operating on the virtual platform of Second Life since 2006. In view of the fact that there is no actual person called Gazira Babeli, and the identity of the person who controls her is unknown, Gazira Babeli is, on one level, a work of art in her own right – an identity construction project in a simulated world. But as an artist, Gazira also produces art: "performances", "installations", "sculptures", "environments" and even "paintings." However, like Umberto Eco's postmodern rose, all of these terms require inverted commas because the different entities that they describe are all actually the result of the same operation: the manipulation and subversion of the codes (3D modeling, scripting languages) that a simulated world is based on. To approach work of this kind we must undoubtedly be familiar with the media world. We have to know what a virtual world is, and what an avatar is; nothing that the *Matrix* saga and James Cameron's recent blockbuster have not illustrated, in abundant detail. Basic knowledge of computers as an operative environment, with their limits of bandwidth and graphics card, languages and conventions is desirable, and a minimum of experience of virtual environments will aid comprehension of certain community dynamics. It also helps to be familiar with the brief tradition of the artistic use of virtual worlds. All of this provides the technological key to access the figure of Gazira Babeli and her work, but is not enough to develop a critical discourse on it. To enter into possession of the "cultural" key needed to understand it, it is equally necessary to be conversant with the theme of identity experimentation that runs throughout the history of contemporary art, from Rrose Sélavy to Matthew Barney.

Works like *Avatar On Canvas*, reproductions of Francis Bacon paintings that the viewer is invited to sit on in order to be subjected to a series of spectacular deformations, can be better understood in the light of the history of performance art and body interventions; while projects like *Grey Goo*, that unleashes a storm of pop icons, require the viewer to have some knowledge not only of the viral strategies deployed by hackers, but also the pop multiplication of images and the invasion of the spectator's visual horizon put into practice by Andy Warhol, for example. [51]

Viewing a practice of this kind against a limited background such as that of New Media Art certainly does not help us to comprehend "its contemporary specificity." What does Gazira Babeli have in common with those who construct impossible architectural structures in virtual worlds? Or with the amateur art that is displayed in the galleries of Second Life? Or with the interactive installations at ZKM? Vice versa, what benefits can be drawn from considering her work critically or curatorially in a discourse on gender ambiguity, alongside Wolfgang Tillmans, or contemporary identity, in a dialogue with Cindy Sherman, or with regard to the manipulation of the body and interventions in public space?

This kind of argument could probably be made for much of the art formerly known as New Media Art, the real power of which today lies in what more and what else, compared to other practices, it can tell us about the destiny and topical nature of abstraction; racial and sexual issues; our globalized world; control and censorship; terrorism and climate change. The art of our time must be measured and assessed in these terms. In order to do so, art criticism must cast off its prejudices on the media nature or the social origin of what it is looking at, and learn to look inside and outside of the art world, and look for art where it is not expected to exist; it must lose that baggage of ignorance (technological on one hand, artistic on the other) that it still carries.

Conclusions

Turin, October 2010. After attending a conference, I head out for a beer with two friends from the School of Art & Media of Plymouth University, UK. They tell me that their department, which till then had been part of the Polytechnic, has just been made part of the university's art faculty. They reckon this is undoubtedly a good thing, but report that it has also sparked something of an identity crisis, with the result that the department is now doing all it can to reassert its unique status. The art school students, they add with a hint of scorn, tend to view the new media as something neutral, which can be merely deployed like any other medium, without dwelling on the critical issues involved. Their department, on the other hand, has always sought to develop a critical vision, based on in-depth knowledge of the media in question.

It is not easy to explain to them how both of these processes, albeit moving in different directions, are positive, and that it is possible to maintain a "postmedia" approach to the new media without rejecting the need for temporarily independent arenas in which the specificity of those media is tenaciously cultivated. It is not even easy to explain what "temporarily" might mean in these circumstances: no-one likes handing the fruits of their labours over to others, above all if there is a divide based on half a century of history, and equipped with its own institutional form. It might take a long time before the relationships between the contemporary art world and the New Media Art world settle according to the outlook presented in this book. For now, any attempts at communication still tend to end in deadlock, when not the stirrings of conflict.

"Aesthetics is to artists what ornithology is to birds" said Barnett Newman. This book is an attempt to follow artists taking off in freedom on their very first flight, and loosen the bars of the cages constructed around them by ornithologists too preoccupied with supporting or contradicting the arguments of other ornithologists.

Notes

[1] Steve Dietz, "Foreword", p. xiv, in Beryl Graham, Sarah Cook, op. cit., 2010
[2] In Emma Quinn, "Live and Media Arts at the ICA", in *New Media Curating*, October 17, 2008.
[3] Cf. www.crumbweb.org.
[4] Cf. the Variable Media Initiative, online at www.variablemedia.net. The initiative also produced the book Alain Depocas, Jon Ippolito, Caitlin Jones (Eds.), *Permanence Through Change: The Variable Media Approach*, The Solomon R. Guggenheim Foundation, New York, and The Daniel Langlois Foundation for Art, Science, and Technology, Montreal, 2003. Cf. also AA.VV., *The EAI Online Resource Guide for Exhibiting, Collecting & Preserving Media Art*, 2006, online at http://resourceguide.eai.org.
[5] Cf. Christiane Paul, "Challanges for a Ubiquitous Museum. From the White Cube to the Black Box and Beyond". In C. Paul, op. cit., 2008, pp. 53 – 75.
[6] In Inke Arns & Jacob Lillemose, "'It's contemporary art, stupid'. Curating computer based art out of the ghetto", 2005, cit.
[7] Valeska K. Buehrer, "Dearest progressive scan loading, on victims of Broadband", in Neural, n° 23, 2006, p. 48.
[8] Olia Lialina, in "Media Art Undone", conference panel at transmediale07, Berlin, February 3, 2007. Full transcript of the presentations is available here: www.mikro.in-berlin.de/wiki/tiki-index.php?page=MAU (last visit March 2013).
[9] Documentation about the project can be found online here: www.showmethecontent.com/115234/135029/all/tft-tennis (last visit March 2013).
[10] Cf. John Schwartz, "Museum Kills Live Exhibit", in The New York Times, May 13, 2008, online at www.nytimes.com/2008/05/13/science/13coat.html?_r=0 (last visit March 2013). More information about Symbiotica can be found here: www.symbiotica.uwa.edu.au (last visit March 2013).
[11] I refer to the article: Gerfried Stocker, "The Art of Tomorrow", in *a minima*, n° 15, 2006, pp. 6 – 19, widely discussed in Chapter 3.
[12] Catherine David, "dx and new media", June 20, 1997, online at http://archiv.documenta.de/archiv/dx/lists/debate/0001.html (last visit March 2013).
[13] In actual fact, Gianni Romano has been using the term "postmedia" since 1994, when he set up the magazine of the same name. After the first three issues, in 1995 the magazine was converted into the site postmedia.net, which is still active; in 2002 it was joined by the publisher Postmediabooks.

According to Romano, «the postmedia condition is the parting shot of the postmodern age, the final warning that the media are not neutral when used politically, while artists favour a neutral use, not conditioned by the medium» (personal communication, October 2010).

[14] In Michael Goddard, "Felix and Alice in Wonderland. The Encounter between Guattari and Berardi and the Post-Media Era", in *Generation-online*, June 1996. Cf. also Félix Guattari, *Soft Subversions*. Edited by Sylvère Lotringer. Semiotext(e) 1996.

[15] José Luis Brea, *La era postmedia. Acción comunicativa, prácticas (post)artísticas y dispositivos neomediales*, Consorcio Salamanca, Salamanca 2002.

[16] Rosalind Krauss, *A Voyage in the North Sea. Art in the Age of the Post-Medium Condition*, Thames & Hudson, London 1999.

[17] Neue Galerie Graz am Landesmuseum Joanneum, November 15 2005 – January 15 2006; Centro Cultural Conde Duque, Madrid, February 7 –April 16 2006.

[18] Peter Weibel, "The Post-media Condition", in AAVV, *Postmedia Condition*, cat., Centro Cultural Conde Duque, Madrid 2006, p. 98.

[19] Cfr. Lev Manovich, "Post-Media Aesthetics", sd (2000 –), online at www.manovich.net/DOCS/Post_media_aesthetics1.doc (last visit March 2013).

[20] Ivi.

[21] Nicolas Bourriaud, *Relational Aesthetics*, Les Presse du Reel, Paris 1998, p. 67.

[22] Nicolas Bourriaud, *Postproduction. Culture as Screenplay: How Art Reprograms the World*, Lukas & Sternberg, New York 2002, p. 13.

[23] Ibidem, p. 19.

[24] Nicolas Bourriaud, "Altermodern Manifesto", 2009, online at www.tate.org.uk/whats-on/tate-britain/exhibition/altermodern/explain-altermodern/altermodern-explainedmanifesto (last visit March 2013).

[25] Nicolas Bourriaud, *The Radicant*, Sternberg Press, New York 2009, pp. 53 – 54.

[26] Ibidem, p. 138.

[27] The original website has been now replaced by the exhibition entry in the museum's Digital Archive, online at http://archive.newmuseum.org/index.php/Detail/Occurrence/Show/occurrence_id/914 (last visit March 2013).

[28] Paul Chan, "The Unthinkable Community", in *Eflux Journal*, Issue 16, May 2010, online at www.e-flux.com/journal/view/144 (last visit March 2013).

[29] In Nicolas Bourriaud, *The Radicant*, cit., pp. 130 – 131.

[30] Rosalind Krauss, *Under Blue Cup*, 2011, cit., pp. 38 – 39.

[31] Boris Groys, "From Image to Image File – and Back: Art in the Age of Digitalization", in *Art Power*, The MIT Press, Cambridge – London 2008, p. 83.

[32] Ibidem, p. 91.

[33] Seth Price, "Dispersion", 2002 – ongoing, online at www.distributedhistory.com/Disperzone.html (last visit March 2013).

[34] Ibid.

[35] Hito Steyerl, "In Defense of the Poor Image", in *eflux journal*, Issue 10, November 2009, online at www.e-flux.com/journal/in-defense-of-the-poor-image/ (last visit March 2013).

[36] Artie Vierkant, "The Image Object Post-Internet", in *jstchillin*, 2010, online at http://jstchillin.org/artie/vierkant.html (last visit March 2013), p. 5.

[37] Lauren Christiansen, cit. in Vierkant 2010, p. 9.

[38] David Ioselit, *After Art*, Cloth 2012, p. xiv

[39] Ibid., p. 1

[40] Ioselit seem to agree with Steyerl, when she writes: «Apart from resolution and exchange value, one might imagine another form of value defined by velocity, intensity, and spread. Poor images are poor because they are heavily compressed and travel quickly. They lose matter and gain speed […] this is precisely why it also ends up being perfectly integrated into an information capitalism thriving on compressed attention spans, on impression rather than immersion, on intensity rather than contemplation, on previews rather than screenings». Cf. Steyerl 2009, cit.

[41] Ioselit 2012, p. 2.

[42] Ibid., p. 12.

[43] And how he also asserts in *The Radicant*: «home computing has gradually spread to all modes of thought and production. At the moment, however, its most innovative artistic applications stem from artists whose practice is quite distant from digital art of any kind – no doubt while waiting for something better to come along.» In Nicolas Bourriaud, *The Radicant*, cit., p. 133.

[44] About digital natives, cf. Don Tapscott, *Grown Up Digital*, McGraw-Hill eBooks 2009; John Palfrey, Urs Gasser, *Born Digital. Understanding the First Generation of Digital Natives*, Basic Books, New York 2008.

[45] Tom Sherman, "Vernacular Video", in Geert Lovink, Sabine Niederer (eds.), *Video Vortex Reader. Responses to Youtube*, Institute of Networked Cultures, Amsterdam 2008, p. 161.

[46] Cfr. Marisa Olson, "Lost Not Found: The Circulation of Images in Digital

Visual Culture", in *Words Without Pictures*, 18 September 2008, online at http://uncopy.net/wp-content/uploads/2011/01/olson-lostnotfound.pdf (last visit March 2013),

[47] Cf. Olia Lialina, Dragan Espenschied (eds.), *Digital Folklore*, Merz and Solitude, Stuttgart 2009.

[48] Cf. Louis Doulas, "Within Post-Internet, Part One", cit. and Gene McHugh, *Post Internet*, Link Editions, Brescia 2012.

[49] Vierkant 2010, p. 3.

[50] Christiane Paul, "Introduction", in C. Paul (ed.), *New Media in the White Cube and Beyond*, University of California Press 2008, p. 5.

[51] For more about Babeli, cf. Domenico Quaranta (ed.), *Gazira Babeli*, Link Editions, Brescia 2012.

Appendix 1

In the following appendix I have collected some responses to the issues discussed in this book, generated by the publication, on Rhizome, of an excerpt in English from the last chapter of the book and by the attention caused by Régine Debatty's generous review published in her blog "We Make Money Not Art" in August 2011. These comments not only document the anomalous life of this book between its Italian release (2010) and the present English edition, but also show what this book really is: not a definitive statement, but a little, modest contribution to an international, live debate that goes far beyond it, that nurtured it as it developed, and that I hope will continue to make me think about these issues in the future and help my ideas evolve and change.

I

In response to D. Quaranta, "The Postmedia Perspective", in *Rhizome*, January 12, 2011, online at http://rhizome.org/editorial/2011/jan/12/the-postmedia-perspective/.

«Orientated "towards new, state-of-the-art computer technology," yes unfortunately this is true of much of the poorer quality work that gets produced by people with no background in art, they can't contextualise the work in a history of art so focus on the immediate, the technology and what has to be learned in order to create the work. These people are routinely spit out from media and design courses where students are challenged to think about new type of forms, media and audiences. The vast majority of this work should never be seen but this is (depending on how you look at it) an unfortunate / liberating result of a 'form' where medium and publication (amongst other things) are merged and so everyone can put their work into the public realm. And the this side-effect of technology is not the only problem, the art world has also contributed by way of Joseph Beuys' famous slogan, "Everyone Is an Artist" – quite literally now everyone can (and is) trying to be an artist and its difficult to navigate through the bad to the good». **Garrett Lynch**, January 12, 2011

«"New Media Art" per se came about later than the sixties, as it came out of artists working directly with computational processes, producing computer code and this reached critical mass in the early to mid 1990's at the time of the introduction of the internet. Prior to that, there was digital media arts which was considered an esoteric practice (if I think back to the students and colleagues I had back then), and it also consisted of practitioners who wrote computer code, assembly language, and built hardware. Begun in the sixties and continuing throughout today is a field called "media art" but it was primarily based on video, analog time-based image and installation work, rather then computationally based as computers were not accessible except under unusual circumstances». **George Legrady**, January 12, 2011

«The idea must precede the object. so called artists killed new media by creating works in complete lack of conceptual content or personal statements. Even in major markets like New York and LA most new media art is nothing more than a bunch of fancy pants gadgetry lacking any kind of content, personal statement or conceptual idea. What ever happened to addressing the human condition? Isn't that why we make art in the first place? To communicate, express or question an idea. Technology for technologies sake does not equal art». **Michael Importico**, January 13, 2011

«I'm in the process of completing a manuscript that examines the gap between what I call mainstream contemporary art (MCA) and new media art (NMA). [...] My goal is to forge a hybrid discourse that joins the best of both worlds, informing each other in a way that is mutually beneficial and fortuitous for art in general. While this merging of NMA and MCA is perhaps inevitable, proactively theorizing the issues and stakes involved may play an important role in informing the ways in which that merger unfolds. Indeed, as historian of photography John Tagg has noted of the reception of an earlier "new media," the more experimental aspects of photography were not well-assimilated and that the impact of the discourses of photography and contemporary art on each other was highly asymmetrical: the latter changed very little, while the former lost its edge in the process of "fitting in." Needless to say, many in the NMA community are wary of losing our edge in the process of assimilation...

At Art Basel in June 2011, I organized and chaired a panel discussion with Nicolas Bourriaud, Peter Weibel, and Michael Grey [...] That occasion demonstrated some challenges to bridging the gap between MCA and NMA. One simple but clear indication of this disconnect was the fact that Weibel, arguably the most powerful individual in the world of NMA and Bourriaud, arguably the most influential curator and theorist in the world of MCA, had never met before. Although Domenico and I (and many others in the NMA artworld) see significant parallels and overlaps between MCA and NMA, these worlds do not see eye-to-eye, no matter how much they may share the rhetoric of interactivity, participation, and avant-gardism.

If MCA curators like Bourriaud genuinely embraced the so-called "post-medium condition," as he suggested at Art Basel, then the exclusionary prejudice against the explicit use of technological media in and as art would not exist. Bourriaud would not favor "indirect influences" of technology on art as he asserted. His discussions and exhibitions of contemporary art would be blind to medium, and there would be no debate. But that is not the case. Peter Weibel astutely picked up on Bourriaud's distinction between direct / indirect influences and pointed out the hypocrisy of valuing the indirect influence of technology while ignoring the explicit use of technology as an artistic medium in its own right. Weibel accurately and provocatively labels this "media injustice." Here I'm picking on Bourriaud, but the same argument applies to the vast majority of MCA curators.

While Domenico traces the roots of the post-medium discourse to Guattari and Brea, it could also be seen as rooted in Dick Higgins' 1966 "Statement on Intermedia." I propose another early touchstone, one that, like Higgins' statement, has the advantage of authorizing the historiography of art and technology / new media art: critic Burnham's embrace of 'post-formalist art' in his influential *Artforum* essay, "Systems Esthetics" (1968) and his magnum opus, *Beyond Modern Sculpture* (1968). Burnham was able to see ideas beneath forms and media, as exemplified in his brilliant exhibition, *Software* (1970), which joined together, without differentiating between them, works of art and works of technology, technological artworks, and artworks associated with conceptual art, happenings, and performance. As I noted in my essay, "Art in the Information Age: Technology and Conceptual Art" (2001), for Burnham, scientific and technological advances (now known as new media) were inseparable from the sweeping economic and social changes associated with the information age. Given the flood of technology and technological modes of exchange into all facets of life in the 2000s, I argue that this inseparability is as true or truer today than it was four decades ago. It is in this context that I agree with Weibel, whom Domenico quotes as stating, "This media experience has become the norm for all aesthetic experience. Hence in art there is no longer anything beyond the media... There is no longer any [art] outside and beyond the media experience."

The debate surrounding medium-specificity and the post-medium condition is fraught with tension both in NMA and MCA circles. Rosalind Krauss refers to post-medium practitioners as "nothing but pretenders" in contrast to Ruscha, Kentridge, Calle, and Marclay, whom she champions as "the genuine avant-garde of our day." (Krauss, *The Guarantee of the Medium*, 2009, p. 42). Bourriaud, on the other hand, seems to embrace the post-medium condition as a positive development, yet refuses to grant art that explicitly uses technological media, like NMA, entry into the high alter of MCA. Regarding medium-specificity and, more particularly, the importance of medium-specific analysis for NMA (which surely must threaten the uninitiated in MCA), Domenico rightly points out that "many works cannot be properly understood without an in-depth knowledge of the medium and its dynamics, and therefore continues to require a specialized critical approach." Later, he hedges on this, arguing against Christiane Paul's "prejudice" that "New media art requires media literacy,'" yet a few sentences later he returns to the Weibelian position that "all contemporary art needs to be media literate."

Citing Inke Arns, Domenico asks, how can we "underline New Media Art's 'specific form of contemporaneity'" in a way that does not "violate th[e] taboos" of MCA? I'm compelled to take issue with the tone of this query. Violating taboos has played an

important role in the history of art. One of the key contributions NMA can make to art in general is in drawing attention to and contesting the status quo. This has a lot to do not just with the explicit use of technological media but with challenging the museum and gallery – or any specific locale – as the privileged site of exhibition and reception. If NMA lies down and accepts assimilation on the terms of MCA, then much of its critical value will have been usurped.

At the same time, I'm compelled to agree with Catherine David's assertion (quoted) that "Much of what today's artists produce with New Media is very boring," but I must add that much of what today's artists produce without New Media is equally boring. While MCA curators and theorists like Krauss, Bourriaud, David make all the usual criticisms of NMA's "vacuous celebration of technology," I agree with Domenico's assertions that some of this work, even if it fails as art, may have "heralded a new development in knowledge" and that "The New Media Art world can potentially generate the energy that powers the other art worlds, giving their respective 'ideas of art' a radical evolution." Moreover, I argue that there may be specific strategic and conceptual advantages to using emerging media in a metacritical way. In other words, if used cleverly, technological media may offer precisely the tools needed to reflect on the profound ways in which that very technology is deeply embedded in modes of knowledge production, perception, and interaction, and is thus inextricable from corresponding epistemological and ontological transformations. I believe that such a metacritical approach is operating in the best NMA (and the best digital humanities scholarship.) Rather than shunning technological media, this method may offer artists the most advantageous opportunities to comment on and participate in the social transformations taking place in digital culture, in order to, as Bourriaud implores, "inhabit the world in a better way."

Early in the excerpt, Domenico summons Manovich's 1996 distinction between "Duchamp Land" and "Turing Land," a distinction that he claims remain "valid to a point" despite considerable changes in both artworlds over 15 years. As a matter of principle, I abhor such simplistic, binary oppositions, which do violence to the subtle layering of ideas and practices by flattening reality into sound-byte categories. Moreover,

Manovich's characterization of Turing Land, as oriented "towards new, state-of-the-art computer technology" misses what is conceptually most interesting about Turing's (and Manovich's!) theories of digital computing: the idea of the universal machine. Writing about the Dynabook (an early multimedia computing system) in their 1977 essay, "Personal Dynamic Media," Alan Kay and Adele Goldberg claimed that "the computer, viewed as a medium itself, can be all other media." This "new 'metamedium,'" as they called it, has "new properties" including "dynamic search" (i.e., random access), simulation, the ability to combine images, animations, and sound, and programmability. Its content, they propose, "would be a wide range of already-existing and not-yet-invented media." Manovich credits these ideas in his later, more nuanced theories, which emphasize the unique properties of meta-media.

From the above considerations, it should be becoming clear that new media theory straddles medium-specificity (the "new properties" of meta-media first proposed by Kay) and medium-generality (the "universal machine" proposed by Turing). In my book, I argue that the history of ideas and practices pertaining to computing and new media as a technological and cultural field cannot be limited to modernist conceptions of medium-specificity propounded by Krauss in her dismissal of the post-medium condition. It appears that neither specific nor universal theories of media are sufficient for the task, just as Domenico rightly suggests that neither new media theory nor contemporary art theory are sufficient for the task of making sense of either NMA or MCA. To their benefit, new media discourses have a remarkable ability to equally embrace universality and specificity, to say nothing of remediation (Bolter and Grusin 1999), convergence (Jenkins 2006), software studies, and a variety of other theoretical models, eroding the binary opposition between specificity and universality. The richly textured conceptual and applied hybridity of NMA practices and theoretical discourses offers great potential for reconfiguring the terms of debate concerning experimental and avant-garde artistic practices in the 21st century». **Edward Shanken**, January 26, 2011

II

Excerpts from Paddy Johnson's *Art Fag City* post on the Italian version of the book, and from the comments it generated. The article and the discussion are both available online at www.artfagcity.com/2011/08/30/is-new-media-accepted-in-the-art-world-domenico-quarantas-media-new-media-postmedia/.

«Do institutions and galleries have a growing interest in New Media? Two weeks ago, I identified the art "internet bubble" at The *L Magazine*, a trend that's currently giving new media the spot light. Not everyone sees new media the same way though. Domenico Quaranta, an Italian writer and curator previously best known to this blog for "Holy Fire", a dubiously themed new media exhibition in Brussels that included only "collectible" work, being one such example. Quaranta's followed up the 2008 exhibition by writing a whole book on the subject of New Media – "Media, New Media, PostMedia" – one core theme being that the field isn't accepted in the contemporary art world. "New Media Art is more or less absent in the contemporary art market, as well as in mainstream art magazines," he writes in his abstract, "and recent accounts on contemporary art history completely forgot it."

This has some truth to it, of course, but as of late these sentiments seem a little out of step with the attention noted above. Past the many New York museums attempting to capitalize on the public's interest in New Media – The Whitney's recently closed Cory Arcangel "ProTools" exhibition, MoMA's design and social media show "Talk To Me", and Ryan Trecartin's "Any Ever" at PS1 – blue chip interest is rearing its head. Pace Gallery just announced the launch of a social media show this September, thus replaying its 2006 attempt to capitalize on a trend: "Breaking and Entering; Art and the Video Game" was launched at the height of the video game art hype bubble. This, too, may be short-lived, but so what? Even if it is Pace's entry is a good sign that there's money to be made in New Media. Cash never fails to draw the attention of the art world». **Paddy Johnson**, August 30, 2011

«It's nice to see Arcangel at the Whitney and Ryoji Ikeda at Park Ave Armory before that, but two isolated shows don't change the fact that this work is barely being shown in the US. And how is Trecartin a "New Media" artist, anyway? Like "Design and the Elastic Mind" before it, MoMA's "Talk to Me" is great because it exposes the general public to new ideas from technology-based art and design practices. But nowhere will you find the exhibited works described properly within an art context. The V&A in London did a similar sleight-of-hand with their DECODE show, subtitling it "Digital Design Sensations" even though none of the works dealt with design concepts.

Sure, a few notable galleries have picked up new media artists. Shockingly the work has even begun to sell a little, which is a huge improvement from 10 years ago. But walk through any art fair (except perhaps ARCO, which has made media art a focus and does fairly well with it) and you'll see precious few works that can be defined as media art. Maybe an Arcangel or a Nicolai here, a Jim Campbell there and the lurking spectre of a Hirschmann [Lynn Hershman Leeson, ndr] or a Lozano-Hemmer. If you happen on a booth from Bitforms or the 4-5 galleries worldwide specializing in New Media you might get a bigger picture.

But this isn't such great news once you consider that easily 90-95% of even moderately successful media artists have no access to the market at all. Instead their work is known (and validated by) the ephemeral European media art festival circuit and public speaking, as well as ceaseless self-publishing (especially in the case of net-based art). In the US media artists would have precious few outlets if they weren't setting up their own project spaces, which is a laudable activity but unfortunately usually lacking in staying power and mainstream validation.

Meanwhile European funding for media art has just been decimated across the board, a move that is likely to have significant repercussions. The large interactive installations of the mid-1990's disappeared overnight the last time funding dropped away like this. It's no secret that many US-based media artists historically have kickstarted their careers by showing in Europe before gaining visibility at home. I'm

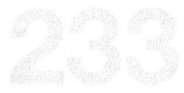

certainly not alone in worrying about the resulting fallout from this development.

I agree that there seems to be more media art writing going on – some of it even serious and well-considered. But most of it is still an internal discourse, and as such marginal to the art world or the larger public. I was amazed to have a recent show in San Francisco covered on Artforum.com, but the show's affiliation with a 'serious' institution like the SF Film Society likely helped a lot. The amount of column space given to media art in mainstream journals is likely to be coverage of a handful of iconic names (Arcangel etc.), stories on emerging artists or shows that don't feature big names are few and far between.

So I'm afraid I'll play devil's advocate and share Domenico's summary: New media artists who want a serious play at the art world might do better to play down the media art rhetoric.The "New Media" label has served to differentiate and promote the field in many ways (not coincidentally by helping it to gain funding), and without that discourse there would be no field at all. But for the artists themselves it can also be an obstacle to be taken seriously.

New Media as Grand Project has already been done, and arguing the transformative potential of technology should be superfluous in a world of smartphones. So let's focus on the good work for its qualities as art, and not because of the rather outdated and frankly meaningless label of "New Media".

Meanwhile, the contemporary art world (with all its inertia and dubious internal agendas) should sit up and pay attention to a field of art that is both vital and important. Not because media artists need a pity fuck, but because their work often address contemporary issues of society and identity better than a lot of what's going on in art in general. That's Quaranta's ultimate agenda after all, to communicate once and for all that is unforgivable for the art world to pretend we're still living in the 1960's.

PS: It feels strange and counter-productive for me to be arguing against the notion of a growing success of New Media, when I personally have much invested in such success. But I'm hearing echoes of the inevitable 5-year hype cycles ("Virtual Reality is the New Shit", "No, It's Net.Art", "Man, Look At Those Kitten

GIFs". Call me cynical, but I worry that we'd be lulling ourselves into another lithium dream. ("Look, we're doing great, there's at least 3 blogs that say so.")

I'll take Quaranta's harsh analysis any day, particularly since his perspective is largely based on actual history going back to the mid-1990's rather than hopeful projections based on the current situation». **Marius Watz**, August 31, 2011

«when I look at the enormous growth in the field over the last five years, it's hard to believe that once the hype dies down that new media will be left in the same place. The market can ignore a lot of things, but it won't ignore an army of art school trained artists now producing new media work (or whatever we decide to call it. I'm not a fan of the term either)». **Paddy Johnson**, September 1, 2011

«I think it's worth mentioning or considering that much of new media art is born of a tradition that eschews the art market and works against commodification. If this kind of work doesn't sell, it doesn't mean it's unsuccessful, just that maybe its success can be measured in other ways. So I think we should focus more on finding ways of showing this kind of work rather than trying to find ways of selling it». **Heather**, September 1, 2011

«In Quaranta's argument it would be fallacious to consider Trecartin (or to some degree Arcangel) "new media." Quaranta is invested in a certain narrative of the new media art world infrastructure – think Ars Electronica, ZKM, and so on – more so than the question of thematics. In fact, I suspect he might add that the contemporary art world has historically selected work like that of Trecartin and Arcangel instead of this older parallel version of new media». **Robin Peckham**, August 31, 2011

«It's true that Trecartin is really a video artist who happens to use themes of the Internet in his work, so I see your point and to that of Arcangel as well. Of course, if we're lamenting over why Jim Campbell and Lozano-Hemmer aren't being shown more, that's not a party I'm going to join. For the most part I don't like the work of either, and have always considered it a poor representative of new media art». **Paddy Johnson**, August 31, 2011

«I wonder if by "older parallel version of new media" you mean to propose that there is another (and newer?) narrative in which Quaranta's argument is invalid? I agree that his reasoning relies on a specific recent history of media art that is somewhat Euro-centric (although full of non-European artists) and possibly biased towards a technology-heavy definition of the field. But I'm not sure that invalidates the basic argument». **Marius Watz**, August 31, 2011

«What i'd like to stress are two things: the first is that the fact that most of the work which was once called "new media art" is designed and developed inside of universities, in one form or the other, is really significative. As it is the fact that the interdisciplinary character of many – many of these works – crossing boundaries in sciences, humanities, journalism, performance, arts, architecture, technology, robotics etc-, multiple times – is possibly one of these works' most significant traits. And the one which more explicitly creates a definite gap between what is called "art" and what is not called "art" (let me oversimplify... I hope it is clear. I'll be happy to clarify, if it's not).

The second element which i'd like to highlight has to do with the fact that it sounds always "bureaucratic" to group things together. I know it is useful and convenient, and it allows to investigate and present things at institutional level, but we have been really out of the "era of classification" for a few years now. Even marketing people understand it». **xdxd (Salvatore Iaconesi)**, August 31, 2011

«When you get a piece of open source software you don't only get "a piece of software", you get something that, in a way, is left "incomplete" on purpose, and it includes a responsibility: to use it and fix anything which you don't like, and to share your efforts with the rest of the planet. This simple act is revolutionary, as it includes a vision on the world. Your revolution is personal, it is an attitude, and it is not complete unless you become a node of a network, and the part "share your revolution" just cannot be left out.

So, while i truly enjoy and adore the works which are starting to find their economic sustainability in the Art Market, I cannot help thinking that we could (and probably already did) define "other" areas, other domains, for that which was once called art and now it's different, as it covers and interconnects many more things. And, of course, we need to find a sustainability scheme for that, too. I just feel that "making a lot of things be called art" is not a "big" objective». xdxd (Salvatore Iaconesi), August 31, 2011

«I remember discussions about the young hip CEO theory as early as 2000, we had big hopes for those dotcom boys as market drivers. The closest I've heard of is the Girls Gone Wild guy buying a piece from Golan Levin, there must be others but the deluge of media art collectors is yet to appear. Too bad Gates etc. seem more concerned with Old World credibility or Warhol cool. I hear Bloomberg has a promising collection, and it's simply idiotic that Google hasn't started one. Fingers crossed!» Marius Watz, September 2, 2011

«Our conversation with Ken Johnson, art critic from the NYTimes, is now up at LISA: http://softwareandart.com/?p=747. In it, Ken talks about why digital art is not respected in the world of high art. To him, it is because people (curators, gallerists, collectors) don't have any way to tell whether the art is the result of individual inspiration or creativity or just a "gimmick".

He also says that much digital art looks to be "part of pop culture" as opposed to "a comment on pop culture". And this is a no-no. With media art these days I guess you have to be "critiquing" something – this explains the heretofore inexplicable popularity of Ryan Trecartin and Cory Arcangel in the high art community.

I guess this is why museums protect themselves by putting digital art in the "design" bucket – since they can't tell whether it is real art or just "design" it's a useful hedge.

[...] So based on our conversation with Ken I'd say what needs to happen is that the High Art world needs more curators who actually know what they are talking about when it comes to technology who also have the pedigree – a few people with Computer Science PhD's and a twin degree in art history? Who aren't flummoxed by technology and have the capacity to tell the difference between something that is unoriginal or made by applying a Photoshop filter / Aftereffects, and something that is based on a personal vision, unique coding, intricate software design that is both beautiful and experiential». **Isabel Draves**, September 6, 2011

«New media (in the United States at least) needs a visionary dealer.» **Paddy Johnson**, September 3, 2011

«[...] there is a very interesting long-term phobia about work made and shown on the computer or the Internet. I think it is most interesting to look at this as phobia. If you were from outer space and went to the last Whitney Biennial, (or any of the recent Biennials?) you would have no idea there was any such thing as a computer or a social network. That's downright strange and out of character with a supposed forward looking world of art. A number of critics and writers have done everything needed to connect this "new media" to preceding artistic history, it's all there if you want to read it. [...] About content versus aesthetics or technique: new media artworks have plenty of content, but this content is often about life on the computer or the net, vs life in the physical world, and up to this point it seems that the latter is the preferred subject of conventional arts. In painting, and especially with the return of abstraction, half the discussion is about painting, not content. But because of the aura accorded to painting, technical issues, in this case, are viewed with the subtext of genius and gravitas (PS. I heart painting).

What is encouraging is that I think this mindset is changing, simply because everyone is more engaged in life on the computer. I am sensing that the next generation of gallerists, artists, critics and historians will have grown up in this "condition" [...] If and when this approach to art making arrives as a recognized art form, I wonder if anyone will acknowledge

just how long it took and reflect on the forces of market conservatism in the so-called experimental art world, a world which I nevertheless deeply appreciate and follow». **Will Pappenheimer,** September 1, 2011

«You make a valid point, although I would point out that the idea that the "content" of new media artworks are primarily "about life on the computer or the net" is a widely spread misunderstanding. I suspect it stems from the fact the new media artwork that is most visible to someone who doesn't follow the field will inevitably be net based works, since they are infinitely more distributable than, say, a large-scale mechanical construction of a cybernetic mechanism in a dialogue with itself». **Marius Watz,** September 3, 2011

«If indeed there is a growing exhibitions that include work by artists who employ new media tools in one way or another, very little has changed. There remains a more or less autonomous new media artworld (what I call NMA) that has its own institutions, galleries critics and historians, journals and university departments. The NMA is rarely invited to the mainstream contemporary artworld (MCA) and when it is, it is generally those works that already obey its rules that get tapped.

MCA does not need NMA; or at least it does not need NMA in order to justify its authority. Indeed, the domination of MCA is so absolute that the term "artworld" is synonymous with it. Despite the distinguished outcomes generated by the entwinement of art, science, and technology for hundreds of years, MCA collectors, curators, and institutions have difficulty in recognizing NMA as a valid, much less valuable, contribution to the history of art. As Magdalena Sawon, co-founder / co-director of Postmaster Gallery notes, NMA does not meet familiar expectations of what art should look like, feel like, and consist of, based on "hundreds of years of painting and sculpture." It is deemed uncollectible because, as Amy Cappellazzo, a contemporary art expert at Christie's observes, "collectors get confused and concerned about things that plug In." (quoted in Sarah Thornton, *Seven Days in the Artworld,* 2009)». **Edward Shanken,** September 5, 2011

«We live in a global digital culture in which the materials and techniques of new media are widely available and accessible to a growing proportion of the population. Millions and millions of people around the world participate in social media, and have the ability to produce and share with millions and millions of other people their own texts, images, sound recordings, videos, GPS traces. In many ways early NMA works that enabled remote collaboration and interaction, such as Ascott's *La Plissure du Texte* (1983), can be seen as modeling social values and practices that have emerged in tandem with the advent of Web 2.0 and participatory culture. Now a YouTube video, like *Daft Hands*, can delight and amaze 50 million viewers, spawning its own subculture of celebrities, masterpieces, and remixers. In this context what are the roles of the artist, the curator, the theorist, and critic? As Brad Troemel provocatively asked in an *Artfag City* essay, "What can relational aesthetics learn from 4Chan?". What do professional artists, theorists and curators associated with NMA or MCA have to offer that is special, that adds value and insight to this dynamic, collective, creative culture? Why care anymore about MCA or NMA, *per se*? What is at stake preserving these distinctions and in distinguishing such artistic practices from broader forms of popular cultural production and reception? Do such distinctions merely serve to protect MCA and NMA from interlopers by preserving a mythical status to their exclusive, lucrative and / or prestigious practices?» **Edward Shanken**, September 5, 2011

Appendix 2
Collecting New Media Art

The following text was written in July 2012 as my opening statement to a discussion on the mailing list "New Media Curating", which I was kindly invited to take part in by Beryl Graham and Sarah Cook. Edited excerpts from the debate can be downloaded from the CRUMB website, URL: http://crumbweb.org/uploads/reports/2012121911312Collecting_July2012.rtf.zip.

Dear List,

it's a great opportunity for me to be invited to participate in this discussion. The issue of collecting has obsessed me for a long time, and still does. At the same time, I'm a little bit overwhelmed by the need to reduce my ideas on this, which are very layered, to the form of a short statement.

For the sake of clarity, I will try to divide the topic in three different areas:

1. collecting new media art;
2. collecting unstable media;
3. collecting the digital.

1. Collecting New Media Art

New media art IS collected, by private collections and institutions, as long as its cultural relevance is accepted in the art market field. That is, not so much, because galleries, art critics and curators didn't do a great job so far in making this cultural relevance a widespread truth in the field of contemporary art; and yet, enough to allow anybody to make a nice "new media art show" with collected or collectable works provided exclusively by private and institutional collectors or commercial galleries. That's what I – together with Yves Bernard – tried to do in 2008, with the show *Holy Fire. Art of the Digital Age* [1]. Budget limitations didn't allow us to provide a veritable snapshot of new media art collecting all around the world at the time, but I still believe that the exhibition was quite well representative of the forms in which new media art entered art collections: mostly in traditional, accepted, stable forms, such as digital prints, editioned videos, byproducts, and sometimes well crafted, artist's designed, plug-and-play "digital objects": from John Simon's art appliances to Boredomresearch's screens, from Electroboutique's self-ironic works to Lialina & Espenschied's touch screen version of the web piece *Midnight* (2006). This is no surprise. Like it or not, digital media – like all unstable, variable media – challenge collecting in many ways. And along the XXth century, radical forms of art had always to face this conundrum: either accept compromise or stay out of the market. Performance art entered the market through documentation; video entered the market through video installations and editioned VHSs or DVDs; conceptual art entered the market through objectification and authenticity certificates.

Many of my friends think that compromise is a bad thing, and they dismiss these "products" as just a bad way to make money. If this argument was true, it would only mean that 99% of new media / performance / video / conceptual artists are just idiots, because they sold their soul to the Devil without actually changing their financial situation at all. The truth is that traditional artifacts often work as a preservation strategy for the artist himself, who doesn't know any other way to ensure his own (digital) artwork to the future. They are also means of dialogue and mediation, that help artists approaching audiences and collectors that may be unfamiliar with digital technologies, but also different spaces and different contexts: a clever choice, when technology is not the core topic but just a tool, or a display, or one of the many possible interfaces to a content.

In terms of quantity, when (in 2009 and 2010) I was curating the Expanded Box section for the Arco Art Fair in Madrid, I counted around 50 commercial galleries all around the world working with at least one out of 136 artists that could be conventionally described as "new media artists", from Vera Molnar to Raphael Lozano-Hemmer. Either these dealers are bad businessmen who find a perverse pleasure in failure, or they have a small but brave network of collectors interested in new media art. So, again: new media art is collected.

2. Collecting Unstable Media

New media art CAN ALSO BE collected in its unstable, computer based, digital form. This is difficult, but not impossible. And it already happened, quite a few times. Why not? In the past, collectors bought conversations, candies, fresh fruit, living and dead flies, dead and badly preserved sharks, performances: why should they be afraid of old computers, interactive installations, websites, softwares, etc.? Also, collectors (especially private collectors) are the kind of people who love challenges and risky businesses. Paradoxically, in the art world it seems to be easier to sell challenges than compromises. What they want in return is cultural and economic value. Collectors can buy almost anything, if it is interesting, highly desirable, and if it can be sold back to somebody else at an higher price tag (not necessarily in this order).

In collecting, the preservation issue always comes later. But both cultural and economic value are not a given. They have to be "created," in a convincing way. That's why collecting new media in its unstable forms is going to be just a funny experiment, and an innocent game, until artists won't start talking to the right people, and until galleries, museums, curators and critics won't be able to persuade the art world about its cultural relevance.

3. Collecting the Digital

The digital is challenging collecting in many ways, but the biggest challenge is probably connected to its reproducible, sharable nature. This turns scarcity into something completely artificial, and abstract. You can keep making limited editions, but you can't lie to yourself: there is no difference between the five certified copies of that video and the sixth one, that somebody uploads to YouTube and that hundreds of people all around the world download on their desktop. No difference except an abstract, ritual act of transferral of ownership. And there is no difference between the 5 collectors who bought the video and the 500 ones who downloaded it for free: the latter don't own a bootleg, a bad copy, but the same file; they just don't own a certificate.

The other problem is sharing. A collector can accept almost everything, if he is rewarded with cultural and economic value. Yet, what most collectors can't still accept is to be the owners of something that is available for anybody else for free. Why should I buy a website and leave it publicly accessible to anybody, as Rafael Rozendaal suggests in his beautiful contract? [2] Why should I have no privileges and no rights, only duties? Why should I buy an animated gif (or a video, or a sound file) and allow it to circulate freely on the internet in the very same form?

It would be easy to conclude that, because of this, traditional forms of collecting won't never apply successfully to digital art forms. Brad Troemel recently [3] wrote:

«The commodification of internet art is not going to happen in the way the art market has traditionally operated or in any way currently being attempted. This all comes down to a simple square-peg-in-a-circular-hole economic dilemma, which is that digital content is infinitely reproducible and free while physical commodities are scarce and expensive».

What's true in this is that the digital allows another form of collecting, free of any money investment and available to anybody: downloading. This form of collecting has been widely practiced for any kind of digital content: from animated gifs to amateur photographs, from videogames to pornographic pictures. For example, a collection that is highly valuable to me is Travis Hallenbeck's *Windows Meta File Collection*, that can be downloaded from his website. [4] Hallenbeck collected more than 3,000 cliparts in an obsolete file format, that doesn't work properly on most modern computers. Most of these images – designed by amateur and professional designers along the 90s – are now rare, so Hallenbeck's collection has an high cultural value. But any time anybody downloads his collection, he becomes the owner of a perfect copy of it – thus making these images less rare. Furthermore, since Hallenbeck is an artist, we should consider his collection a work of art: a work of art we can "collect" just clicking on the link to the zipped folder. Is my act of collecting less legitimate because I didn't pay, and I didn't get a certificate in return? Hallenbeck is not selling his work of art on DVD, and he is not writing certificates of authenticity for those who buy it. There is no other way to collect this work of art: you can just download it for free.

Suppose that, in 50 years, Hallenbeck's website won't be online anymore. Net art will be an highly respected form of art. And you, who downloaded this file and made your best to preserve it, will be the unique owner of a great net art masterpiece. Will museums consider you a legitimate collector?

What I mean here is that, even if a digital file can be reproduced infinite times with no loss of quality, scarcity is always around the corner. With the digital for the first time, art preservation can become a social, distributed thing, not something regulated only by those in power, such as institutions and economic elites. And thus do collecting.

And yet, this doesn't mean that traditional forms of collecting won't never apply successfully to digital art forms. Art collectors should be brave enough to confront the challenge, and accept the idea of a shareable property. When they will, they'll realize that becoming the legal, unique owner of something that can still be enjoyed, played, stolen, remixed by hundreds of people every day is an immense pleasure. Owning and sharing: isn't it what God is doing with his own property, after all?

Thank you for your patience,
My best,
Domenico

Notes

[1] iMAL, Bruxelles, April 18 – 30, 2008. More info at www.imal.org/HolyFire/ (last visit March 2013).
[2] Cf. www.art websitesalescontract.com (last visit March 2013).
[3] Brad Troemel, "Why Your .JPEGs Aren't Making You A Millionaire", in *The Creators Project,* May 14, 2012, online at http://thecreatorsproject.com/blog/digart-why-your-jpegs-arent-making-you-a-millionaire (last visit March 2013).
[4] Cf. http://anotherunknowntime.com/wmf.html (last visit March 2013).

Appendix 3
What's (Really) Specific in New Media Art? Curating in the Information Age

This text has been written for the proceedings of the international conference "New Perspectives, New Technologies", organized by the Doctoral School Ca' Foscari – IUAV in Arts History and held in Venice and Pordenone, Italy in October 2011. It was published on Rhizome on December 6, 2012. The essay recalls and expands some issues discussed in the paragraph "A Few Notes About Curating", featured in the last chapter of this book.

The "new media art" label consolidated in the late Nineties and along the first decade of this century to define that broad range of artistic practices that encompasses artworks created, or somehow dealing with, new media technologies. Providing a more detailed definition here would inevitably mean addressing topics that may go far away the scope of this paper, and that this author already discussed extensively in his book *Media, New Media, Postmedia* (Quaranta 2010). What should be added here, as a premise to the issues discussed in this paper, is the main thesis suggested by the mentioned book: that this label, and the practices it applies to, developed mostly in an enclosed social context, sometimes addressed as the "new media art niche", but that would be better described as an art world in its own, with its own institutions, its own professionals, its own discussion platforms, its own audience, its own economic model, its own idea of what art is and should be; and that only in recent years, the practice was able to escape its own world, and to be presented on the wider platform of contemporary art.

It's at this point in time, and mainly thanks to curators who were actively involved in the presentation of new media art in the contemporary art arena, that a debate about "curating new media (art)" took shape. This debate was triggered by the pioneering work of curators – from Steve Dietz to Jon Ippolito, from Benjamin Weil to Christiane Paul – who at the turn of the Millennium curated seminal new media art exhibitions for contemporary art museums; and it was – and still is – mainly nurtured by CRUMB, an acronym for "Curatorial Resource for Upstart Media Bliss": a platform – and a mailing list – founded by Beryl Graham and Sarah Cook in 2000 within the School of Arts, Design, Media and Culture at the University of Sunderland, UK. As early as 2001, CRUMB organized the first ever meeting of new media curators in the UK as part of BALTIC's pre-opening program – a seminar on Curating New Media held in May 2001.

In the context of this paper, our main reference texts will be CRUMB-related publications, from the "Curating New Media" proceedings (2001) to *Rethinking Curating. Art After New Media* (2010), a recent book by Beryl Graham and Sarah Cook; and *New Media in the White Cube and Beyond*, a book edited by Christiane Paul in 2008. Instead of addressing specific issues and curatorial models discussed in these publications, we will try to focus on the very foundations of the "curating new media" model. Specific questions raised in the following will be: does new media art require a specific curatorial model? Does this curatorial model follow the way artists working with new media are currently presenting themselves on the contemporary art platform? How much could "new media art" benefit from a non specialized gaze? Are we curating "new media" or curating "art"?

A Medium Based Definition

"A lowest common denominator for defining new media art seems to be that it is computational and based on algorithms." (Paul 2008: 3)

"[...] in this book, what is meant by the term new media art is, broadly, art that is made using electronic media technology and that displays any or all of the three behaviours of interactivity, connectivity and computability in any combination." (Graham, Cook 2010: 10)

Whatever you may think about new media art, when it comes to curating the definition becomes strictly technical and medium-based. New media art is the art using new media technologies as a medium – period. No further complexity is allowed. For example, Beryl Graham and Sarah Cook, in the continuation of the quoted paragraph, seem to be well aware of the sociological complexity of new media art, but they willingly put it aside, focusing on all art that displays "the three behaviours of interactivity, connectivity and computability", wherever it is shown and whatever it has been labeled [1]. This is no surprise, because – especially when it comes to museum departments – curating has always been medium-based. This model generally works, even if sometimes curators criticized it, especially when the complexity of the medium used doesn't allow oversimplification. In 2005, writing about video art, David A. Ross said: "Most often, at this point in time, video art is a term of convenience valued by museum conservators who have a professional need to devise proper storage and conservation standards for this specific medium, but even in this situation it is inadequate" (Gianelli, Beccaria 2005: 14 – 15). It's inadequate, Ross goes on, because video became an ubiquitous medium, that often makes its appearance in what should be better defined as "mixed media sculptural installations." The same may be said as well for other contemporary art forms such as performance and installation, but it fits even more to new media – a definition that, even in its strictly technical sense, applies to a wide range of forms and behaviors, from computer animation to robotics, from internet based art to biotechnologies.

Of course, both Paul and Graham / Cook – and, generally speaking, any good new media art curator – are fully aware of this complexity, and this awareness shapes their theoretical writing. It's exactly because of it that Graham and Cook, in their book, focus on behaviors rather than on specific forms and languages. At the same time, they are fully aware of new media art's resistance to the white cube and the specific kind of space it provides. As Christiane Paul puts it: "Traditional presentation spaces create exhibition models that are not particularly appropriate for new media art. The white cube creates a "sacred" space and a blank slate for contemplating objects. Most new media is inherently performative and contextual." (Paul 2008: 56) Paul goes even further, arguing that new media art does not just resist the white cube, but even the kind of understanding provided by the contemporary art world: "New media could never be understood from a strictly art-historical perspective: the history of technology and media sciences plays an equally important role in this art's formation and reception. New media art requires media literacy." (Paul 2008: 5).

Paul responds to this situation invoking a curator that is less a caretaker of objects and more a mediator, an interpreter or a producer (Paul 2008: 65). But what does this mediation applies to? Paul implicitly responds to this question when she talks about the average museum / gallery audience, and its common criticism to the new media art they encounter there. According to Paul, "the museum / gallery audience for new media art might be divided roughly into the following categories: the experts who are *familiar with the art form*; the fairly small group of those who claim a "natural" *aversion to computers and technology* and refuse to look at anything presented by means of them; a relatively young audience segment that is highly *familiar with virtual worlds, interfaces and navigation paradigms* but no necessarily accustomed to art that involves these aspects; and those who are *open to and interested in the art but need assistance* using it and navigating it." (Paul 2008: 66, my italics). This paragraph already shows that, in most of the cases, what's at stake is the different level of familiarity with technology in the audience. This becomes more clear when Paul starts considering "recurring criticisms" against new media art – well summed up by the titles of the following chapters: "it's all about technology" [2]; "it doesn't work"; "it belongs in a science museum"; "I work on a computer all day – I don't want to see art on it in my free time"; "I want to look at art – not interact with it" [3]; "where are the special effects?"

Paul concludes that "the intrinsic features of new media art ultimately protect it from being co-opted by the art establishment" (Paul 2008: 74). Yet, what she wrote so far may lead to another, as well (and maybe even more) legitimate conclusion: that technology ultimately prevents new media art from being understood by the contemporary art audience.

Moving the Focus

"The hype surrounding the technology driving new media art hasn't helped its long term engagement with the art world..." (Graham, Cook 2010: 39)

This is where a strictly medium-based definition obviously leads. If new media art is rooted in the active use of technology as a medium, there is no way to do without it; and if technology is the main obstacle between new media art and the art audience, what's left to new media curating is just to make this encounter less shocking, and the art more artificially "at home". Or, as Vuk Cosic puts it talking about net-based art: "In my view, when you show online stuff in a gallery space, which is not online, you essentially put it in the wrong place. It's not at home. It's not where it is supposed to be. It's decontextualized; it's shown in a glass test-tube. So whatever you do is just an attempt to make it look more alive. You either move the test-tube or have some fancy lighting. And this is how it works for me." (Cook, Graham, Martin 2002: 42).

An easy argument against this could be that technology won't be always new. We got used to TV monitors and projectors in the gallery space; we will got used to computers as well. Young people who made their first drawing on an iPhone at the age of two will finally grow up, and new media art will look more natural to them than it is to us. This is true only to some point. The "new media hype" didn't fade in the last two decades, quite the contrary: it grows any time a new gadget is launched on the market, to an even wider audience. And so far, the art world's resistance against new media art wasn't that much affected by the fact that every living human in developed countries knows Google, and that half of them have a Facebook account.

So, the questions at stake are: if technology is the problem, can curating allow the art audience to access new media art without technology, or at least reducing technology's impact on the perception of the work? Can the curator become not a mediator between technology and the art audience, as in the model described by Paul and Graham / Cook, but between an art interested in the social, political and cultural implications of technology and the art audience? If this is possible, it can only happen, of course, out of the strictly medium-based definition outlined before, and in the frame of a definition that focuses more on new media art's critical engagement with new media and the information age, and on its ability to reach, in different forms, different audiences: not just the contemporary art audience, but also, on the one side, the more specialized audience attending new media art events and, on the other side, the "bored at work network" [4] that can be reached online.

In other words, if new media curating wants to better serve the practice it supports and the audiences it addresses, it has to move its focus from the use of technology to other features that are intrinsic to new media art, but that have been sidestepped by the debate around new media curating so far. In other words, it has to be more about curating the art that deals with new media, and less about curating new media in themselves. Furthermore, it has to take advantage of the intrinsic variability of new media and of the adaptability of artists who are able to speak different languages (something that should not be misunderstood as conformism) in order to facilitate the presentation of their art to different audiences, and generate a better, broader understanding.

Intermezzo: Against Specialization

> "The professional tends to classify and to specialize, to accept uncritically the groundrules of the environment. The groundrules provided by the mass response of his colleagues serve as a pervasive environment of which he is contentedly unaware. The 'expert' is the man who stays put." (McLuhan, Fiore 1967 (2001): 92)

But why did the debate around new media curating, that involved – as said before – curators active within the field of contemporary art, and well aware of the problems that the art audience may experience in front of technologies, didn't get this point yet? Probably, they are just uncritically accepting the groundrules of the environment, namely of the new media art world. Probably, their ideal audience is still the one depicted by Paul as "the experts who are familiar with the art form" – that is, the niche audience of new media art. Probably, they are still valuing media literacy more than art literacy, as a condition to understand a piece of new media art.

Unfortunately, this approach doesn't go along with their declared mission, that is to bring new media art to a broader audience and to generate a dialogue with other forms of contemporary art. Of course, this mission also includes increasing the audience's familiarity with technology as a medium for art, but it's not limited to that. We could go even further, and say that this is just the last stage of a long journey taken to show to the contemporary art audience the extraordinary impact of media and technologies on the world we live in, the importance of increasing awareness around them for a better understanding of contemporaneity, and so the topicality of an art that engages them critically both as a medium and as a content of the work.

This may bring us to say that there is no need of a specific figure of "new media curator": a contemporary art curator open to new languages and with a good level of media literacy can do an even better job, in terms of picking out what can be relevant for a contemporary art audience, working with the artist to find out a good way to "translate" the work for the white cube, and generating a dialogue with other forms of contemporary art. This may be true in the future. At the moment, the cultural insularity of new media art and the existence of two different art worlds still makes a specialized figure of curator necessary at some point. But new media curating should be rethought in terms of a practice of mediation between two artworlds and two different cultures, instead of between the art audience and technology. It should be about bringing new media art to the art audience in a way that can be accepted by it as art, but that can also force it to reconsider its own prejudices about what can be accepted as art. With or without technologies.

Follow the artists

"My interest in technology is in its relationship with culture and its effects on society, and in many cases that can be communicated in things other than code." (O'Dwyer 2012: 7)

Along this path, artists are already showing the way to curators. At some point, artists formerly known as new media artists started taking the problem of how to present their art in the white cube more seriously, and realized that sometimes, putting technology aside wasn't just a compromise with the market [5], or a way to weaken their work and make it more digestible to the masses, but the right thing to do it. It was a process that took time, it required to proceed by trials and errors and ultimately to accept failure, and it was finally facilitated by the emergence of a new generation of artists who did enjoy both bits and atoms, and who didn't see "new" and "old" media in opposition, but as lines of inquire that should be pursued together, and that can some time converge, some time diverge, some times criss-cross. Providing a complete, or at least representative, list of examples would go far beyond the possibilities of this short paper, so I will provide just two random, recent examples. When I started writing this texts, I was reached by two press releases: the first announcing that Berlin based artist Oliver Laric, in conjunction with The Collection and Usher Gallery in Lincoln, just won the Contemporary Art Society's £60,000 "commission to collect" award; and the second announcing a new work by US born, Paris based artist Evan Roth, currently on display at the Science Gallery in Dublin. Even if the "new media artist" label would be problematic for both, it would be hard to question that the two artists originally attracted the interest of a community of "experts" with their (mostly net based) early practice. Thanks to the CAS' grant, Laric would now be able to create a new work of art for The Collection and Usher Gallery's permanent collection. According to the press release, the work "will employ the latest 3D scanning methods to scan all of the works in The Collection and Usher Gallery's collections – from classical sculpture to archeological finds – with the aim of eliminating historical and material hierarchies and reduce all the works to objects and forms. These scans will be made available to the public to view, download and use for free from the museum's website and other platforms, without copyright restrictions, and can be used for social media and academic research alike. Laric will use the scans himself to create a sculptural collage for the museum, for which the digital data will be combined, 3D printed and cast in acrylic plaster." [6] The commission allows Laric to bring his ongoing project *Versions*, started in 2009 with a video essay and developed in following years with other videos, sculptures, installations, to a new level. Versions focuses on issues of copyright, originality and repetition along history, up to the digital age. With the project for The Collection and Usher Gallery, he will be able to make the gallery's audience think and learn about 3D scanning, digital manipulation, sharing and the shifting relationship between the physical and the digital, addressing it in the familiar form of a sculptural installation. The online audience, on the other side, will be able to fully enjoy and interact with that amazing mass of digital material.

Angry Birds All Levels (2012) is the telling title of Evan Roth's last work, consisting of 300 sheets of tracing paper and black ink fixed on wall in a grid with small nails. According to the Science Gallery website, "it's a visualization of every finger swipe needed to complete the popular mobile game of the same name. The gestures exist on a sheet of paper that's the same size as the iPhone on which it was originally created. Angry Birds is part of a larger series that Roth has been working on over the last year called Multi-Touch Paintings. These compositions are created by performing simple routine tasks on multi-touch handheld computing devices [ranging from unlocking the device to checking Twitter] with inked fingers. The series is a comment on computing and identity, but also creates an archive of this moment in history where we have started to manipulate pixels directly through gestures that we were unfamiliar with just over 5 years ago." [7] Even if it's shown in a science museum, nobody would ever say it belongs to there.

In both works, technology is part of the creative process and one of the issues at stake (but not the only one). In both works, technology is put aside from the gallery display, not for convenience or marketing reasons, but because this is the way it works best for the artwork itself.

In most of the cases, artists got to this point on their own feet, with little help from curators. Are new media curators ready to help them taking the next step? If so, they should probably start from taking care of their art, and not of their media.

Notes

[1] "Artworks showing these behaviors, but that may be from the wider fields of contemporary art or from life in technological times are included, however." (Graham, Cook 2010: 10)

[2] As Paul explains: "If a museum visitor is unfamiliar with technology, it automatically becomes the focus of attention – an effect unintended by the artist." (Paul 2008: 67)

[3] "Art that breaks with the conventions of contemplation and purely private engagement shocks the average museumgoer, disrupting the mind-set that art institutions so carefully cultivated." (Paul 2008: 71)

[4] The "bored at work network" has been theorized by artist and researcher Jonah Peretti in the frame of the Contagious Media Project. Cf. http://contagiousmedia.org/.

[5] A take on the way new media art circulates in the art market was the exhibition *Holy Fire. Art in the Digital Age* I curated together with Yves Bernard for the iMAL Centre for Digital Cultures & Technologies in Bruxelles, Belgium (April 18 – 30, 2008). Cf. Bernard, Quaranta 2008.

[6] The press release is available in the News section of the website of the Contemporary Art Society: "Rising star Oliver Laric scoops Contemporary Art Society's prestigious £60,000 Annual Award 2012 with The Collection and Usher Gallery, Lincoln", November 20, 2012, www.contemporaryartsociety.org/news.

[7] Cf. http://sciencegallery.com/game/angrybirds.

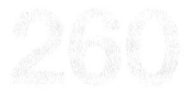

Bibliography

Essays, books and catalogues

VVAA, *Deep Screen. Art in Digital Culture*, exh. cat., Stedelijk Museum, Amsterdam 2008.

VVAA, *Eva & Franco Mattes: 0100101110101101.ORG*, Charta, Milano – New York 2009.

VVAA, *Mediascape*, exh. cat., Guggenheim Museum Publications, New York 1996.

VVAA, *Postmedia Condition*, exh. cat., Centro Cultural Conde Duque, Madrid 2006.

VVAA, *Olafur Eliasson. Colour memory and other informal shadows*, Astrup Fearnley Museet for Moderne Kunst, Oslo 2004.

VVAA, *XLII Esposizione Internazionale d'Arte La Biennale di Venezia. Arte e scienza. Biologia / Tecnologia e informatica*, exh. cat., Electa, Venezia 1986.

VVAA, *010101: Art in Technological Times*, exh. cat., SFMoMA, San Francisco 2001.

VVAA, "Media Art Undone", conference panel at transmediale07, Berlin, February 3, 2007. Full transcript of the presentations is available here: www.mikro.in-berlin.de/wiki/tiki-index.php?page=MAU

ALLEN, J., "From Media to New Media", in *Mousse*, Issue 26, December 2010, pp. 196 – 200.

ALTSHULER B. (ed.), *Collecting the New*, Princeton University Press, Princeton & Oxford 2005.

ATKINS R., "State of the Art – On-line – art on the World Wide Web", in *Art in America*, April 1999.

AYERS R., "Code in a Box", in *Artinfo*, 3 August 2007, online at www.artinfo.com/news/story/25445/code-in-a-box/.

BALZOLA A., MONTEVERDI A. M. (eds.), *Le arti multimediali digitali. Storia, tecniche, linguaggi, etiche ed estetiche delle arti del nuovo millennio*, Garzanti,

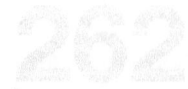

Milano 2004.

BARBENI L., *Webcinema. L'immagine cibernetica*, Costa & Nolan, Milano 2006.

BARRAGAN P., *The Art Fair Age*, Charta, Milano 2008.

BAUMGAERTEL T., *net.art. Materialien zur Netzkunst*, Verlag für moderne Kunst Nürberg, 2000.

_, *net.art 2.0. Neue Materialien zur Netzkunst*, Verlag für moderne Kunst Nürberg, 2001.

BAZZICHELLI T., *Networking. The Net as Artwork*, Digital Aesthetics Research Center, Aarhus University 2008.

BECKER H. S., *Art Worlds*, University of California Press, Berkeley – Los Angeles – London 1982 [1984].

BERRY J., "The Unbearable Connectedness of Everything", in *Telepolis*, 28 September 1999, online at www.heise.de/tp/artikel/3/3433/1.html.

BERWICK C., "New Media Moguls", in *Art & Auction*, June 2006.

BISHOP C., "Digital Divide. Claire Bishop on Contemporary Art and New Media", in *Artforum*, September 2012, online at http://artforum.com/inprint/issue=201207&id=31944&pagenum=0.

BITTANTI M., QUARANTA D. (eds.), *GameScenes. Art in the Age of Videogames*, Johan & Levi, Milano 2006.

BLAIS J., IPPOLITO J., *At the Edge of Art*, Thames and Hudson, London 2006.

BLISTÈNE B., "Les Immatériaux: A Conversation with Jean-François Lyotard", in *Flash Art*, Issue 121, March 1985, online at www.kether.com/words/lyotard/index.html.

BOLOGNINI M., *Machines. Conversations on Art and Technology*, Postmediabooks, Milano 2012.

BOLTER J. D., GRUSIN R., *Remediation. Understanding New Media*, 1999.

BONAMI F., *Lo potevo fare anch'io. Perché l'arte contemporanea è davvero arte*, Mondadori, Milano 2007.

BORDINI S., *Arte Elettronica*, Giunti, Firenze – Milano 2004.

BOURRIAUD N., *Relational Aesthetics*, Les presses du réel, Paris 1998.

_, *Post Production. La culture comme scénario: comment l'art reprogramme le monde contemporain*, 2002. *Postproduction*, Lukas & Sternberg, New York 2007.

_, "Altermodern Manifesto", 2009, online at www.tate.org.uk/whats-on/tate-britain/exhibition/altermodern/explain-altermodern/altermodern-explainedmanifesto.

_, *The Radicant*, Lukas & Sternberg, New York 2009.

BOWDITCH L., "Driven to distraction – multimedia art exhibition by the Guggenheim Museum Soho", in *Afterimage*, January – February 1997.

BREA J. L., *La era postmedia. Acción comunicativa, prácticas (post)artísticas y dispositivos neomediales*, Consorcio Salamanca, Salamanca 2002.

BROCKMAN J., *Digerati. Encounters with the CyberElite*, Hardwired, New York 1996.

BUEHRER V. K. , "Dearest progressive scan loading, on victims of Broadband", in *Neural*, n° 23, 2006, p. 48.

BUXMANN A., DEPRAETERE F. (Eds.), *Argos Festival*, argoseditions, Brussels 2005.

CASTELLS M., *The Information Age*, Blackwell, Cambridge, MA – Oxford, UK, 1996 – 1998.

_, *Internet Galaxy*, Oxford University Press 2001.

CAMPANELLI V., *Web Aesthetics*, Institute of Network Cultures / NAi Publishers, Rotterdam 2010.

CELANT G., *Artmix. Flussi tra arte, architettura, cinema, design, moda, musica e televisione*, Feltrinelli, Milano 2008.

CHANDLER A., NEUMARK N. (Eds), *At a Distance. Precursors to Art and Activism on the Internet*, The MIT Press, Cambridge and London 2005 [2006].

CLARKE A., MITCHELL G. (Eds.), *Videogames and Art*, Intellect Books, Bristol – Chicago 2007.

CHAN, J., "From Browser to Gallery (and Back): The Commodification of Net Art 1990-2011", in *Pool*, December 28, 2011, online at http://pooool.info/from-browser-to-gallery-and-back-the-commodification-of-net-art-1990-2011/.

CHAN P., "The Unthinkable Community", in *Eflux Journal*, Issue 16, May 2010, online at www.e-flux.com/journal/view/144.

CHRISTOV-BAKARGIEV C., *I Moderni / The Moderns*, exh. cat., Castello di Rivoli Museo d'Arte Contemporanea, Rivoli – Torino. Skira, Milano 2003.

CONT3XT.NET (Eds.), *Circulating Contexts. Curating Media / Net / Art*, Books on demand GmbH, Norderstedt 2007.

COOK S., GRAHAM B., MARTIN S. (Eds.), *Curating New Media*, B.READ / SIX, Baltic, Gateshead 2002.

COOK S., GRAHAM B., GFADER V., LAPP A. (Eds.), *A Brief History of Curating New Media Art: Conversations with Curators*, The Green Box, Berlin 2010.

_, *A Brief History of Working with New Media Art: Conversations with Artists*, The Green Box, Berlin 2010.

COOK S., "An interview with Christiane Paul", in *Crumbweb*, 28 March 2001, online at http://crumbweb.org/getInterviewDetail.php?id=10&ts=1241707558&op=3& sublink=9.

CORBY T. (ed.) *Network Art: Practices and Positions*, London, Swets & Zeitlinger / Routledge 2005.

ĆOSIĆ V. (ed.), *Net.art Per Me*, cat., Venezia, Santa Maria del Soccorso, June 2001. MGLC 2001.

CRITICAL ART ENSEMBLE, *Electronic Civil Disobedience*, Autonomedia, New York 1995.

DAL LAGO A., GIORDANO S., *Mercanti d'aura. Logiche dell'arte contemporanea*, Il Mulino, Bologna 2006.

DANTO A., *The Abuse of Beauty. Aesthetics and the Concept of Art,* Open Court Publishing 2003.

DAVENPORT T. H., BECK J. C., *The Attention Economy: Understanding the New Currency of Business*, Harvard Business School Press, 2001.

DAVID C., "dx and new media", 20 June 1997, online at www.documenta12.de/archiv/dx/lists/debate/0001.html.

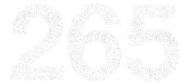

DEBATTY R., "Book review – Media, New Media, Postmedia", in *We Make Money Not Art*, August 27, 2011, online at http://we-make-money-not-art.com/archives/2011/08/media-new-media-postmedia.php.

_, "Holy Fire, art of the digital age", in *We Make Money Not Art*, 22 April 2008, online at www.we-make-money-not-art.com/archives/2008/04/holy-fire.php.

DEITCH J. (Ed.), *Post Human*, exh. cat., Cantz / Deste Foundation for Contemporary Art, 1992.

DELSON S., "If Picasso Were A Programmer", in *Forbes*, Best of The Web, 25 June 2001.

DEPOCAS A., IPPOLITO J., JONES C. (Eds.), *Permanence Through Change: The Variable Media Approach*, The Solomon R. Guggenheim Foundation, New York, and The Daniel Langlois Foundation for Art, Science, and Technology, Montreal, 2003.

DESERIIS M., MARANO G., *net.art. L'arte della connessione*, Shake, Milano 2003 [2008].

DESERIIS M., LAMPO L. QUARANTA D., *Connessioni Leggendarie. Net.art 1995 – 2005*, cat., Ready Made, Milano 2005.

DIETZ S., "Curating New Media", August 2000, in *Yproductions*, online at www.yproductions.com/writing/archives/curating_new_media.html.

_, "'Just Art': Contemporary Art After the Art Formerly Known As New Media", October 27, 2006, in *Yproductions*, online at www.yproductions.com/writing/archives/just_art_contemporary_art_afte.html.

DRAVES, I., "Interview with Ken Johnson", in *Leaders in Software and Art*, September 4, 2011, online at http://softwareandart.com/?p=747.

DOULAS L., "Within Post-Internet, Part One", in *Pool*, April 6, 2011, online at http://pooool.info/within-post-internet-part-i/.

EVERETT A., CALDWELL J. T. (Eds.), *New Media. Theories and Practice of Digitextuality*, Routledge, New York 2003.

FOSTER H., KRAUSS R., BOIS Y., BUCHLOH B. H. D., *Art since 1900. Modernism, Antimodernism, Postmodernism*, Thames & Hudson, London 2004.

FRASCINA F., HARRISON C. (Eds.), *Modern Art and Modernism: A Critical Anthology*, Sage Publications 1982.

FROHNE U., SCHIEREN M., GUITON J.F. (Eds.), *Present Continuous Past(s): Media Art. Strategies of Presentation, Mediation and Dissemination*, Springer-Verlag, Vienna 2005.

GALLO F., *Les immateriaux. Un percorso di Jean-Francois Lyotard nell'arte contemporanea*, Aracne 2008.

GALLOWAY A. R., *Protocol. How Control Exists After Decentralization*, The MIT Press, Cambridge – London 2004.

GALLOWAY A. R., THACKER R., *The Exploit. A Theory of Networks*, University of Minnesota Press, Minneapolis – London 2007.

GERE C., *Digital Culture*, Reaktion Books, London 2002 (2008).

GOODYEAR A. C., "From Technophilia to Technophobia: The Impact of the Vietnam War on the Reception of "Art and Technology"", in *Leonardo*, April 2008, Vol. 41, No. 2, pp. 169-173.

GRAHAM B., *Curating New Media Art: SFMoMA and 010101*, University of Sunderland 2001.

GRAHAM B., COOK S., *Rethinking Curating: Art After New Media*, MIT Press 2010.

GRANT T., "How Anti-Computer Sentiment Shaped Early Computer Art", in *Refresh!*, September 2008.

GRAU O. (Ed.), *Media Art Histories*, MIT Press (Leonardo Books), Cambridge and London, England, 2007.

GREENE R., *Internet Art*, Thames & Hudson, London – New York, 2004.

GROYS B., *Art Power*, The MIT Press, Cambridge – London 2008

GUATTARI F., *Soft Subversions*. Edited by Sylvère Lotringer. Semiotext(e) 1996.

HALL D., FIFER S.J. (Eds.), *Illuminating Video. An Essential Guide to Video Art*, Aperture / BAVC, New York 1990.

HABER J., "Medium Rare", 1996, online at www.haberarts.com/tvscape.htm.

HANSEN M., *New Philosophy for New Media*, The MIT Press, Cambridge 2006.

HEARTNEY E., *Art & Today*, Phaidon Press, London 2008.

HIGGINS D., "Statement on Intermedia", 1966. Published in: VOSTELL W. (Ed.), *Dé-coll/age (décollage) * 6*, Typos Verlag, Frankfurt - Something Else Press, New York, July 1967. Online at http://artpool.hu/Fluxus/Higgins/intermedia2.html.

HIMANEN P., *The Hacker Ethic and the Spirit of the Information Age*, Random House 2001.

HUGHES P. K., *Breaking and Entering: A User's Guide*, Pace Wildenstein, New York 2005.

JODI, "dx webprojects", 9 July 1997, online at www.documenta12.de/archiv/dx/lists/debate/0010.html.

JOSEPH B.W., "Engineering Marvel: Branden W. Joseph on Billy Klüver", in *Artforum*, March 2004.

JOHNSON P., "Is New Media Accepted in the Art World? Domenico Quaranta's Media, New Media, PostMedia", in *Art Fag City*, August 30, 2011, online at www.artfagcity.com/2011/08/30/is-new-media-accepted-in-the-art-world-domenico-quarantas-media-new-media-postmedia/.

_, "Interview with Aron Namenwirth of artMovingProjects", in *Rhizome*, April 9, 2008, online at http://rhizome.org/editorial/2008/apr/9/interview-with-aron-namenwirth-of-artmovingproject/.

JONES C., "The Function of the Studio (when the studio is a laptop)", in *Art Lies*, Issue 67, 2010, online at www.artlies.org/article.php?id=1996&issue=67&s=0.

KLÜVER B., MARTIN J., ROSE B. (Eds), *Pavilion: Experiments in Art and Technology*, New York, E. P. Dutton 1972.

KLÜVER B., "E.A.T. – Archive of published documents", 2000, online at www.fondation-langlois.org/html/e/page.php?NumPage=306.

KRAUSS R., *A Voyage in the North Sea. Art in the Age of the Post-Medium Condition*, Thames & Hudson, London 1999.

_, "Reinventing the Medium", in *Critical Inquiry*, n. 25, Winter 1999, pp. 289 – 305.

_, *Under Blue Cup*, The MIT Press, Cambridge – London 2011.

_, "The Guarantee of the Medium", In ARPPE T., KAITARO T., MIKKONEN K. (Eds.), *Writing in Context: French Literature, Theory and the Avant-Gardes. Studies across Disciplines in the Humanities and Social Sciences*, Helsinki, Helsinki Collegium for Advanced Studies 2009, 139–145. Online at http://www.helsinki.fi/collegium/e-series/volumes/volume_5/005_09_Krauss.pdf.

KRYSA J. (Ed.), *Curating Immateriality. The work of the curator in the age of network systems*, Data Browser 03, Autonomedia, New York 2006.

KUO M., "Art's New Media", in *Artforum*, September 2012, online at http://artforum.com/inprint/id=31950 (last visit March 2013).

IOSELIT D., *After Art*, Cloth 2012.

LACERTE S., "Experiments in Art and Technology: a Gap to Fill in Art History's Recent Chronicles", in *Refresh!*, September 2008. Online at www.fondation-langlois.org/html/e/page.php?NumPage=1716.

LAERA M., "Arte Digitale: Collezionisti, fatevi avanti!", in *Wired.it*, 22 April 2009, online at http://daily.wired.it/news/cultura/arte-digitale-collezionisti-fatevi-avanti.html.

LAMUNIÈRE S., "dx webprojects", 10 July 1997, online at www.documenta12.de/archiv/dx/lists/debate/0014.html.

LEOPOLDSEDER H., SCHÖPF C., STOCKER G., *1979 – 2004 Ars Electronica*, Hatje Cantz Verlag 2004.

LIALINA O., ESPENSCHIED D. (Eds.), *Digital Folklore*, Merz and Solitude, Stuttgart 2009.

LIESER W. (Ed.), *Digital Art*, h.f.ullmann 2009.

LISTER M., DOVEY J., GIDDINGS S., GRANT I., KELLY K., *New Media: a Critical Introduction*, Routledge, New York 2009.

LOVINK G., *Zero Comments, Blogging and Critical Internet Culture*, Routledge, New York 2007.

_, "New Media Arts: In Search of the Cool Obscure. Explorations beyond the Official Discourse", in *Diagonal Thoughts*, 2007. Online at www.diagonalthoughts.com/?p=204.

LOVINK G., NIEDERER S. (Eds.), *Video Vortex Reader. Responses to Youtube*, Institute of Networked Cultures, Amsterdam 2008.

LUDOVICO A. (ED.), *UBERMORGEN.COM – MEDIA HACKING VS. CONCEPTUAL ART. HANS BERNHARD / LIZVLX*, Christoph Merian Verlag, Basel 2009.

LUNENFELD P., *Snap to Grid: A User's Guide to Digital Arts*, Media, and Cultures, MIT Press, Cambridge 2000.

MANOVICH L., *The Language of New Media*, The MIT Press, Cambridge 2001.

_, "The Death of Computer Art", 1997, , 1997. Online at www.manovich.net/TEXT/death.html.

_, "Post-Media Aesthetics", sd (2000 –), online at www.manovich.net/DOCS/Post_media_aesthetics1.doc

_, "Don't Call it Art: Ars Electronica 2003", in *Nettime*, September 22, 2003. Also available at http://manovich.net/DOCS/ars_03.doc.

_, "From Borges to HTML", in *Intelligent Agent*, 2003, online at http://intelligentagent.com/CNM200/manovich_new_media.doc.

MEDOSCH A., *Technological Determinism in Media Art*, 2005. A dissertation submitted in partial fulfilment of the requirements of Sussex University for the degree of MA Interactive Digital Media. Online at www.thenextlayer.org/files/TechnoDeterminismAM_0.pdf.

MASON C., *A computer in the Art Room: the Origins of British Computer Arts 1950 – 80*, Norfolk, JJG Publishing 2008.

MACGREGOR B., "Cybernetic Serendipity Revisited", undated (2008), online at http://design.osu.edu/carlson/history/PDFs/cyberserendipity.pdf.

MCHUGH G., *Post Internet*, Link Editions, Brescia 2012.

MCLUHAN M., *Understanding Media. The Extensions of Man*, 1964. MIT Press, Cambridge 1994.

MICHAUD Y., *L'artiste et les commissaires*, Hachette Pluriel Reference 2007.

MIRAPAUL M., "Museum Puts Internet Art on the Wall", in *The New York Times*, 16 September 1999, online at http://theater.nytimes.com/library/tech/99/09/cyber/artsatlarge/16artsatlarge.html.

_, "Selling and Collecting the Intangible, at $1,000 a Share", in *The New York Times*, 29 April 2002, online at www.nytimes.com/2002/04/29/arts/arts-online-selling-and-collecting-the-intangible-at-1000-a-share.html.

MORRIS S., "Museums and new media art", New York, Rockefeller Foundation, October 2001, online at www.cs.vu.nl/~eliens/archive/refs/Museums_and_New_Media_Art.pdf.

NICHOLS J., "Documenta X", October 1997, online at www.artdes.monash.edu.au/globe/issue7/doctxt.html.

NIDEFFER R. F., "SHIFT-CTRL. Mediating the process of academic exhibitionism", 2000, online at www.nideffer.net/classes/135-09-W/readings/nideffer.html.

OLSON M., "Lost Not Found: The Circulation of Images in Digital Visual Culture", in *Words Without Pictures*, 18 September 2008, online at http://uncopy.net/wp-content/uploads/2011/01/olson-lostnotfound.pdf.

PACKER R., JORDAN K. (Eds.), *Multimedia: From Wagner to Virtual Reality*, New York, W. W. Norton & Company 2001.

PALFREY J., GASSER U., *Born Digital. Understanding the First Generation of Digital Natives*, Basic Books, New York 2008.

PAUL C., *Digital Art*, Thames & Hudson, London 2003 [2008].

PAUL C. (Ed.), *New Media in the White Cube and Beyond. Curatorial Models for Digital Art*, University of California Press, Berkeley 2008.

PERNIOLA M., *L'arte e la sua ombra*, Giulio Einaudi Editore, Torino 2000.

PERRA D., *Impatto digitale. Dall'immagine elaborata all'immagine partecipata: il computer nell'arte contemporanea*, Baskerville, Bologna 2007.

PIRO N. (Ed.), *Etoy – Cyberterrorismo. Come si organizza un rapimento virtuale*, Castelvecchi, Roma 1998.

POLVERONI A., *This is contemporary! Come cambiano i musei di arte contemporanea*, Franco Angeli, Milano 2007.

PONZINI P., "DiVA Digital Video Art Fair", in *Digimag 33*, April 2008, online at www.digicult.it/digimag/article.asp?id=1125.

POPPER F., *Art of the Electronic Age*, Thames & Hudson, London 1997.

_, *From Technological to Virtual Art*, MIT Press, Cambridge, Massachusetts – London, England 2007.

PRICE S., "Dispersion", 2002 – ongoing, online at www.distributedhistory.com/ Disperzone.html.

QUARANTA D., *Net art 1994-1998. La vicenda di Äda'web*, Vita e Pensiero, Milano 2004.

_, "Let's Get Loud! Interview with Helen Thorington, director of TURBULENCE.ORG", in *Cluster. On Innovation*, n. 5, 2005, pp. 12 – 17.

_, "Don't Say New Media!", in *FMR Bianca*, n° 4, Franco Maria Ricci, Bologna 2008.

_, "We Are All Ready for a Change. Interview with Steven Sacks", in *Rhizome*, 28 June 2007, online at http://rhizome.org/discuss/view/26364#4889.

_, *Media, New Media, Postmedia*, Postmedia Books, Milan 2010

_, "The Postmedia Perspective", in *Rhizome*, January 12, 2011, online at http://rhizome.org/editorial/2011/jan/12/the-postmedia-perspective/.

QUARANTA D. (Ed.), *Gazira Babeli*, Link Editions, Brescia 2012.

_, *Playlist. Playing Games, Music, Art*. Exh. Cat., LABoral Centro de Arte y Creación Industrial, Gijon, Spain, December 18, 2009 – May 17, 2010. Online at: http://domenicoquaranta.com/public/pdf/LABoral_Revista_PLAYLIST.pdf (last visit March 2013).

_, *Collect the WWWorld. The Artist as Archivist in the Internet Age*. Exh. cat. Brescia, Spazio Contemporanea, September 24 – October 15, 2011. LINK Editions, Brescia 2011. Online at http://editions.linkartcenter.eu/ (last visit March 2013).

QUARANTA D., BERNARD Y. (Eds.), *Holy Fire. Art of the Digital Age*, cat., iMAL, Bruxelles, 2008. Brescia, FPEditions 2008.

QUINN E., "Live and Media Arts at the ICA", in *New Media Curating*, October 17, 2008.

RASTAS P., "Alien Intelligence", 2000, in *Kiasma Magazine*, 5 -99.

REAS C., FRY B. (Eds.), *Processing: A Programming Handbook for Visual Designers and Artists*, MIT Press, 2007.

RINEHART R., "The Media Art Notation System: Documenting and Preserving Digital/Media Art", in *Leonardo*, April 2007, vol. 40, No. 2, pp. 181-187.

RINDER L., SINGER D. (Eds.), *Bitstreams*, exh. cat., Whitney Museum of American Art, New York 2001.

ROMANO G., *Artscape. Panorama dell'arte in Rete*, Costa & Nolan, Ancona – Milano 2000.

ROSENBAUM L., "guggenheim soho to go high-tech", in *Artnet*, 29 March 1996, online at www.artnet.com/magazine_pre2000/news/rosenbaum/ rosenbaum3-29-96.asp.

RUSH M., *New Media in Late 20th-Century Art*, Thames & Hudson, London 1999 [2001].

SALTZ J., "My Sixth Sense", in *The Village Voice*, 2000.

SCHNEIDER I., KOROT B. (Eds.), *Video Art*, New York, Harcourt Brace

Jovanovich, 1976.

SCHOLDER A., CRANDALL J. (Eds.), *Interaction. Artistic Practice in the Network*, Eyebeam / D.A.P., New York 2001.

SCHWARTZ J., "Museum Kills Live Exhibit", in *The New York Times*, May 13, 2008, online at www.nytimes.com/2008/05/13/science/13coat.html?_r=0.

SCUDERO D., *Manuale del curator. Teoria e pratica della cura critica*, Gangemi Editore, Roma 2004.

SHANKEN E. A., *Art and Electronic Media*, Phaidon Press, London 2009.

_, "Art in the Information Age: Technology and Conceptual Art", 2001. Online at http://artexetra.files.wordpress.com/2009/02/shankenartinfoage.pdf.

SHANKEN, E. A. (Ed.), "New Media, Art-Science and Contemporary Art: Towards a Hybrid Discourse?". *Artnodes*, No. 11, p. 65-116. UOC. Online at http://artnodes.uoc.edu/ojs/index.php/artnodes/article/view/artnodes-n11-shanken/artnodes-n11-new-media-art-science-and-contemporary-art-eng (last visit March 2013).

SLATON J., "Museum Offers Webby Art Award", in *Wired*, 18 February 2000, online at www.wired.com/culture/lifestyle/news/2000/02/34414.

SLOCUM P., "New Media and the Gallery", in *Artlies*, Issue 67, 2010, online at www.artlies.org/article.php?id=1993&issue=67&s=0.

SMITH R., "A Museum's Metamorphosis: The Virtual Arcade", in *New York Times*, 18 June 1996.

SPINGARN-KOFF J., "010101: Art for Our Times", in *Wired*, 28 February 2001, online at www.wired.com/culture/lifestyle/news/2001/02/41972.

SYMAN S., "Bell Curves and Bitstreams. Stefanie Syman on the beginning of the end of digital art", in *Feed*, 27 March 2001.

STALLABRASS J., *Art Incorporated. The Story of Contemporary Art,* Oxford University Press 2004.

STEYERL H., "In Defense of the Poor Image", in *eflux journal*, Issue 10, November 2009, online at www.e-flux.com/journal/in-defense-of-the-poor-image/.

STOCKER G., "The Art of Tomorrow", in *a minima*, n° 15, 2006, pp. 6 – 19.

TAPSCOTT D., *Grown Up Digital*, McGraw-Hill eBooks 2009.

TERRAROLI V. (Ed.), *Art of the Twentieth Century*, 5 vv, Milano, Skira 2006 – 2010.

THORNTON S., *Seven Days in the Art World*, W. W. Norton & Company 2009.

TRIBE M., JANA R., *New Media Art*, Taschen, Köln 2006.

TROEMEL B., "What Relational Aesthetics Can Learn From 4Chan", in *Artfagcity*, September 9, 2010. Online at http://www.artfagcity.com/2010/09/09/img-mgmt-what-relational-aesthetics-can-learn-from-4chan/.

_, "Why Your .JPEGs Aren't Making You A Millionaire", in *The Creators Project*, May 14, 2012, online at http://thecreatorsproject.com/blog/ digart-why-your-jpegs-arent-making-you-a-millionaire.

_, *Peer Pressure*, Link Editions, Brescia 2012.

VANDERBILT T., "The King of Digital Art", in *Wired*, issue 13.9, September 2005, online at www.wired.com/wired/archive/13.09/sacks.html.

VERSCHOOREN K. A., *.art. Situating Internet Art in the Traditional Institution for Contemporary Art*, 2007. Master of Science in Comparative Media Studies, Massachusetts Institute of Technology, online at http://cms.mit.edu/research/theses/KarenVerschooren2007.pdf.

VICENTE J. L., "Una historia del arte y la tecnología en ARCO", in *El Cultural*, February 2008. Available online in *Elastico*, at http://elastico.net/archives/2008/02/post_59.html.

VIERKANT A., "The Image Object Post-Internet", in *jstchillin*, 2010, online at http://jstchillin.org/artie/vierkant.html.

VOROPAI L., "Institutionalisation of Media Art in the Post-Soviet Space: The Role of Cultural Policy and Socioeconomic Factors", in *Re:place*, November 2007, online at http://pl02.donau-uni.ac.at/jspui/handle/10002/449.

WANDS B., *Art of the Digital Age*, Thames & Hudson, London – New York, 2006.

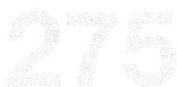

WARDRIP-FRUIN N., MONTFORT N. (Eds.), *The New Media Reader*, The MIT Press, Cambridge – London 2003.

WEIBEL P., DRUCKREY T. (Eds.), *net_condition: art and global media*, The MIT Press, Cambridge (Massachussets), 2001.

WISHART A., BOCHSLER R., *Leaving Reality Behind. The Battle for the Soul of the Internet*, 4th ESTATE, 2002 (Ecco – Harper Collins 2003).

WOLFE T., *The Painted World*, New York 1975. Trad. it. *Come ottenere il successo in arte*, Torino, Allemandi 1987 (2004).

Online Resources and Magazines

http://resourceguide.eai.org/

The EAI Online Resource Guide for Exhibiting, Collecting & Preserving Media Art, produced by the Electronic Art Intermix, New York.

http://www.nettime.org/

Mailing lists for networked cultures, politics, and tactics. In its archives you can find hundreds of texts, interviews and discussions about New Media Art.

http://rhizome.org/

Rhizome, mailing list and no-profit organization "dedicated to the creation, presentation, preservation, and critique of emerging artistic practices that engage technology."

http://www.yproductions.com/

Steve Dietz's website.

http://www.fondationlanglois.org/

Daniel Langlois Foundation for Art, Science, and Technology, Montreal (Canada).

http://www.mediaarthistory.org/

Conference series on the Histories of Media Art, Science and Technology.

http://www.nytimes.com/library/tech/reference/indexartsatlarge.html

Arts At Large, Matthew Mirapaul's column on art and technology in the *New York Times*.

http://crumbweb.org/

CRUMB, Curatorial Resource for Upstart Media Bliss. It hosts the mailing list *New Media Curating*.

http://www.we-make-money-not-art.com/

Regine Débatty's blog.

http://gallery9.walkerart.org/

Gallery 9, the online gallery of the Walker Art Center, Minneapolis.

http://www.tate.org.uk/intermediaart/

The "Intermedia Art" section of the Tate Gallery, London.

http://variablemedia.net/

The Variable Media Initiative.

http://www.aec.at/

Ars Electronica Center, Linz.

http://www.mediaartnet.org/

An "online encyclopedia" on New Media Art, edited by Rudolf Frieling and Dieter Daniels.

http://www.archimuse.com/

The international conference *Museums and the Web*.

http://switch.sjsu.edu/

Switch, "Online Journal of New Media".

http://vagueterrain.net/

Vague Terrain, an online magazine on digital culture, art and technology.

http://www.laudanum.net/cream/

Cream, a newsletter on digital culture (active between 2001 and 2002).

http://www.kurator.org/

The online curatorial platform Kurator, developed by Joasia Krysa.

http://www.intelligentagent.com/

Intelligent Agent, an online magazine edited by Christiane Paul and Patrick Lichty.

http://pooool.info/

Pool Magazine, "an online platform and publication dedicated to expanding and improving the discourse between online and offline realities and their cultural, societal and political impact on each other", edited by Louis Doulas.

http://www.artfagcity.com/

Art Fag City, an independent New York-based art blog dedicated to providing exposure to emerging contemporary art and under-known artists, edited by Paddy Johnson.

http://www.e-flux.com/journals/

The magazine developed by the international network e-flux.

http://dismagazine.com/

DIS Magazine, "a post-Internet lifestyle magazine about art, fashion and commerce."

LINK Editions

http://editions.linkartcenter.eu/

Clouds

Domenico Quaranta, *In Your Computer*, 2011
Valentina Tanni, *Random*, 2011
Gene McHugh, *Post Internet*, 2011
Brad Troemel, *Peer Pressure*, 2011
Kevin Bewersdorf, *Spirit Surfing*, 2012
Mathias Jansson, *Everything I shoot Is Art*, 2012
Joanne McNeil (Ed.), *Best of Rhizome 2012*, 2013
Domenico Quaranta, *Beyond New Media Art*, 2013

Catalogues

Collect the WWWorld. The Artist as Archivist in the Internet Age, 2011. Exhibition Catalogue. Edited by Domenico Quaranta, with texts by Josephine Bosma, Gene McHugh, Joanne McNeil, D. Quaranta
Gazira Babeli, 2011. Exhibition catalogue. Edited by Domenico Quaranta, with texts by Mario Gerosa, Patrick Lichty, D. Quaranta, Alan Sondheim.
Holy Fire. Art of the Digital Age, 2011. Exhibition catalogue. Edited by Yves Bernard, Domenico Quaranta.

In My Computer

Miltos Manetas, *In My Computer # 1*, 2011
Ryan Trecartin, *Ryan's Web 1.0. A Lossless Fall*, 2012
Chris Coy, *After Brad Troemel*, 2013

LINK Editions is a publishing initiative of the **LINK Center for the Arts of the Information Age.** LINK Editions uses the print on demand approach to create an accessible, dynamic series of essays and pamphlets, but also tutorials, study notes and conference proceedings connected to its educational activities.
A keen advocate of the idea that information wants to be free, LINK Editions releases its contents free of charge in .pdf format, and on paper at a price accessible to all. Link Editions is a not-for-profit initiative and all its contents are circulated under an Attribution-NonCommercial-ShareAlike 3.0 Unported (CC BY-NC-SA 3.0) license.